AUDREY COHEN COLLEGE LIBRARY
75 Varick St. 12th Floor
New York, NY 10013

Second Home

Second Home

Orphan Asylums and Poor Families in America

Timothy A. Hacsi

Harvard University Press

Cambridge, Massachusetts
London, England
1997

Copyright © 1997 by the President and Fellows of Harvard College
All rights reserved
Printed in the United States of America

Library of Congress Cataloging-in-Publication Data

Hacsi, Timothy.
    Second home: orphan asylums and poor families in America /
Timothy Hacsi.
      p.   cm.
    Includes bibliographical references and index.
    ISBN 0-674-79644-6
    1. Orphanages—United States—History. I. Title.
HV983.H33   1997
362.73'2'0973—dc21   97-17063

*With love and gratitude,
this book is dedicated to the people who raised me:
Papa, Mom, Jon, and most of all, my mother*

Contents

Acknowledgments   ix

Introduction   1

1. The Growth and Triumph of an Institution   11
2. The Changing Nature of Orphan Asylums   54
3. Managers and Funding   75
4. Through the Asylum Doors   104
5. Routine, Discipline, and Improvements in Asylum Life   148
6. Education and Building Character   173
7. Play, Holidays, and Vacations   196

Conclusion   213

Appendix: Supplementary Tables   225

Notes   231

Bibliography   269

Index   283

Acknowledgments

Small moments can have surprisingly large outcomes, and the story of this book began when I was the beneficiary of one such moment. In the winter of 1988, Michael Katz and I spoke on the phone about my application to the University of Pennsylvania's graduate history program. That conversation led to my visiting Penn even though I'd thought I was going elsewhere; my visit led to my enrolling there. It was one of the best decisions of my life. While at Penn I learned a great deal from my fellow history graduate students, and I want to especially thank George Barnett, Dana Barron, Rose Beiler, Debbie Block, Celia Cusson, Sherman Dorn, Thomas Heinrich, Lara Iglitzen, Alison Isenberg, Mary McNear, Max Page, Sue Schulton, Marc Stein, Victoria Thompson, and Monica Tetzlaff. In addition, I owe a great debt to Steve Conn, Jim Heinzen, Jeff Horn, Dave Kerans, Mark Meier, John Noakes, Liam Riordan, Rubin Sinins, Dave Smith, and Tim Waples.

Of course, I also benefitted from studying with a number of superb professors at Penn. Richard Dunn generously volunteered to teach a class on writing dissertation proposals that helped shape my questions. Two years later, Michael Zuckerman gave what was then the first chapter such a thorough reading that the rest of the manuscript was vastly improved. Mark Stern read most of the dissertation and gave me a great deal of useful advice, not the least of which was his warning against getting bogged down in case records in a study that was intended to be broad. Walter Licht gave the dissertation a thorough and incisive reading, in the process giving me the key to turning it into a book. Finally, Michael Katz was my adviser. Few historians can match Michael's understanding of the complexities of history. Just as importantly, he maintained a high level of intellectual rigor for his students while helping to create the collegial, supportive, non-competitive atmosphere that helps make Penn's graduate history program a special place. I could not have asked for a better mentor—or a better friend.

As an undergraduate at Oberlin College, I was fortunate to study under a number of dedicated teachers. I would like to thank Geoffrey Blodgett, Carol Lasser, and the late Robert Neil for encouraging my interest in history. Gary Kornblith was my undergraduate thesis adviser, and he became a friend as well as a mentor. His understanding of the contours of American history, and his dedication to teaching his students how to think for themselves about history, are benchmarks to which we should all aspire. At Harvard University Press, Aida Donald and Elizabeth Suttell have been consistently helpful and have given me good advice throughout an unfamiliar process. I would also like to thank Linda McLatchie for greatly improving the manuscript. At Chapin Hall, I would like to thank Harold Richman, Larry Stanton, Rebecca Stone, and Liz Hurley for providing a supportive environment and different viewpoints on many things. I would especially like to thank Joan Costello, and my fellow Fellows in Chicago: Kathy Hall, Sudhir Venkatesh, and Sam Whalen. I owe Bernadine Barr and Ann Brown special thanks for managing to keep me in academia, at least for now. I would also like to thank Allan Brandt and Alberta Siegel for encouraging my work when it was most needed. The two readers for Harvard University Press made a number of suggestions that helped improve the manuscript noticeably, for which I am grateful.

There are a number of other people I would like to thank, though in some cases for reasons only marginally related to this book: Dana Barron and Tom Sugrue, Kelly and Henry Kingdon, Joy Kammerling and Dave Smith, Paul, Mari, Katie, and Tommy O'Neill, Chris Hunter, Robin Jaslow, Debby Levy, Linda Lowenthal, Mark Meier, Beth Fordham-Meier, and especially Christy Goldfinch, who had to put up with me when this, in its dissertation form, dominated my life. Finally, I want to thank the four members of my family who raised me, and did so in the least "institutional" manner imaginable. My maternal grandmother ("Mom" to the whole family) passed away a few months before I received my Ph.D., and my father passed away while I was trying to turn the dissertation into a book. I wish they had lived to hold this in their hands. My older brother Jon was, among many other things, the best of friends and a role model for life. I cannot imagine what my life would have been like without him. Finally, I want to thank my mother, for all the usual reasons and many more. This book is dedicated to them.

Second Home

Introduction

From before the Civil War to the Great Depression, more of America's dependent children—children whose families, including extended families, were for a time unable to care for them—were helped in orphan asylums than by any other means.[1] Perhaps because orphan asylums are not very common in the late twentieth century, they have received little attention from scholars. Historians have spent much more effort studying other institutions, such as juvenile reformatories. In fact, there were far more orphan asylums than reformatories, and they cared for many more children than did reformatories. Indeed, from the 1830s, when a cholera epidemic led to the founding of dozens of new asylums across the young nation, to the 1920s, when public pensions finally helped more mothers keep children in their homes than were being helped in asylums, orphan asylums helped shape more poor children's lives than any other American social institution except public schools and churches.

Despite the name "orphan asylum," relatively few children cared for in these institutions were actually full orphans who had lost both parents. Throughout the nineteenth century, most children in orphan asylums were half-orphans, children who had lost one parent through death and had one living parent. As mortality rates fell, the number of full orphans and half-orphans being cared for in orphan asylums declined, and the percentage of dependent children in asylum populations increased. Consequently, an increasing percentage of the children who entered orphan asylums had families to which they could hope to return, and most asylum children did in fact rejoin their families after being institutionalized for a few years. By the end of the nineteenth century, many asylum wards were dependent or destitute children with two living parents who were, either temporarily or permanently, unable to care for them due to the strains caused by a family illness, lengthy unemployment, or other problem. Reunification was usually a real possibility for such children. Most other asylum children were half-orphans who also had families with which they could hope to reunite.

In some ways, orphan asylums were representative of American institutions designed for the poor. Their spread across the nineteenth century was similar to that of other institutions, especially hospitals: they were rare at the start of the century, had become common by the Civil War era, and continued to experience rapid growth in the decades leading up to 1900. In the early twentieth century, when hospitals changed from religiously motivated welfare providers to secular, scientifically managed, profit-oriented businesses, orphan asylums, most of which were religious institutions, began to be challenged by more secular methods of child care, chiefly varying versions of mothers' pensions and foster care. These changes would eventually force them either to close or to shift their focus away from caring for poor but basically healthy children.

Throughout the one-hundred-year period when orphan asylums were a highly visible part of the American landscape, the vast majority were local institutions, managed by private groups and serving a specific clientele. They received both private and public funding, but most asylums remained under private control and relied on extensive fundraising efforts to survive. Like other institutions such as old-age homes, orphan asylums were usually founded by, and for, members of a specific religious group. Orphan asylums were touted by their managers as "homes," and probably did succeed in being more "homelike" than other institutions, such as insane asylums, whose managers made similar claims. However, most failed to be homes to their children in the most positive senses of the word. Finally, like most other institutions, they were continuously molded by their clients' needs as well as their managers' wishes.[2]

But it would be a mistake to assume that orphan asylums were like other nineteenth-century institutions, such as schools, hospitals, and poorhouses, in every important way. It would also be a mistake to assume orphan asylums all fell into one mold; there was a tremendous variety in how they functioned. As Gerald Grob has pointed out, it is just as important to recognize the differences between various institutions as to note their similarities.³ Unlike many other parts of the fragmented American relief system, orphan asylums recognized that there were short-term poor and long-term poor, and to some extent they developed methods designed to help members of each group. More than most social welfare institutions, orphan asylums performed the duty that their clientele wished them to by helping poor families survive harsh times through temporarily caring for children.

Unlike reform schools and prisons, orphan asylums did not change from optimistic, reform-oriented institutions to pessimistic, custodial ones between the Civil War and the turn of the century; instead, orphanages became more humane as time passed. The main reason for this fundamental difference was their clientele. Prisons and other antebellum institutions hoped to reform their inmates, but orphan asylum managers rarely thought their children needed reform nearly as much as they needed shelter, sustenance, and moral education. Juvenile reformatories often mixed delinquent children with children who were simply poor, and viewed them all as in need of reform. As Eric Schneider points out, the powerful belief that those receiving assistance should never live better than the poorest worker, known as "less eligibility," meant that delinquent children "could not be treated more favorably than nondelinquent children." In orphan asylums, however, dislike of poor parents led some managers to try to break ties between children and parents, but it did not lead to intentionally harsh treatment of the children themselves. A major reason for this different viewpoint is that, unlike prisons and reformatories, orphan asylums were not publicly managed institutions but rather were private ones affiliated to a greater or lesser degree with a church. And because many asylum managers recognized that poor parents suffered from unemployment, illness, and spousal death more than from character flaws, many asylums did not even try to split up families but instead looked forward to reuniting children with their families; this attitude became increasingly common among asylum managers after 1900.[4]

There were other important ways in which asylums were unusual or even unique. Most early reformatories focused on boys, but most early orphan asylums were founded to help girls.[5] And children in orphan asylums were treated very differently from another group defined by age, the elderly. Carole Haber found that by the early twentieth century, "American physicians had developed a conception of old age that legitimated the complete separation of the aged from the rest of society." The elderly poor were in poorhouses, and old-age homes won the approval of social workers as appropriate for the middle-class elderly.[6] But social workers treated dependent children very differently. They supported foster care over institutions for children, who, unlike the elderly, were not supposed to be separated from society. At the same time, in the decades before and after 1900, orphan asylum managers themselves became more and more likely to send their children out to mingle with other children and adults.

From the 1830s to the 1880s, orphan asylums were widely, though not unanimously, viewed as the best way to care for poor children outside of their own homes. In the 1890s, attacks on asylums multiplied, usually coming from advocates of placing children in homes.[7] Critics of orphan asylums argued that they were overcrowded, impersonal institutions that failed to treat children as individuals while at the same time allowing undeserving parents to shirk their parental duties. These criticisms reached their climax at the White House Conference on Dependent Children of 1909, which called for aid to poor widows and other destitute mothers in their own homes, so that they could continue to care for their own children despite their family's poverty. The conference also declared that foster care, the temporary placement of dependent children in homes other than their own, was the second-best option, when maintaining family homes was for some reason impossible. Orphan asylums were to be employed only as a last resort, and even then only as temporary homes. Yet in most states, orphan asylums continued to care for more children than were aided by either mothers' pensions or foster care until at least the 1920s. In the 1930s, when the depression strained asylum budgets to the breaking point and federal involvement in an improved version of mothers' pensions, Aid to Dependent Children, made home care more widely available, orphan asylums finally moved away from their long place at the center of child welfare in the United States. Some, especially Catholic asylums, struggled on caring for poor children into the 1950s or 1960s; others became foster care agencies or residential treatment centers for troubled children, or closed their doors.

Asylums spread so widely and lasted so long because different groups—various churches, ethnic communities, secular charitable organizations, fraternal societies, and city, county, and state governments—

could all adapt them to their own purposes. They were flexible institutions that could keep children for short periods of time or for years, educate children on-site or send them out to public schools, control their religious training, and decide whom to accept or reject for admission. In most cases, orphan asylums functioned as community-based institutions that helped preserve the culture and values of ethnic and religious groups.[8]

Starting with less-lofty and more-attainable goals than other Jacksonian era institutions, most orphan asylums throughout the century had a clearly defined, if not easily attained, mission: to clothe, house, and educate children; provide them with a specific moral and religious code; and otherwise care for children until they could be indentured, placed in a family, or returned to their own homes. Unlike some other institutions that began as private corporations serving public functions and then evolved into more clearly public institutions, orphan asylums remained largely private. Even in the early twentieth century, government involvement in most orphan asylums was limited to annual inspections by state boards of charity, or to no involvement at all. Because orphan asylums were private institutions, their managers enjoyed greater control over them than did their counterparts in public institutions, and local asylums that enjoyed the support of their communities were able to continue in the face of extensive criticism from outsiders on the national stage.

The literature on poverty and American responses to it has grown dramatically, both in quality and quantity, over the past decade.[9] But its greatest weakness remains children: for example, the literature on indenture, foster care and its predecessors, and the actual practice (as opposed to creation) of Aid to Dependent Children (ADC) is scanty and uneven. The published literature on the history of orphanages has grown dramatically in the mid-1990s but remains limited. It focuses chiefly on Jewish orphanages, which barely existed in the nineteenth century and, even at their peak in the 1920s, made up only a small percentage of all orphan asylums.[10] Since the mid-1980s, a few dissertations focusing either completely or partially on orphan asylums have appeared.[11] There are also a number of articles on orphanages, many of which are quite insightful.[12] In addition, there are several good studies of child welfare in a region or time period, although their arguments about orphan asylums are generally less sophisticated than the works cited above.[13]

Not surprisingly, each author takes a somewhat different approach and argues that orphan asylums have certain characteristics based on the one or two institutions they examine. Yet none allows for much generalization about what was common among most orphan asylums, what made asylums of one kind different from another, and how different kinds of asylums changed over time.

Despite considerable diversity among orphan asylums, almost all did share some common features: a focus on providing a secular education similar (or superior) to what most working-class children of the day might expect; an emphasis on giving children a set of moral values, usually tied to a specific religion; and a desire to make the institution a "home" for its children. But other things varied. Some asylums wanted to return children to their parents, while others tried to block children off from their former lives. Some children were educated in asylum schools, others in public schools. Some were encouraged to interact with the broader community, while others were shielded (or imprisoned) from the world outside asylum walls. By taking a national perspective, this work attempts to discover the commonalities and distinctions between asylums of different religious backgrounds and different regions. By looking at orphan asylums from before the Civil War to the 1930s, it also attempts to understand how these similarities and differences changed over time.

The most useful way to distinguish one type of orphan asylum from another may be to examine how much contact the children had with the broader society—with their families, with other children, with other adults, and with institutions such as schools and churches—and the specific nature of those contacts. Individual orphan asylums functioned in ways best described by three ideal types: *protective*, *isolating*, and *integrative* asylums. In practice, most asylums were mixtures of two of these types. Protective and integrative asylums hoped to act as temporary replacements for children's own parents, while isolating asylums wanted to permanently replace poor children's parents with what they considered superior parenting and socialization tactics. Isolating and protective asylums both kept fairly tight control over their children's lives, while integrative asylums allowed their children much more contact with the outer world. However, protective asylums and isolating asylums had very different reasons for seeking to control their children, just as integrative and protective institutions had different ways of trying to pass a poor parent's heritage on to his or her children. For example, in protective institutions, children were carefully guarded from the outside world in an effort to preserve an ethnic or religious heritage, which was usually either Catholic or Jewish.[14] Isolating asylums, on the other hand, kept children completely inside the institution, educating them there and blocking off contact with whatever family remained in the hopes of breaking children away from their parents' world and making them into "Americans." (It is this type of orphan asylum, sometimes avowedly nonsectarian but usually basically Protestant in nature, that comes closest to the social control model so often used when discussing nineteenth-century institutions.) For most of the nineteenth century, the majority of orphan asylums were very much like the protective asylum described above, though many others were isolating institutions. By the early twentieth century, the majority of orphan asylums were gradually becoming integrative institutions that helped their children interact with the world outside asylum walls, though often the change was slow and uneven.

Scholars have offered a number of theories to explain the nature of the American welfare state. One argues that the "logic of industrialism" is the driving force behind the growth of welfare states. The extent and nature of a particular nation's economic development is supposed to explain how its welfare capacities and programs have developed, with little weight given to political processes.[15] Another explanation focuses on national values. It accepts many of the tenets of the logic-of-industrialism argument but adds ideology to the mix to better explain differences among various industrialized nations. By this theory, a nation's cultural values can speed or hinder the development of the welfare state; in the United States, in particular, a widespread commitment to individualism is seen to have slowed the growth of welfare programs.[16]

Another argument places private business people and government officials at the center of the story. The private sector provided models upon which the public sector was based at the beginning of the American welfare state. Later, as the central government grew and its bureaucrats gained experience and confidence, they eventually became the most important actors in expanding the welfare state.[17] Scholars with less sympathy for capitalists argue that business interests have always tended to resist the growth of the welfare state, which they see as developing out of a class struggle pitting capitalists against labor. In particular, the weakness of American labor unions, and the complete lack of a labor political party, allowed capitalists to dominate the debate in the United States more than they were able to elsewhere, causing the American welfare state to lag behind European counterparts.[18]

But that is only a brief sketch, and only of the beginning. Margaret Weir, Ann Shola Orloff, and Theda Skocpol have argued that a focus on politics is appropriate, but that it must take much more into account than just the actions of business people and labor. They assume that "political struggles and policy outcomes" are "jointly conditioned by the institutional arrangements of the state and by class and other social relationships, but never once and for all." The likelihood of any new policy being enacted is powerfully affected by current state capacities and by previous policies. Politics creates policies, which in turn affect politics. More recently, Skocpol has moved further back in time to look at events from the Civil War to the 1920s. However, her focus remains similar: "Governmental institutions, electoral rules, political parties, and prior public policies" are what matter. For Skocpol, private charity and ideology carry little weight.[19] Nor is that all; the list of interesting arguments about the welfare state goes on and on. The most important recent addition is a feminist perspective on the welfare state that argues for the central role of gender in shaping welfare, thus broadening the debate even further.[20]

Each of these theories has merit, especially if one pays attention to their basic arguments rather than every detail. For example, it is not necessary to accept everything about the logic-of-industrialism argument to recognize that industrialization has a very definite impact on a nation's welfare policies. But there is more to the story than business, industrialization, and politics, however broadly defined. This is especially true when trying to understand programs for poor children. Current explanations of the welfare state do not illuminate why (or in most cases even recognize that) public programs for poor children are shaped much more powerfully by a distrust of the poor than by a desire to protect innocent children. To understand the reasons varied groups receive such different treatment under the American welfare state, it is necessary to look at the treatment of the poor in the nineteenth century. As Michael Katz writes, "American public welfare has a very old history."[21] Twentieth-century welfare policies have built on that history, and nowhere is this more true than in the case of poor children.

Ann Shola Orloff writes that "ultimately, it was the larger obstacles produced by the legacies of U.S. state building, state structure, and past policy that prevented the achievement of a more complete welfare state in New Deal America."[22] But most past policy had in fact been created by *private* groups, not government bureaucracies. Orphan asylums, along with other private agencies, played a role in the development of the American welfare state. Opposition to institutional care in the early twentieth century was inextricably linked to support for foster care and, in many cases, to approval of aid to poor mothers to allow them to keep their families together. When government intervention to aid poor mothers and/or their children developed, it came in the form of mothers' pensions, and later ADC; instead of taking over private asylums, these new systems assisted the exact clientele orphan asylums had long cared for, thereby forcing asylums to either adapt or perish. Furthermore, attitudes toward the poor that shaped nineteenth-century policies remained largely unchanged in the twentieth century and continued to shape new policies. The welfare state's treatment of children repudiated the nineteenth century's use of institutions while maintaining the underlying principle of child-placing advocates, such as Charles Loring Brace, that poor parents were largely to blame for their own poverty. No one can understand the roots of today's discussions about reforming welfare or revamping the foster care system without understanding the history of charity and the conflicting ideologies that drove it, and orphanages played a large role in this story.

Attitudes toward the poor have helped shape policies toward the families of poor children in remarkably similar ways ever since the 1820s. Without an understanding of how poor children have been cared for by charity and welfare, no study of politics or economic development can fully explain what the American welfare state does *not* do very well. And of all the welfare state's failures, none is more glaring than its inability to provide for poor children. Understanding what orphanages were, and were not, can shed considerable light on this question. In particular, as we search for new methods of child care at the end of the twentieth century, as we did at its start, we need to understand what was gained and what was lost when orphanages fell out of favor more than half a century ago.

As events in the mid-1990s once again show, the strengths and failings of the American welfare state are powerfully influenced by two running debates. The first concerns whether poor families unable to raise their own children should be aided to do so, or instead should have their children taken from them and placed elsewhere. The second concerns who should be aiding, or separating, poor families: should it be private charity or the government, and if the latter, what level of government? Orphanages were a large part of American society's response to these questions in the nineteenth century. When orphanages were widespread, it was generally agreed that aid should be chiefly private, whether or not families were to be separated. At the same time, families that needed help but were not so completely desperate that they were willing to give up their children to an institution received little or no aid, while the children who did spend time in orphan asylums received little emotional attention. The shift toward public pensions to keep families together, while addressing these two flaws in a system based on asylum care, has itself had different weaknesses, most especially payment levels so low that families remained mired in poverty even when being "helped." America has yet to develop a system of caring for dependent children that works well for the majority of the children in it. If we are ever to do so, perhaps we need to begin by better understanding what we have tried in the past.

1

The Growth and Triumph of an Institution

Several orphan asylums were founded in North America before the American Revolution, and the early Republic saw the gradual spread of institutions for orphaned children in cities on the eastern seaboard. But orphan asylums did not become a widespread method of caring for dependent children in the United States until the 1830s. In colonial America, orphans and other children whose parents were for one reason or another unable to care for them were usually apprenticed or indentured. Indenture continued to be widely employed to care for poor children in the early Republic, but at the same time, two different forms of institutional care for orphaned and dependent children began to spread across the nation. One was public and the other private, and each had been used sparingly in colonial America. The former, publicly managed almshouses, were built in a number of states to care for children as well as ill, aged, poor, and even criminal adults.

After 1800, privately managed orphan asylums also began to be founded in many of the nation's largest cities. In the 1830s, asylums spread much more rapidly, opening in cities across the growing nation to care for children left orphaned by epidemics. Asylums continued to be founded at a rapid pace throughout the 1840s and 1850s, especially after the cholera epidemic of 1849. Many orphan asylums took in poor children with one living parent, known as half-orphans, as well as caring for full orphans; some antebellum institutions even accepted children with two living parents if the family's need was seen as desperate. Antebellum orphan asylums often successfully fulfilled their relatively modest goals: they took in poor children and supplied them with shelter, food, education, and moral and religious guidance.

After the Civil War, the growth of orphan asylums continued to outpace the tremendous growth of the national population. From the 1832 cholera epidemic onward, Catholic institutions were at the forefront of the asylum-building movement. This remained true after the devastation wrought by the Civil War led to an even faster spread of asylums. Between the Civil War and 1890, the number of orphan asylums in the United States tripled. Almost half of the nearly fifty thousand children in asylums at the end of 1890 were in Catholic institutions. By then, thousands of children also lived in Protestant and publicly managed orphan asylums, and Jewish and fraternal asylums had begun to appear. In fact, by 1890 asylums existed in every state where there was significant urban growth. Some of these orphan asylums were small, housing just a few dozen children; others, particularly in New York, were large congregate institutions caring for hundreds of children. Throughout the period, orphan asylums were the nation's main method of caring for dependent children.

Government involvement in asylums, previously limited to occasional grants of money or land, increased greatly in a handful of states in the last decades of the nineteenth century. California and New York paid private asylums to care for children, while Ohio, Indiana, and Connecticut supported county-managed asylums. Michigan founded a large state-run asylum that broke all ties between parents and children before placing children in homes; a number of other states followed suit. Many northern states responded directly to the Civil War's tremendous death toll by founding homes for soldiers' orphans, where the children of dead or disabled Union veterans could be cared for. Private asylums continued to flourish in these states, caring for thousands of children in need, and in most cases eventually returning children to their families.

Throughout the nineteenth century, orphan asylums across the nation remained community institutions, controlled by local groups and serving local interests. Most children within asylum walls after the Civil War were half-orphans or children with one living parent, but many had two parents; the majority returned to their families when they left the asylum. In the postbellum era, asylums continued to raise children, educate them, provide them with religious training, and then either return them to their families or send them into the world prepared to support themselves, just as they had done before the Civil War. Some began to encourage modest contact between their children and the outside world, by allowing them to take day trips, by sending them to outside churches or Sunday schools, and in some cases even by enrolling them in public schools. More than any other late-nineteenth-century institution, orphan asylums helped poor families by caring for their children, for months or years.

By the 1890s, reformers who favored other methods of child care were regularly criticizing orphan asylums as regimented, harsh institutions that failed to develop children's individuality. Despite these attacks, orphan asylums continued to spread across the nation well into the twentieth century. During the first three decades of the twentieth century, more children were cared for in orphan asylums than ever before. Institutions for dependent children appeared in every state that enjoyed—or suffered from—rapid population growth, even as a national consensus was reached, among almost all child welfare reformers other than asylum managers, that asylums should be used only for temporary care and as a last resort.

While this consensus against children's institutions had little immediate impact on most orphan asylums, the alternative methods of care that had come into favor—mothers' pensions and foster care—would supplant asylums as the most common method of caring for dependent children between the 1920s and 1940s. In response to the fact that many widows could now receive state aid to keep their children at home, as well as to the anti-institutional attitude of social work, in the 1920s some asylums began to care for specialized groups of troubled children, while others shifted their focus to placing children in homes and away from providing institutional care. Many eventually became foster care agencies or residential homes for children with emotional or psychological problems; many others closed. Although institutional care continued on as part of the foster care system, the era of the orphan asylum being at the center of the care of dependent children came to an end in the 1930s and 1940s. For nearly a century, however, most children in need of a home relied on orphan asylums.

Poor Relief in the Colonies and Early Republic

Certain themes run throughout the history of poverty, charity, and welfare in the United States. Perhaps the most important of these is the consistency of attitudes toward the poor. For more than two centuries, the majority of Americans have believed that most of the poor were largely to blame for their own poverty, though some important shifts have occurred in how the poor have been viewed and treated. In colonial times, the poor were seen as two separate groups: the deserving poor and the undeserving poor. Poverty was not, by itself, seen as a sign of immorality for all poor individuals. Orphans, elderly widows, and adults made infirm by age or other causes were usually viewed as deserving of aid. Adults who were not regularly employed, but who were seen as capable of working, were widely considered undeserving of any help; their poverty was their own doing.

While the line between worthy and unworthy in colonial thinking was not always absolute and rigid, it clearly existed. Neighbors, especially orphans and aged widows, were worthy of society's help, while strangers and healthy adult males were not. But in colonial America this harsh view of the poor was softened in practice in ways that it is not in the twentieth century. In the colonies, all the poor, whether deserving or not, were considered to be part of a society that was ordered by God's will. Some people were poor and others wealthy because God had decided the world should be that way. The wealthy had a duty to aid their less fortunate neighbors, and even the undeserving poor were treated with a certain amount of charity and dignity.[1]

Specific methods for aiding dependent people developed within local communities in colonial America and remained under local control well into the nineteenth century. These methods were heavily influenced by the somewhat contradictory ideas that there were deserving and undeserving poor and that society had been ordered by God. The fact that severe poverty was still fairly rare in the largely rural seventeenth century also influenced how communities dealt with their poor. The limited need for aid often meant that the needy were treated well, or at least with basic respect. Across the eighteenth century, the extent of poverty increased only gradually, and it remained a fairly minor problem in most communities in 1800. Small amounts of private charity and public welfare were able to care for most of the elderly, sick, impaired, and orphaned. Severe poverty was barely a problem in small towns and rural areas, and was not yet too widespread even in major urban centers like New York City. Most people who needed help received small amounts of aid, such as firewood or coal in the winter, but the number of people who needed more substantial assistance was quite low. Those who received aid were cared for on an individual basis: the elderly and widows with children usually received outdoor relief, which allowed them to stay in their own homes, while orphans were apprenticed. In both cases, the worthy poor remained a part of society. But they were also often stigmatized, though not nearly so harshly as were the supposedly "unworthy" poor. For example, in colonial New Jersey, town paupers were required to wear a letter "P" on their sleeves as well as the initial of their town.[2]

The colonial view of mankind as inherently flawed, and of society as being ordered by the will of God, gradually weakened in the early Republic, while the belief that humans, though flawed, had considerable control over their own characters and actions gained prominence. Individuals could change for the better if they had proper guidance and were willing to try to improve themselves. The categories of deserving and undeserving poor subtly changed. By the early nineteenth century, the undeserving poor were increasingly likely to be blamed for their poverty, and even the deserving poor were often viewed as suspect. The new view of man as perfectible meant that poor people should be encouraged—or forced if necessary—to change the way they acted and, presumably, lift themselves from poverty in the process. The poor, now to blame for their poverty, had become a social problem. This new, harsher view of the poor was widespread in the North. In the more rural South, relatively generous colonial attitudes toward the poor remained prevalent in the early nineteenth century.[3]

Changing ideas about the causes of poverty went hand in hand with other changes in society, particularly the rapid growth of urban centers in the North and the spread of wage labor, each of which fueled increasingly concentrated, and therefore increasingly visible, poverty. As small towns grew into urban communities, a wide variety of public and private institutions aimed at preventing or easing poverty were founded. Public outdoor relief was widely attacked as urban relief rolls grew, but it usually survived, and continued to play an important role in the survival of the poor throughout the century. As public relief became more formalized, many of its recipients were isolated from their communities, usually in institutions, in ways they were not when receiving outdoor relief. More and more dependent children were placed in almshouses, though indenture remained the most common way of dealing with orphans and other dependent children in the 1810s and 1820s. At the same time, numerous private charity organizations formed and attempted to reduce or ease poverty. During the first three decades of the nineteenth century, private benevolent groups multiplied in northeastern cities and began to spread along with the frontier. They too sought to help dependent and destitute people who were "worthy," while refusing aid to the "unworthy" such as criminals and vagrants.[4]

Indenture, also called apprenticeship or binding out, was widely used in colonial society and was particularly adaptable to aiding needy orphans. Orphans were regularly bound out to an adult employer, who was also expected to act as a parental figure. Indentured children worked on farms, in artisanal shops, or as household servants, and were to be provided with skills, fed, and clothed until they came of age. They would presumably receive some religious training. But it was not just orphans who were bound out. In colonial Virginia, children with parents who were deemed "idle" or "dissolute" could be legally removed from their parents and bound out by church wardens. Public officials in Massachusetts had the same power to interfere with a family by removing its children.[5]

Laws passed in the early Republic continued to promote indenture as the best approach for dealing with dependent children. Its terms remained similar to those of the colonial era, though a requirement that children be provided a basic education had become fairly widespread by 1800. For example, New York's poor law of 1788 required the "Master" or "Mistress" to ensure that the apprenticed child learned to read and write. Laws passed in Illinois in 1826 and 1833 made probate judges partially responsible for investigating and enforcing apprenticeship contracts and required that children receive decent treatment and an education.[6]

Until at least the 1830s, indenture remained the most widely used method of providing for children without parents able to raise them, but it was not the only method. In colonial America, as has already been noted, some dependent children were placed in almshouses, where they mixed with the ill, the insane, the elderly, and the criminal. This practice became more common in the first half of the nineteenth century. Prior to the establishment of New York City's first orphan asylum in 1806, the city's only institution caring for poor children was an almshouse. Though generally a last option, almshouses would continue to house large numbers of dependent children until after the Civil War in most northern states, and into the twentieth century in some southern and western states.[7]

The belief that poverty was usually the result of character flaws and that poor people were perfectible had particularly strong implications for poor children. Of all dependent groups, children seemed the least deserving of blame for their condition, which was after all their parents' fault rather than their own. When childhood came to be seen as a separate and distinct phase of life in the early nineteenth century, children were increasingly viewed as unformed innocents. Poor children were seen "as a separate category of worthy dependents." Unlike their parents, poor children seemed likely to benefit from intervention by the government or private charity organizations, since they had presumably not yet developed the character flaws of poor adults.[8] In the eyes of most charity workers, dealing with poor children was less a question of reform than of prevention. In the first few decades of the nineteenth century, intervention in poor children's lives came in the form of indenture and placement in almshouses, just as it had in the eighteenth century. More and more, however, especially from the 1830s on, dependent children were being placed in orphan asylums.

Orphan Asylums Prior to 1830

The first orphanage in the area that would eventually become the United States was established in New Orleans in 1729 under French auspices. The Ursuline convent had begun caring for one orphan soon after its establishment in 1727. When Indian attacks left more children orphaned, the Ursuline nuns, who had already been running a day school and a hospital in connection with their convent, decided that it also needed to serve as an orphan asylum. They cared for dependent children for more than a century, until the city transferred their children to the Poydras Orphan Asylum in 1834.[9] This pattern—individuals with strong religious convictions, often women, seeing children who desperately needed help, and responding by creating an orphan asylum—would be repeated time and again over the following century.

The first orphan asylums begun in the British colonies of North America both seem to have started in 1738. A Lutheran asylum was opened at the Ebenezer Colony in January 1738. It was modeled on an orphan home in Halle, Germany, that had been managed by one of the colony's pastors before he moved to North America. The asylum at Ebenezer does not seem to have lasted very long, but in its first months of existence it was visited by George Whitefield, a prominent British Methodist preacher. He in turn opened a home in Bethesda, Georgia, later that year that was modeled on both the Ebenezer asylum and its inspiration in Halle. According to Elizabeth Wisner, Whitefield was "moved by the miserable situation of the orphans and of the many children living in poor families" in Georgia. He quickly lost control of the asylum, however, after attempting to remove children from families whenever he thought they would be better off in the Bethesda home.[10]

The only publicly managed orphanage built in the United States in the eighteenth century, and the first begun in the new nation, was in Charleston, South Carolina. When the Revolutionary War ended, the city government took on the responsibility of caring for poor orphans. Children were boarded out in families at first, and the city apparently paid for both board and the children's educations. By 1790, Charleston had decided to build an orphan asylum and care for all its needy children in one place. When completed, the Charleston Orphan House was promptly filled with 115 orphans.[11]

Following the creation of the Charleston Orphan House, private associations founded to care for dependent children began to appear in a few northern cities. One association to care for orphans was created in New York City in 1797. Another began in Philadelphia in 1798, established by a Catholic priest to help children orphaned by yellow fever. Both groups soon decided to establish institutions. In 1799, an asylum opened in Baltimore for the care of destitute girls, and the next year an asylum for orphan girls was incorporated in Boston.[12] Thus, at the dawn of the nineteenth century, there were a half-dozen orphan asylums in cities stretching up and down the Atlantic coast.

Before the 1830s, most orphan asylums were Protestant institutions, but Catholic orphan asylums also were founded in a number of cities in the first few decades of the century. In 1801, the Poor Clares, a French religious community, opened an academy for girls in the District of Columbia that also offered a day school for poor children and cared for a few orphans. By 1806, Philadelphia had a second Catholic asylum, joining the one founded eight years earlier. The Sisters of Charity opened St. Joseph's Academy in Emmitsburg, Maryland, in 1809. It functioned as "a boarding school, day school, and orphanage."[13] This was not unusual. The earliest Catholic asylums were often begun by nuns with a mission to educate poor children or care for the ill.[14] Several orders of nuns were forbidden from educating boys, or at least older boys, and most focused on helping girls first. Indeed, the first Catholic asylums in New York City, Boston, Cincinnati, and Troy, New York, all cared only for girls.[15]

Groups of middle-class Protestant women were particularly active in establishing asylums in the Northeast. By 1810, they had created institutions for poor children in Troy, Salem, Newburyport, and Portsmouth. In 1815, a group of women opened an asylum in Philadelphia, "partly in response to the War of 1812, which left many youngsters without one or both parents." In 1817, a group of women founded a Protestant asylum for girls in New Orleans; in 1824, a group of men did the same for boys. By 1830, there were over thirty institutions for dependent children in the United States, almost all of which were either Protestant or Catholic. Some vanished within a few years, but most of the earliest orphan asylums would survive for many decades and become important institutions within their communities.[16] They were built in an era in which, as Anne Firor Scott writes, "voluntary associations of all kinds proliferated, to supplement the old institutional structures of family, church, and local government."[17]

In 1830, the vast majority of asylums in existence were being managed by members of specific neighborhood churches. When some were created by various Protestants working together, they viewed themselves as nonsectarian because their trustees and boards of managers mingled together members of Presbyterian, Methodist, Episcopalian, Baptist, and other Protestant churches. Partly because of this, Table 1.1 underestimates the number of Protestant asylums, which undoubtedly outnumbered Catholic asylums prior to the 1830s. In fact, many of the asylums whose management type is listed as "unknown" during the nineteenth century were this kind of "nonsectarian," but actually Protestant, asylum. In addition, since Table 1.1 only includes asylums still in existence in 1910, it obviously does not include asylums that had existed early in the nineteenth century but at some point had gone out of existence. This does not seem to have happened very often; most orphan asylums were desperately needed and flourished from their founding into the twentieth century. But it should be kept in mind that Table 1.1 underestimates the total number of asylums in existence before 1830, probably by between six and ten asylums. Despite these problems, Table 1.1 shows several important things, including the fact that throughout the first half of the nineteenth century the rapid expansion of asylums was both a Catholic and a Protestant phenomenon, and that asylums began appearing at a much faster rate in the 1830s.[18]

Not surprisingly, the largest cities had multiple asylums. By 1830, four orphan asylums had been founded in New York City, and a number of other cities also had two or three asylums, including Philadelphia, Boston, and Albany in the North, Baltimore and Washington in the middle Atlantic region, and New Orleans and Savannah in the South. The same pattern held true through the Civil War era. More than half of the first two hundred orphan asylums existed in just eighteen cities, and most of the rest were also in large or midsize urban centers such as Buffalo, Charleston, Detroit, Memphis, Milwaukee, Rochester, San Francisco, Syracuse, and Utica.

Epidemics, Urban Poverty, and the Founding of Orphan Asylums, 1830–1860

A number of factors helped fuel the rapid spread of orphan asylums across the nation from the early 1830s onward. Some of these, such as religious beliefs, urban growth, and an increased emphasis on the importance of environment in shaping children, were also important in the creation of other institutions. Some societal changes were particularly important in the spread of orphan asylums, especially the growing belief that childhood was a separate, distinct stage of life. According to Carl Degler, by 1830 families had become far more child-centered than they had been half a century before. In part, the creation of large numbers of orphan asylums reflected this development. As middle-class men and women nurtured their own children more carefully, they also opened orphan asylums for other people's children. And for native-born reformers concerned about the influx of millions of immigrants, children were, as David Ward writes, "regarded as critical targets of reform."[19]

The spread of mercantile capitalism in the first half of the nineteenth century and the wage labor that was its central feature were also important societal changes that furthered the development of orphan asylums and other institutions designed to "deal with" or care for the poor. In the first few decades of the nineteenth century, mercantile capitalism was already changing the class structure of American cities. After the Civil War, industrialization and the increased poverty it brought to urban centers would help fuel the continued multiplication of orphan asylums.[20] In the 1830s, however, it was the combination of wage labor, which left many workers and their families unable to deal with any calamity they might face, and the prevalence of cholera, yellow fever, and other diseases that led orphan asylums to spread across the nation.

But it is important to note that this spread occurred within a specific economic and cultural setting. A variety of ethnic and religious groups, fairly recent arrivals to the United States who were concerned with their own survival and their relationship with American society, chose to build orphan asylums. And they made this choice in a society undergoing rapid and extensive economic change. Ira Katznelson and Margaret Weir write that "early capitalist industrialization created a potential for disorder that was managed by the creation of public schools as one way to protect the political regime and the economic order." Unlike public schools, most asylums were not conscious attempts to protect the political regime, although they often did deliberately train children to fit into the prevailing economic order. More fundamentally, asylums were responses to disorder at the local level in the form of parental death, illness, or unemployment. Many of the groups that founded orphan asylums did so to protect themselves and their community's future.[21]

Another important factor leading to the spread of orphan asylums was the tremendous growth that most urban centers experienced in the first few decades of the nineteenth century, growth fueled by increasing immigration from Europe. The overall population of the nation rose from 13 million in 1830 to 31 million in 1860; during the same period, the growth in urban areas was even faster. In 1830, less than 10 percent of Americans lived in "urban" areas of 2,500 or more people, but by 1860, 20 percent of the population were urban dwellers. Furthermore, the number of foreign-born people living in the United States had risen dramatically by 1860, when over four million immigrants lived in the mid-Atlantic states alone.[22] Within these growing, and increasingly immigrant, cities, as a result of the increasing prevalence of both manufacturing and wage labor, the lower ranks of the poor and working class grew. In addition, tremendous improvements in the nation's transportation system also spurred asylum growth, though less directly than immigration, urban growth, and the spread of wage labor. Canals and railroads made travel easier with every passing decade, and facilitated the spread of people and of diseases such as cholera. Movement from one place to another in response to the labor market was a part of American life by the middle of the century, particularly for the poor.[23] This constant movement in search of jobs reduced the chances that a family would have relatives nearby if an emergency arose, for native-born people as well as for immigrants.

Largely confined to cities, orphan asylums appeared in states across the nation. By 1850, they could be found in at least twenty-one states and the District of Columbia. Four more states saw the birth of their first asylums in the 1850s, including California, which had five asylums founded in that decade. By 1860, only eight states were without at least one orphan asylum. Five of those—Arkansas, Florida, Iowa, Oregon, and Texas—were very young states, having entered the Union after 1835. Of the three remaining states, one (New Hampshire) was very small, and the other two (North Carolina and Vermont) had almost no urban population to speak of. In fact, of these eight states, all but New Hampshire had a much smaller percentage of their people living in urban areas than did the United States as a whole. In 1860, Iowa's population was only 8.9 percent urban, and of the other six states without asylums, the highest urban percentage was Oregon at 5.7 percent. For the nation as a whole in 1860, the urban population was a much higher 19.8 percent.[24]

In the early 1830s, a savage cholera epidemic struck across urban America, leading to the rapid proliferation of orphan asylums in the early and mid-1830s. The Sisters of Charity arrived in St. Louis in 1828 to open a hospital; just six years later, the bishop also provided them with a building for a coed orphan asylum. The Sisters of Charity opened a day school in Albany in 1829. Cholera struck the city in 1831, and by the next year the sisters had also opened an orphan asylum.[25] By 1840, there were at least two dozen Catholic orphan asylums in the United States, most of which apparently also operated day schools for poor children. The 1832 cholera epidemic ravaged Philadelphia, Baltimore, New Orleans, and cities throughout New York and New Jersey. However, it only lightly touched most of New England, which may partially explain Boston's failure to move heavily toward institutional care of dependent children in a decade when so many other cities did so.[26] Boston's Irish Catholic community, while poor, did not face the immediate need in 1832–1833 that cities like New Orleans and Cincinnati did. The first Catholic orphan asylum in Boston opened in 1832—the year of the cholera epidemic—but its founders had been raising money in hopes of opening an asylum since at least 1823.[27]

Ethnicity played an important role within the Catholic Church's charity works. Most of the Catholic orphan asylums begun before 1840 were Irish in origin; were run by an order with its origins in Ireland, such as the Sisters of Charity of Emmitsburg; and served a largely Irish clientele. With the arrival of large numbers of German Catholic immigrants over the next two decades, this began to change. When Cincinnati was ravaged by cholera in 1832, German Catholics saw their children cared for in St. Peter's Orphan Asylum, an Irish institution. While this was clearly preferable to German Catholic children receiving no care at all or being raised in a Protestant institution, the city's German Catholics did not like having to rely on an Irish Catholic institution. In 1837, Cincinnati's German Catholics organized the St. Aloysius Orphan Society, which purchased a building just two years later. In 1849–1850, a German Catholic asylum was opened in St. Louis, again because cholera had led to many of that city's German Catholic children being placed in Irish Catholic asylums (there were already three Catholic asylums in St. Louis in 1845, presumably all Irish in origin). Over the next decade, German Catholic orphan asylums were established in Buffalo, Louisville, Pittsburgh, New York City, Baltimore, and Philadelphia.[28]

Whether founded by Catholics or Protestants, orphan asylums outside the major northeastern cities were particularly likely to be responses to epidemics. All three of the orphan asylums in New Orleans that Priscilla Clement studied, established between 1817 and 1835, "were founded for the same instrumental reason—to cope with orphanage caused by disease and immigration." New Orleans was hit harder by epidemics during the nineteenth century than any other southern city, and largely because of this, it also had more orphan asylums than any other southern city throughout the century. In 1860, only Philadelphia and New York City had more orphan asylums than New Orleans. The outbreak of cholera in Louisville in 1832 led the Sisters of Charity of Nazareth to open St. Vincent's Orphan Asylum that year. Cholera hit Cincinnati hard in 1832 and was partially responsible for the founding of the Cincinnati Orphan Asylum the next year. In the early 1830s, St. Peter's Orphan Asylum, also in Cincinnati, expanded greatly to care for children orphaned by cholera. Though hardly the only disease that led to the founding of orphan asylums, cholera may have been responsible for the creation of more asylums than any other single cause prior to the Civil War.[29]

Other diseases also led to many children's need for help from an asylum. In this era, tuberculosis probably accounted for more deaths in the United States than any other disease. People living in crowded, poorly ventilated housing (particularly women) were especially vulnerable. In addition, yellow fever "took on a new ferocity in American seaports" between 1790 and 1860. Asylums cared for numerous children who had lost one or both parents to these diseases as well.[30]

The 1832 cholera epidemic was neither the last to occur nor the last to lead to the founding of orphan asylums.[31] To cite just a few examples, asylums were founded in response to children orphaned by the 1849–1850 cholera epidemic in Buffalo, San Francisco, Milwaukee, Sandusky, St. Louis, and Chicago. In 1848, the Sisters of Charity arrived in Buffalo to care for children left parentless by the cholera epidemic of that year. In 1850, Milwaukee's Catholic community opened an asylum for "a score or more of dependent boys left destitute by the [cholera] epidemic." The same disease struck San Francisco in 1850; early in 1851 a small group of Presbyterians formed a society to care for orphan and half-orphan Protestant children. By 1853, the society had purchased land in the city and erected an institution. The Chicago Orphan Asylum, the first institution of its kind in that city, was founded in 1849 largely in response to cholera, which had left the city's almshouse "so badly overcrowded that cholera victims and their children were being turned away."[32]

Just as religious groups responded to epidemics by building orphan asylums, they also built institutions to care for children left orphaned or destitute by accidents, desertion, and other causes. In 1829, a difficult winter left many Catholic immigrant families in Philadelphia "reduced to dire need," and St. Joseph's Orphan Asylum was already full. The pastor of St. John's Church led a movement that quickly established St. John's Orphan Asylum, which like St. Joseph's was run by the Sisters of Charity.[33] Other Catholic leaders also responded to the poverty in their communities. A priest in Pittsburgh, aroused to sympathy by the growing number of dependent children in that city, organized St. Paul's Orphan Society in the late 1830s.[34]

Like Catholics, Protestant groups responded to children's poverty, usually by building an institution. The Female Beneficent Society of

Hartford, Connecticut, was founded in 1819 to aid friendless and indigent girls. It later merged with the Hartford Orphan Asylum, which opened to aid indigent boys in the early 1830s. A few years later the New Haven Orphan Asylum was begun by a physician and the pastor of Trinity Church, who had found themselves caring for four children left orphaned by their mother's death just a few months after cholera killed their father. In New York City, members of the Protestant Episcopal church gathered in 1851 to decide how to care for three children "who had been baptized in St. Paul's Chapel." The group soon established the Orphans' Home and Asylum after "numerous cases were brought to light, where the same charity could have been as properly extended, had there been means to do so."[35]

There were a few orphan asylums founded before 1860 that were neither Catholic nor Protestant. As has already been mentioned, the first public asylum was founded in Charleston in 1790. The first association to care for dependent Jewish children in the United States was apparently the Hebrew Benevolent and Orphan Asylum Society, which began in New York City in 1822. The second did not follow until 1855, when institutions for Jewish children opened in Philadelphia and New Orleans. A few orphan asylums designed to care for nonwhite children also opened before the Civil War. The Association for the Benefit of Colored Orphans in the City of New York was founded in 1836. The association's attempts to rent a house failed, apparently due to prejudice against the idea of aiding black children, so a house was purchased. In 1842, the city provided a large plot of land, upon which a "plain, substantial building was erected." The Thomas Asylum for Orphan and Destitute Indian Children was incorporated in New York in 1855.[36]

Orphan asylums also appeared outside the northeastern states as responses to poverty. Marian J. Morton has argued that the founding of orphan asylums in Ohio in the 1850s was "an outgrowth of the conviction that dependent children and adults should not be housed together in an undifferentiated facility." Instead, dependent children were to be removed from almshouses and placed in institutions where they would be cared for more properly.[37] The fear of poor but basically innocent children mixing with adult paupers and criminals in almshouses would serve as an even more important impetus to orphan asylum creation (and to the growth of some already existing asylums into huge institutions) after the Civil War. Throughout the first half of the nineteenth century, most orphan asylums began as temporary homes for a handful of orphans and half-orphans, whatever the reasons for their parents' deaths. In many cases, orphan asylums founded to care for children orphaned by cholera or another disease quickly became homes for children with living, but poor, parents.[38]

In California, orphan asylums appeared almost immediately after the gold rush of 1849. Families that journeyed to the Pacific coast in the mid–nineteenth century often had no relations within two thousand miles. The isolation of early migrants to California was similar to, or worse than, that of European immigrants in eastern cities. They might know a few other people in the city they lived in, but those people were probably also poor. Decent housing was difficult to find as the state's population grew at a tremendous pace. Sundered from broader family and community ties, families that lost a parent to serious illness or death were unable to care for their children. Children left homeless and fatherless quickly became a problem. Orphan asylums run by religious bodies were California's response, as they had been in eastern states. San Francisco had a Protestant and a Catholic orphan asylum by 1852, and the first orphan asylum in Los Angeles opened in 1856. Other asylums followed quickly and remained an important part of California's system of child care into the 1920s.[39]

Although they were far less common in southern states than in the Northeast during the first half of the nineteenth century, as we have seen, some orphan asylums appeared quite early in the South. They continued to be built in or near cities up to the eve of the Civil War. As elsewhere, Catholic care of dependent children often began in connection with schools or hospitals. When the Sisters of Charity converted a church into a hospital in Nashville in 1848, the hospital included an orphan asylum. In Memphis, the St. Agnes Academy began caring for orphans in 1851. In the middle of the Civil War, St. Mary's Orphanage was founded in Nashville, apparently the state's first institution solely for the care of dependent children.[40]

Like ethnic immigrant groups in northern cities, free blacks responded to poverty within their community by creating and supporting charitable organizations. New Orleans's free black community established numerous benevolent societies in the antebellum years, including a Catholic orphan asylum. This process continued after the Civil War. Black communities faced much harsher discrimination from public relief sources than any ethnic immigrant group and responded by creating a wide variety of community organizations, including orphan asylums.[41] There were also white groups seeking to aid poor blacks, usually for religious reasons. For example, in the 1830s, two Quaker women founded the Association for the Benefit of the Colored Orphan in New York City after learning that none of the city's institutions would accept two black orphans they were trying to help.[42]

From the Civil War to the Progressive Era

After the Civil War, orphan asylums were founded in even greater numbers than in the antebellum period. They were built in every region, centering largely in the Northeast but also multiplying or appearing for the first time in many western and southern states. The devastation caused by the war flooded asylums with requests for help and led a number of states to create large, publicly managed "Soldiers' Orphans' Homes" in the 1860s and 1870s; as the century moved on, the effects of the war itself became less important, but as the nation continued to grow both more urban and more industrial, and as immigration continued to grow, the need for orphan asylums increased. As before the Civil War, most new asylums were founded in or near urban centers. The number of Catholic and Protestant asylums skyrocketed, and public asylums appeared in meaningful numbers for the first time.[43] The number of new Catholic and Protestant asylums built each decade was similar, and the rate of growth stabilized between 1850 and 1870 at approximately three dozen new asylums of each kind. During the 1870s, county-based asylums began to appear, a trend that greatly increased in the 1880s, the same decade when eight new state-managed asylums were founded. Jewish and fraternal asylums were still rare in 1890, while the number of new asylums of unknown management type skyrocketed in the 1880s. This may represent a real growth in the number of nonsectarian asylums in existence; it is more likely that these asylums, managed by private corporations, still retained clear religious viewpoints even though they were not actually built or run by churches or religious groups by the time of the census in 1910 (see Table 1.2).

Not surprisingly, when asylums had meaningful help from a state or county government, a higher percentage of the state's population was within asylums than would otherwise have been expected. The most important factor, however, in determining the percent of children in orphan asylums at any given time seems to have been the state's level of urbanization. Highly urbanized states almost always had a relatively high percentage of their population in orphan asylums in 1890; rural states had few children in asylums. In fact, the fit between urban population and asylum population was very tight, especially if one discounts states where public funding for asylums was widely available.[44] While the exact relationship between urban growth and poverty remains unclear, it seems very clear that urban growth and the creation of large numbers of orphan asylums were closely linked in the late nineteenth century.[45]

One reason for the connection between urbanization and high orphan asylum populations is that most cities included multiple ethnic communities. These communities often centered around a church, and such churches were important in the creation of charity institutions. Olivier Zunz writes about Detroit in 1880 that "class affiliations were secondary to people's ethnic attachments." These ethnic attachments often played a key role in the founding of orphan asylums.[46] By the 1880s, large cities such as New York and Philadelphia were likely to have orphan asylums run by a variety of Protestant churches, a number of parish-based Catholic asylums, some nonsectarian asylums, and often one Jewish asylum. In densely populated cities, many families, particularly those of immigrants, were without relatives financially able to help them through hard times or take in children after a death or during a serious illness. Community institutions such as orphan asylums filled this need. Because orphan asylums had become a widely accepted response to the poverty of children, when a specific religious group became concerned about its own dependent children, opening an orphan asylum probably seemed the obvious action to take. It was not just a matter of ethnic or religious survival; for some groups, building their own orphan asylum might also be a matter of ethnic or religious pride.

In many northern states, the Civil War and its immediate aftermath saw an increase in the involvement of state governments in the care of orphans. In some cases, the children of soldiers were placed in private asylums at state expense when their mothers were unable to support them. In Pennsylvania, for example, during the war children were kept in Protestant and Catholic asylums, and the state paid $100 per child annually.[47] In the 1870s, Pennsylvania also opened a number of orphan asylums for the children of Union soldiers who had died in the Civil War. By 1876, the state government "had cared for more than 8,000 soldiers' orphans, almost all of them in orphanages."[48]

Few states responded as strongly as Pennsylvania to the problem of war orphans, but most northern states did build at least one home for soldiers' orphans in the years after the war. The Illinois Soldiers' Orphans' Home opened in 1865, to care for children whose fathers had died or become disabled during the war. In the 1870s, its admissions policy broadened to include the children of any Civil War veterans, whatever the cause of their children's need for shelter. Eventually, the home accepted dependent children whether or not they had any connection to a Civil War veteran. In the late 1920s, veterans' groups succeeded in changing the home's policy back to accepting only the children of veterans.[49] Illinois was unusual; state-run homes for soldiers' orphans were a short-lived phenomenon in most northeastern states, and few survived by 1900. Even so, they were emblematic of the response by state governments to the war's destruction and of the increased willingness of state governments during this period to become at least somewhat involved in child welfare.

Some states became more directly involved in providing funding to private orphan asylums after the war. This was usually the result of the broad interest state legislatures began to take in public institutions such as prisons and poorhouses. No state developed a tighter connection between state government and public and private institutions, including orphan asylums, than New York. As early as 1856, a state senate committee recommended that children should be removed from poorhouses and placed either in private orphan asylums at state or county expense, or in public asylums built specifically to hold dependent children. When the legislature did not act in the 1850s, the problem of children kept in poorhouses continued to grow. The number of children in New York's poorhouses more than tripled between 1861 and 1866, helping to lead to the creation of a State Board of Public Charities, whose members had authority to inspect public institutions and make recommendations about improving them. The State Board pushed for the removal of children from almshouses, with eventual success. The New York Children's Act of 1875 mandated that children be removed from almshouses and placed in homes or institutions of their parents' religious backgrounds.[50]

The Children's Act of 1875 added several thousand children to New York's orphanage population. But the orphan asylums were able to accept this increased load partly because of another change. In 1874, a new constitutional amendment had prohibited state aid to private agencies. There were exceptions, but not for orphan asylums. This amendment put an end to the lump-sum state payments that had often helped asylums erect new buildings. Filling the void created by the cessation of state payments, a loose but reliable system of per capita payments from counties and towns to private asylums developed over the second half of the 1870s, which came to include not just children moved directly from almshouses to orphan asylums, but most children already in orphan asylums. Throughout the 1880s, the state mandated that local aid be given to orphan asylums. The availability of this money had substantial long-term effects on the state's orphan asylums: because New York's asylums could now accept a higher percentage of applicants than they did before 1875, the population of the state's orphan asylums doubled between 1875 and 1885.[51]

Some historians have credited the various laws mandating the removal of children from almshouses with leading to "the primacy of the orphan asylum" after the 1870s.[52] In fact, orphan asylums were already the nation's chief method of caring for dependent children before the Civil War. When children were removed from almshouses, they often did wind up in orphan asylums; in many instances, orphan asylums were the best available place to put them. In some states, such as New York and Ohio, when children were banned from public almshouses, it led to increased government funding for orphan asylums.[53]

It is worth noting that the drive to remove poor children from almshouses was part of a larger reform movement that sought to take a number of different groups, including children and the mentally ill, out of almshouses and place them in more specialized, and presumably more humane, institutions. In addition, in the late nineteenth and early twentieth centuries, institutions were built in a number of states to care for children with disabilities; homes for crippled children, for blind children, for deaf and dumb children all appeared, allowing these children to receive better care than they had previously received in almshouses. Orphan asylums only dealt with children who were poor; they had never been willing to care for children with more severe individual problems.

Public funding for New York's orphan asylums did not go unchallenged. Opposition to public funding of private (particularly Catholic) institutions had existed for several decades before it reached its peak in the early 1890s. At New York's 1894 Constitutional Convention, a petition was presented, with 200,000 signatures, asking for a constitutional amendment banning both the state and local governments from giving aid to any sectarian charity, including orphan asylums. The main argument used against public funding was that the money given to private institutions had largely gone to build Catholic asylums, which made up almost half of New York's orphan asylums in the 1890s. This was seen as favoring one religious group over others; that the favored group was Catholic was probably the real source of hostility to state funding. (Most of the numerous "nonsectarian" asylums that also received public money were Protestant institutions in both their outlook and religious teaching.) The convention examined both public and private institutions and decided that greater regulation of orphan asylums was necessary, so it increased the State Board of Charities' supervisory powers. The state legislature also lost the power to force local governments to contribute to children's institutions. But aside from these minor victories, the opposition to public funding failed: no constitutional amendment banning it was passed. Sectarian asylums, including Catholic institutions, could still receive public funds from any level of government that chose to distribute them. Per capita grants, which had been mandated by the state, were now given out at local discretion. In practice, local governments continued to help fund privately managed orphan asylums.[54]

Governments in several other states were also giving money to children's institutions in the late nineteenth century. In the last two decades of the century, Connecticut began acknowledging a public responsibility for its dependent children. Unlike New York, it created public institutions. In 1883, the Connecticut legislature passed a law that prohibited the placement of children over two years of age in almshouses and established a series of county homes for children. There had been only a few hundred children in the state's almshouses, so their removal did not greatly increase the population of the state's orphan asylums, nor did the movement of the children necessitate the creation of public asylums.

A few years later, Connecticut's State Board of Charities claimed that the reason for establishing county homes had been "the increase of the foreign population and the numbers of destitute children overlooked by private charities." As elsewhere, Connecticut's private orphan asylums cared for children they agreed to accept from parents. Private asylums also accepted children committed by town selectmen as destitute, who were then supported in the asylum at public expense. Either of these kinds of children could be removed from privately run orphan asylums by their parents at any time. However, the new county homes only received children from the courts. If a child was separated from his or her parents due to their being "vicious" or "cruel," then legal guardianship was awarded to the county home and state funds were supplied. This led to a dual system of care that, in theory, refused to provide public funds for any child whose parents' only flaw was poverty, but provided public funds and management for children who had "unworthy" parents.[55] Because a family's poverty was often seen as a sign that parents were unworthy, in practice the line of distinction between poor and "vicious" was often blurred, and the county homes undoubtedly held many children whose parents were poor rather than "cruel."

Between the 1860s and the 1890s, Ohio and Indiana also developed dual systems consisting of county-run public asylums for wards of the state and private asylums for all other dependent children. By 1880, nine county homes had been established in Ohio. After an 1883 law mandating that children under three could not be mixed with adult paupers in almshouses, county-run asylums began to appear much more rapidly.[56]

In the South, public aid to orphan asylums, while rare, did occur in some urban centers. Charities in New Orleans received more public aid than those in any other southern city, except perhaps the public orphan asylum in Charleston. Subsidies from the city government regularly aided the orphan asylums that had developed in response to New Orleans's frequent epidemics. In the late nineteenth century, these city subsidies continued, but state subsidies were ended in 1870 and became unconstitutional in 1879. Other southern states gave varying amounts of aid to orphan asylums. North Carolina, for example, regularly gave money to the Masons' Oxford Orphan Asylum, including $10,000 in 1890, and gave smaller amounts to an asylum for "colored orphans." But most of North Carolina's and South Carolina's orphan asylums relied completely on private funding.[57]

As in the South, most midwestern governments gave little aid to private asylums in the late nineteenth century. Illinois, for example, did fund a home for soldiers' orphans, but the state had little to do with private asylums or the children in them. By 1890, private charities and county governments did occasionally work together to help support dependent children sent to industrial schools by county courts. Some asylums, such as the Angel Guardian Orphanage in Chicago, eventually reconfigured themselves into industrial training schools to become eligible for these funds. And though some counties in Illinois had contracts with private asylums and paid them a per capita fee to care for children, most did not. For most children in orphan asylums in Illinois, public money was unavailable, and asylums were completely dependent on private donors.[58]

Michigan also left privately managed orphan asylums, and the children in them, completely alone. A dual system of care developed: public care for state wards and private care for poor children who retained some sort of family ties—in other words, for the vast majority of dependent children. The Michigan system was more hostile to poor families on public support than Connecticut's, however, and the line between private and public asylums was much clearer. In 1871, Michigan decided to create a large, state-run asylum. The Michigan State Public School opened in 1874 and accepted only children who were legally given over to the state. The main focus of the school, which soon became quite large, was to educate children briefly before placing them in family homes. In the process, all ties between the children and their own families were broken. In the 1880s, Minnesota copied the Michigan method and created its own public school, which also served as a placing-out agency. In both states, private orphan asylums were left to their own devices.[59] A number of other states adopted the Michigan plan over the next few decades. Parents who were unable to care for their children, and who could not find a private asylum to help them, were forced to turn to the large state public schools, which would permanently separate them from their children.

California, still a young state with a small population in the late nineteenth century, did more to support its dependent children than any other state, with the possible exception of New York. During the 1850s and 1860s, several asylums had been granted lump-sum subsidies. In 1870, California's legislature provided for annual payments to be made to private orphan asylums. This was done out of a sense of responsibility toward dependent children and also partly to end the special lobbying for appropriations that asylums had been conducting in the legislature.

Four years later, the grants were raised from $50 to $75 for each full orphan and from $25 to $50 for each half-orphan. By the 1880s, California was paying institutions $100 for each full orphan cared for, and $75 for each half-orphan or abandoned child. From July 1, 1886, to June 30, 1887, more than half of the $400,000 the state paid to charities went to orphan asylums.[60]

By 1890, eighteen of the nation's forty-two states had passed some form of law regarding caring for dependent children.[61] In many of these states, however, such laws affected only children who became legal wards of the state and could be placed out. Many poor families survived on limited incomes and small amounts of outdoor relief. For those destitute families who were unable to secure outdoor relief, or for whom it was inadequate, there were few options. One was to completely give up rights to their children. Another, widely preferred by many families, was to use orphan asylums. Only New York and California provided public money to help private institutions that were serving a recognized public good.

Even in New York, state government involvement with orphan asylums was less extensive than with some other institutions. For example, the 1870s saw "the growth of a statewide asylum system" for the mentally ill, within which asylums were built, funded, and managed by the government.[62] The reason for the difference was not that helping poor children was seen as less of a public duty than aiding the mentally ill. Instead, it was a difference in how much private care was available for each group when the state became involved. As the state moved into mental health care, there were few private institutions in existence, so the state began building its own. But when the state decided that dependent children were a public responsibility, dozens of private orphan asylums already existed, and paying them to care for public wards made more sense than building new, publicly run institutions.

From 1890 to the mid-1920s, asylums continued to be built all across the nation.[63] The number of both Catholic and Protestant asylums rose steadily from 1890 to 1923, and each declined somewhat between 1923 and 1933. (The total number of asylums in 1933 was only slightly smaller than it had been in 1923, while the number of asylums with unknown management increased by almost one hundred between 1923 and 1933. Thus, the seeming decline in Catholic and Protestant asylums during that decade may just be an artifact of the limited information offered by the 1933 institutional census.) Between 1890 and 1933, the number of Jewish asylums rose from nine to forty, while the number of fraternal asylums rose from four in 1890 to eighteen in 1910, then skyrocketed to eighty by 1923. County and city asylums, which had begun a rapid growth period in the 1870s, continued to appear, although more slowly, as did state-managed asylums. The total number of institutions for dependent children in the United States probably peaked sometime in the 1920s, at between 1,300 and 1,350 (see Table 1.3).

The number of children held by asylums also varied notably over time and by management. The mean population of all orphan asylums was just under 85 children per asylum in 1890 and had risen to almost 110 children by 1910. By 1923, the mean asylum population had dropped back down to 91 children, probably influenced by the increasing use of foster care as well as the creation in most states of limited mothers' pensions programs. Finally, in 1933, when orphan asylums were about to start receding from the American scene (as they had from child welfare theory over two decades earlier), the depths of the depression had driven the average population of orphan asylums over 115. Catholic asylums, always accused of being far too large, were in fact quite big, peaking, at least so far as institutional census years go, at an average of 173 children each in 1910. But Jewish asylums were larger than Catholic asylums in three of the four census years listed in Table 1.4, and state-managed asylums were larger than Jewish asylums after 1890. Protestant asylums were smaller. County and city asylums were fairly small, until the depression drove their populations up dramatically in the early 1930s, as it did for state-managed asylums (see Table 1.4).

As they had been earlier in the century, black children continued to be largely excluded from orphan asylums built by whites. After the Civil War, the Catholic Josephite Fathers, a group concerned with "the conversion and care of the colored people," opened the St. Francis School and Colored Orphanage in Baltimore. When Chattanooga, Tennessee, suffered from a harsh yellow fever epidemic in 1878, black children continued to be excluded from the local orphanage. A white northern woman tried to get the city or county to found an orphanage for black children, but when they resisted she opened a private asylum herself.[64] In 1890, just twenty-seven asylums existed to care exclusively for black children. They were rare or nonexistent in New England states, the West, and the deep South. Pennsylvania and Maryland each had four orphan asylums for black children, New York and Missouri each had three, and there were two asylums for black children in Indiana, Louisiana, and Tennessee.[65] In addition, 120 asylums for white children occasionally accepted black children as well. But most of these "mixed" asylums held very few blacks. For example, in 1890 only one of California's "mixed" asylums held more than two black children: a Catholic asylum that was caring for 566 boys, 32 of whom were black. The majority of mixed asylums were in New York and Ohio; in the latter state, a number of county asylums held a dozen or more black children. In the South, it was especially rare for children of different races to be in the same orphan asylum. Louisiana, Kentucky, Mississippi, and Tennessee each had one mixed asylum in 1890, holding a total of just five black children.[66]

While many asylums built in the 1890s and 1900s were relatively large, often holding more than one hundred children right from the start, small asylums continued to be founded, especially in rural areas. For example, in 1896 two Ohio Mennonites opened an orphanage on their farm, which then moved to Liberty, Ohio in 1900. This orphanage was described in Mennonite publications, and partly as a result, in 1909 some Pennsylvania Mennonites decided to found their own institution. The Children's Home opened in Millersville, Pennsylvania, in 1911. By September of that year, twenty-four children lived in the home.[67]

Despite the conclusions of the White House Conference of 1909 against institutional care, discussed in the next section, asylums continued to appear virtually everywhere between 1910 and 1923. Even more than a decade after the conference, the only states that had fewer asylums in 1923 than they had had in 1910 were Indiana, which dropped from forty-two to thirty-three, Maryland (from thirty-three to thirty-one), and New Hampshire (from seventeen to fifteen). From 1923 to 1933, more states showed a drop in the number of asylums: California, Massachusetts, New Jersey, New York, Ohio, and Pennsylvania (all of which had relied heavily on orphan asylums for decades), as well as nineteen other states and the District of Columbia. But in most of these states the decline was quite small. Many states already had a dozen or more asylums in 1890; others, such as Arkansas, Colorado, Iowa, Kansas, North Carolina, Texas, and Virginia, saw a dramatic increase in the number of their orphan asylums between 1890 and 1910. In a few states, especially relatively young ones, orphan asylums were much more widespread in 1933 than they had been in 1923: Arizona went from three asylums in 1923 to ten in 1933, Florida from ten to eighteen, Oklahoma from fourteen to twenty-three. Clearly, orphan asylums as homes for dependent children flourished in many parts of the nation long after they had fallen out of favor with state child welfare officials. As state populations grew and became more urbanized, orphan asylums continued to be built.[68]

The White House Conference of 1909

The complaints made against orphan asylums in the late nineteenth century escalated in the Progressive Era.[69] One speaker at the National Conference of Jewish Charities in 1904 responded to a speech praising orphan asylums by stating that "there is one side perhaps that many of you have not considered; the individuality is destroyed in an institution of that kind with a thousand children, and how? The child is reared by the bell. The bell rings in the morning to rise, the bell rings to dress, the bell rings for prayers. . . The consequence is that the child is reared to do only something in the world that it has its attention called to. . . Believe me, ladies and gentlemen, there is no Ideal Orphan Asylum, because the Orphan Asylum is not the ideal of the rearing of fatherless and motherless children."[70]

The idea that huge institutions were far too regimented, and inherently incapable of fostering independence and individuality in children, was widely accepted after the turn of the century. Not everyone agreed, though. In 1903, the supervisor of Catholic Charities in Brooklyn admitted that the greater the size of an asylum, the more difficult encouraging individuality in its children would be. But he also argued that "number is not always a foe to the process, else our public school system in this respect is fundamentally wrong since individual training is not attempted."[71] Other complaints that had surfaced regularly in the 1880s and 1890s also continued to be made after the turn of the century.[72] Child-placing advocates were particularly likely to argue that more children were institutionalized than really needed aid. They claimed that an excess of institutions led poor parents to give up their children, even when they were actually still able to support those children. And public funding of private asylums remained a regular target.[73]

Attacks on orphan asylums found their greatest forum at the 1909

White House Conference on Dependent Children. President Theodore Roosevelt called the conference at the urging of several prominent reformers, none of whom was an advocate of orphan asylums. The membership of the conference reflected this. There were far more placing-out advocates and state board members present than orphan asylum superintendents; while the first two groups did not agree on everything, they usually agreed in disliking orphan asylums. Beginning with the idea that "home life" was the most desirable situation for rearing children, the conference's debates took for granted that asylums were an inherently inferior method of caring for poor children.

The members of the White House Conference came to a number of conclusions. The most important, and in the long run the most influential, was that children should not be removed from their parents simply because a family was poor. When it was necessary to remove children, they should be placed in carefully selected foster homes, which were deemed superior to institutions. Orphan asylums were a distant third choice; institutions, when used, should be for temporary care of children only, and if possible in small cottages rather than crowded congregate asylums. Annual state inspections should be made of every kind of agency that cared for dependent children. In effect, orphan asylum managers were told that they were the last resort.

While the conference's critique of orphan asylums had little immediate impact on asylums themselves, it did stimulate the use of other methods of child care, which would eventually lead to a movement away from institutional care for poor children. Even though the conference had endorsed privately funded mothers' pensions, not publicly funded ones, the passage of mothers' pensions laws in most states in the 1910s was partially due to the conference. So was the increase in children placed out in boarding homes, increasingly known as foster care.[74] The White House Conference's conclusions were the definitive statement of Progressive child welfare: children should be kept in homes, either their own or foster homes, and not in institutions.

Managers of Catholic institutions for dependent children quickly responded to the White House Conference. At the first National Conference of Catholic Charities the following year, the superior of the Sisters of Charity of Emmitsburg, Maryland, whose order had been in charge of dozens of asylums for decades, defended orphan asylums. He pointed out that comparing asylums to ideal homes, as asylum critics almost always did, was unfair and unrealistic. He argued that in "Catholic institutions the child receives instruction and inspiration or stimulus in faith, in religion, in obedience, in justice, and in purity—the pillars of real character—more than he or she could receive, in many cases, from home training." While he admitted that asylums were not the best place for developing children as individuals, he also thought that American society placed too much emphasis on individuality. Important virtues such as obedience and respect for the rights of others were often sacrificed in the process of encouraging individuality. Other speakers at the conference were more willing to admit the superiority of homes to institutions, particularly for small children, but the tone at Catholic charity gatherings was notably friendlier to institutions than that of the White House Conference or than what would be found at the National Conference of Charities and Corrections.[75]

Some historians have seen the 1909 White House Conference as marking the end of orphan asylums as an important part of the nation's system of child welfare. One calls it a "watershed" that led to "a smaller and more marginal role" in child welfare, while another writes that "more than any other single event, [it] represented a turning point in the history of care for the nation's dependent children."[76] But all the changes that the conference endorsed had been called for by reformers for years, or even decades, and none, except for the passage of mothers' pensions (which were often meager in amount or limited to a relatively small number of the needy), had much impact over the next decade—and the conference had *not* endorsed public pensions.

Asylums continued to be a crucial part of the nation's child welfare system into the 1930s. Furthermore, in some states, such as North Carolina, asylums were becoming more important in the early twentieth century, while in others, such as Massachusetts, their importance had already been declining before the turn of the century. Rhetoric and reality would take several decades to converge. In the mid-1920s, the authors of the Duke Endowment's report on orphans in North and South Carolina echoed the conference in viewing mothers' aid as the best method of care for poor children, foster care as next best, and orphanages as the last resort—even as the Duke Endowment doled out money to dozens of orphan asylums throughout both states. In the Carolinas in 1926, three-quarters of the children being supported by people other than their families were in orphanages.[77] Just as the rise of orphan asylums had varied from place to place, so too would their gradual replacement by mothers' pensions and foster care. The creation of a federal program, Aid to Dependent Children (ADC), more widely available across the nation than mothers' pensions had been, would lead to the rapid, and relatively uniform, decline of institutions for dependent children. To the extent that ADC was the successor to mothers' pensions, and to the extent that pensions could be traced to 1909, that gathering did have a powerful impact on the future of child welfare. But it took more than three decades to take full effect.

The Continued Spread of Asylums, 1910–1933

Despite the criticisms leveled at them in the Progressive Era, in the 1910s and 1920s orphan asylums continued to be founded in large and midsize cities across the nation. One of the justifications given for this by asylum managers was that, whatever other methods might be seen as preferable, orphan asylums were the centerpiece of child welfare in the United States and were likely to remain so for the foreseeable future. They existed because of widespread poverty; as one Catholic charity worker in New York stated in 1910 about all Catholic institutions, "They are because they must be. It was the demand for them which created the supply." At the turn of the century, at least half of the nation's working-class families were poor, and a third were extremely poor.[78] The loss of one job or a serious illness to either parent might force any such family to seek temporary care elsewhere for at least one child, and orphan asylums continued to serve that purpose.

Another defense of orphan asylums that was often used, especially by Jewish and Catholic asylum managers, was that while good private homes might be better for children than institutions, finding such homes was very difficult. Orphan asylums were needed to temporarily care for children while their families weathered harsh economic times, or while the asylum or another agency was trying to place them in homes. Finally, at least some reformers attending national meetings recognized that the vast majority of institutions and agencies across the nation were not represented at, nor particularly affected by, gatherings such as the White House Conference.[79]

The four different systems of caring for dependent children—public subsidies to private asylums, county-based public asylums, large state-managed asylums, and private asylums without any meaningful government involvement—that had appeared in various states in the postbellum decades continued past the turn of the century. New or developing states adopted one or another of them. All depended to some extent on private asylums, either as the only option or as a parallel system to public asylums. California and New York continued to provide per capita public payments to private institutions. Many state legislatures still resisted any public involvement other than mothers' pensions, relying on private orphan asylums to care for many of their state's needy children. Ohio, Indiana, and Connecticut continued their county-based system of public asylums, which coexisted with private asylums. It was this system that relied least heavily on private orphan asylums, though California and New York relied the least on private funding of asylums.[80]

The Michigan system, which relied on one large, public asylum that functioned chiefly as a placing-out agency, spread to other states around the turn of the century. However, many of the states that adopted the Michigan system placed far less emphasis on breaking up families and placing children out than Michigan did. For example, Montana had opened a State Orphans' Home by 1900. Montana's counties were too sparsely populated to make a county-based system such as Ohio's feasible, and the state's lack of private asylums led to government involvement in child welfare. But most children leaving Montana's home returned to family members, often within a year or two.[81] In heavily populated states such as Michigan, the vast majority of dependent children in institutions remained in private orphan asylums, and the children often returned to their families. However, most leaving Michigan's State Public School were placed with other families.

Asylums for children of color also continued to be built. By 1923, the number of asylums for black children was approaching one hundred; a few of these institutions also cared for Native American children. Georgia had seven asylums for black children, Pennsylvania eight, Maryland seven, Louisiana six; Illinois, Texas, and Tennessee each had five asylums for black children. There were also thirteen asylums for Native American children in 1923, most in the West and northern Midwest. California had two asylums for Japanese children, two for Chinese children, and one that accepted both Japanese and Korean children.[82]

Orphan asylums continued to be founded because they were flexible institutions that local groups could bend to serve their own needs.

Asylums could provide temporary care to the children of working families, or long-term care to children without families. They could be all-encompassing institutions, or integrative homes that sent their children out to school, to church, and to play. Any religious, ethnic, or fraternal group could run an asylum, either for its own people or for a wider clientele. While far from a perfect way to raise children, asylums continued to serve the needs of both their founders and their clientele in an era when private funding to maintain poor children within their own homes was rare and public funding for the same purpose was still severely limited.

Mothers' Pensions

The idea of financially aiding a widow with children so that she could continue to raise her children herself had a long history in American society. A few private organizations had provided cash and goods to widows with children for more than a century before the passage of mothers' and widows' pensions laws in most states during the 1910s. New York's Ladies Society for the Relief of Poor Widows with Small Children, founded in 1797, gave allowances to supplement widows' incomes. Outdoor relief, provided by many cities and states throughout the nineteenth century, often went to families without a male provider. Though orphan asylums by definition removed children from their parents, in many cases this was at a parent's request and was done with the hope that the children would be reunited with their parents in short order.[83]

In 1902, the committee on dependent children of the National Conference of Jewish Charities recommended that subsidies or pensions to poor families in which both parents were alive were desirable, so that such families could be returned to their "normal condition at the first opportunity." Some charitable societies agreed, though an emphasis on aiding families in which only the mother was present was far more common than a desire to help families with a father present. The Orphan Guardian Society of Philadelphia was already providing private mothers' aid to dozens of Jewish families by this time. At the 1906 New York State Conference of Charities, Homer Folks stated approvingly that New York City's charities were trying to "increase the giving of home relief to widows and deserted wives." Children should be more readily maintained with destitute parents, he argued, but more readily removed from "parents who are morally unfit to care for them."[84] The problem in practice, as it had always been, was to care adequately for the former without giving undeserved aid to the latter.

All of the examples listed above involved private charities helping poor mothers keep their children at home. But the mothers' pension movement that swept the nation in the 1910s called for public funds to care for dependent children within their own homes, assuming their mothers were "worthy." Much of the resistance to mothers' pensions came from reformers opposed to government funding for charitable purposes; social work agencies in particular opposed making public money available to poor women, especially since it was in the form of a right rather than charity.[85] This is hardly surprising, since mothers' pensions had much in common with outdoor relief, which had been widely attacked throughout the nineteenth century, and since public funding of private orphan asylums had come under heavy criticism in both New York and California. Even so, as Michael Katz writes, "Once family breakup was rejected, the campaign against outdoor relief, which already had run out of steam, was doomed, and, even more, some sort of mothers' pensions had to follow."[86]

Some state governments acted on this issue before the 1909 White House Conference. After the 1906 fire that virtually destroyed San Francisco, California's state government began providing de facto widows' pensions. State per capita payments for children boarded in homes were granted because there was not enough space in institutions to care for everyone in need. Some children were boarded in their own homes, thus creating what amounted to widows' pensions. In short order, a number of counties began applying to the state for widows' pensions through this mechanism, which had originally been created to provide for asylum children. In 1913, the law was amended to provide direct payments to mothers. California was unusually willing to help the poor by providing pensions, just as it had been concerning public funding of private asylums; in the former case, however, the rest of the nation would soon follow California's lead, whereas on the latter California had been almost alone. By the 1920s, mothers' pension laws were one of a number of programs that might be identified as "family welfare," including workingmen's compensation, regulations on child labor, and juvenile courts.[87]

The first official mothers' pension laws were passed in Illinois and

Missouri in 1911. By the end of 1913, twenty states had passed them; by 1919, thirty-nine states had some sort of mothers' pension laws.[88] James Patterson has written about mothers' pensions that they "could 'prevent' nothing except hardship; they were outdoor relief to a needy class of people."[89] Patterson is right in arguing that pensions were outdoor relief, but it is important to remember that, despite almost always being given in small amounts, outdoor relief was a more humane method of helping people than were institutions. Pensions certainly did not move poor people out of poverty, but they helped prevent something else: the breakup of poor families simply due to poverty. To be more exact, they helped "deserving" white widows keep their children. In some places, and perhaps throughout the nation, blacks, Mexicans, and other disadvantaged groups did not receive mothers' pensions despite high poverty rates.[90] Of course, this was hardly a new pattern in child welfare. As Chapter 4 shows, few orphan asylums accepted nonwhite children.

Many Catholics also approved of maintaining families with dependent children rather than institutionalizing children. In 1916, Patrick Mallon stated that Catholics should direct their resources "to the maintenance of dependent families and to the retention of the children at home where they belong." He thought that "many Catholics would give $100 to an orphan asylum rather than $10 to us to help to keep a family together," and that this had to change. Children who needed only temporary care should not be institutionalized unless it was absolutely necessary, and even then asylums needed to start distinguishing between children who would need long-term care and those who needed care briefly "on account of illness in one or another parent or a similar passing emergency." Mallon believed that "the whole organization of life is different for the two types."[91]

One sign of states' increasing preference for mothers' pensions over institutional care came in New York State in 1922. The state legislature passed a law allowing (though not requiring) counties to transfer all public duties dealing with dependent children to the county boards of child welfare that had been created specifically to administer mothers' allowances. Thus, children committed to institutions by courts were under the jurisdiction of a board that by its nature and origins preferred noninstitutional care. The passage of New York's mothers' allowance law in 1915, combined with these administrative changes, led to a decrease of roughly 30 percent in the number of institutionalized dependent children in New York between 1915 and 1925, while the number of children cared for in homes—their own, boarding homes, and free homes—tripled, surpassing the number of asylum children in the process. For the entire nation, the number of children receiving state aid through mothers' pensions exceeded the number receiving state aid in institutions in the early 1920s. At some point in the late 1920s, the number of children being helped by mothers' pensions surpassed the total number of children in *all* orphan asylums, including those supported solely by private funds. In 1933, slightly more than 150,000 children were in orphan asylums. Two years earlier, in 1931, the number of children being helped by mothers' pensions was somewhere between 250,000 and 300,000.[92]

Mothers' pensions allowed many of the families that received them to survive without the aid of charity groups or public agencies. They also allowed many women who might have had to turn to an orphan asylum a few years before to keep their children. But even at the start of the depression, many states still failed to make adequate provisions for widows with children. In 1923, North Carolina passed a Mothers' Aid Law but appropriated only $50,000 per year to it. A 1933 study of North Carolina's asylum facilities for African-American children argued that if widows' pensions were more widely available, the majority of institutionalized children would instead be with their mothers.[93] The lack of sufficient funds found in most mothers' pension laws would be continued in ADC, the New Deal program that grew out of mothers' pensions. As always, the desire to avoid rewarding the unworthy poor—mothers who didn't truly need help from the state—would diminish programs such as ADC that were aimed at the worthy poor.

The Decline of Asylums for Dependent Children

Although orphan asylums remained a vital part of child welfare in the 1920s, the handwriting was on the wall. The depression and the government response to it combined to shift the care of dependent children dramatically away from institutional care. The depression also strained the resources of all child-care institutions and agencies. Some asylums kept functioning in the 1930s either by reducing the size of their staffs and cutting salaries or by reducing the number of children cared for in the institution and placing out many more children. The Chicago Orphan Asylum did both. It virtually stopped admitting new children in 1933 and "eliminated most of such extras as raincoats, dancing lessons, special tutoring for our children" in the attempt to continue caring for "the children for whom we felt morally responsible." But by then, the number of children in the asylum had already dropped dramatically. Starting in 1928, the asylum's managers had been shifting toward boarding home care for its children. The asylum's annual report noted in 1933 that boarding home care was actually proving less expensive than institutional care. The asylum was also helping a few families stay intact in their own homes, but boarding home care was clearly now its main function. At the end of 1933, 37 children were being cared for in the asylum's main building and two cottages, 39 were being supported with family members, and 124 were in foster homes, 116 of which were boarding homes.[94] Many asylums had to start tapping into the principal of endowment funds that they had previously only drawn interest from, or even borrowing on the credit of donors or trustees, to keep functioning.

Some asylums had begun down a different path in the 1920s, choosing to continue to provide institutional care but to a different clientele. These asylums' managers redefined their mission in response to the changing availability of alternative forms of care and the tenets of social work. Due to falling mortality rates, there were now relatively few full orphans, and most could probably be adopted. Children whose only problem was their parents' poverty were now to be maintained in their parents' homes, at public expense, if they could qualify for mothers' pensions; when they could not, many such children were being placed in homes, often at state expense. Thus, the orphan asylums' traditional clientele were much less likely to be in need of institutional care. Many orphan asylums responded by shifting away from caring for dependent children toward caring for children with behavioral problems. In keeping with the new psychiatric view at the core of social work, these would be children with emotional or psychological problems. Just as changes within the medical profession had transformed hospitals, the needs and methods of the social work profession helped shift the purpose of many orphan asylums.[95]

By 1930, Cleveland's Protestant Orphan Asylum had shifted to caring for children with emotional and behavioral problems. In 1924, the superintendent of the Cleveland Jewish Orphan Asylum brought psychiatric help into the asylum to aid children "experiencing behavioral or personality problems." This was the beginning of a gradual shift of the asylum's purpose; by the early 1940s, under the name Bellefaire, it had become a residential treatment center for emotionally disturbed children.[96] While this change was well underway in many cities by the 1920s, it would be decades before some asylums shifted away from caring for poor children and toward caring for troubled children. Ken Cmiel found that the managers of the Chicago Nursery and Half-Orphan Asylum, by then known as Chapin Hall, resisted changing until the late 1940s. It was not until then that Chapin Hall underwent "changes so extensive that the institution would no longer be an 'orphanage' in any meaningful sense of the word" as it shifted toward becoming a residential treatment center. In the 1950s, Denver's Jewish orphanage "changed its mission to the challenge of childhood asthma." The Mennonite Children's Home of Millersville, Pennsylvania, finally found in the 1960s that it was receiving "fewer young children and more troubled teens." By 1975, the home was concentrating on helping teenage males and had stopped caring for any girls or boys younger than eleven.[97]

Between 1920 and 1950, some orphan asylums followed the path taken by the Chicago Orphan Asylum and became foster care agencies. Placing out and adoption had been widespread in Massachusetts much earlier than in most states. During the 1910s, faced with an institution "badly in need of repair" and the conviction that placing children in homes was a superior method of child care, Boston's Church Home changed from an asylum to a foster care agency. Most orphan asylums that took this route did so later, especially during the depression. In 1935, the Michigan State School closed its doors as Michigan shifted even more strongly toward foster placements as state policy. In 1942, St. Mary's Home for Children began a "gradual increase in foster home care" that made it possible to continue without an institution by 1946. Though St. Mary's managers were sure they would soon have a new institution, it would be as an "auxiliary to a boarding home program" rather than a replacement of the old asylum. By the mid-1940s, the Duke Endowment was encouraging North Carolina's and South Carolina's orphan asylums to place children in foster homes.[98]

From the 1930s onward, both foster care and institutions would be used as parts of a system designed to maintain children in, or restore children to, their own homes.[99] Although technically a different kind of relief (foster care was for abused or neglected children, ADC for poor children), ADC was the centerpiece of the system, and the part that would expand the most over the next half century. Within just a few years of its creation, ADC already supported far more children than institutions and foster care combined ever had. Foster care and institutions shifted more and more toward "troubled" children, with institutions very much in a subsidiary role, relegated to caring only for the most troubled. While most early placing-out advocates, and some asylum managers, had hoped to remove poor children permanently from their homes, many other orphan asylum managers had tried to serve as temporary caretakers of children until they could be restored to their families. It was this view that triumphed in the twentieth century. It did not, however, triumph through the continued spread of orphan asylums.

Instead, state governments provided direct aid to parents, and orphan asylums either closed, became foster care agencies, or shifted to the care of abused or otherwise troubled children, thus becoming a subsidiary part of the foster care system, which, not coincidentally, led to their receiving large amounts of government funding. By 1950, most asylums that still functioned did so as subsidiaries to state child welfare departments. In June 1948, Indiana had 13,772 child welfare cases open. Almost half were children being supervised in their own homes, while 2,938 were in board homes and 1,779 in free or adoptive homes; 2,093 were living in institutions. In 1960 in Louisiana, just 155 foster children "for whom there were no suitable state facilities" were being cared for "in private institutions under the Exceptional Children's Act." The majority were "retarded children who are on the waiting list for State Colony and Training School. Others are seriously emotionally disturbed and some have physical handicaps." At the same time, 1,481 children were in board homes. By the middle of 1966, 4,735 children were in board homes in Louisiana, while just 562 children under state supervision were in institutions.[100] Care of dependent children had shifted from a religious act performed in nineteenth-century asylums to a more secular act carried through by ADC, later AFDC, and by foster care. At the same time, institutions had shifted from caring for children whose main problem was poverty to caring for children labeled as emotionally, psychologically, or physically damaged.[101]

Conclusion

Though still fairly rare before 1830, orphan asylums spread rapidly as a response to the cholera epidemics of 1832 and 1849. From 1830 to 1860, the population of the United States rose from 13 million to 31 million, an increase of roughly 140 percent. During the same period, the number of orphan asylums in the nation shot from about thirty-three to nearly two hundred, increasing at *more than three times* the rate of population growth. Asylums for poor children succeeded where other antebellum efforts to deal with or care for the poor had failed. Lori Ginzberg writes that the antebellum period was "an era of institutional innovations without parallel in American history."[102] Orphan asylums were a central part of that era for many communities, particularly immigrant communities. In part, this was because orphan asylums, while they often had a certain "moral reform" quality, were not chiefly about changing people. Even more important to their success was the fact that, unlike many reform efforts, they were usually built and managed by the community to care for its own, not imposed by people seen as outsiders.

Orphan asylums continued to play a central role in child welfare for the rest of the century, but important changes occurred after the Civil War. Public funding, and sometimes public management, of orphan asylums developed in New York, California, Ohio, Connecticut, and Indiana. In those states and others, government boards of charity appeared that slowly began to assume limited regulatory powers over orphan asylums. However, in most states child welfare continued to be dominated by privately managed institutions controlled at the local level well into the twentieth century, leaving orphan asylums to do as their managers saw fit. Asylums continued to be built across the nation at a rapid rate. From 1860 to 1890, the national population doubled, from 31 million to 63 million. At the same time, the number of orphan asylums roughly tripled, from just under two hundred to approximately six hundred.[103]

By the time of the 1909 White House Conference, reformers had reached agreement that children should be in homes rather than institutions. Over the next decade, orphan asylums continued to be founded despite this consensus. Foster care was becoming more common as state governments became more active in caring for children without homes, or whose parents were considered unfit, but it did not by any means replace institutional care in the 1910s and 1920s. In fact, from 1910 to 1933, the national population rose from 92 million to 125 million, while the number of asylums rose at about the same pace, going from 972 to 1,321.[104] And the orphanage population in the early 1930s was still overwhelmingly poor children, not troubled children as it would increasingly be during the 1940s and 1950s. At the same time, the passage of mothers' pension laws undoubtedly allowed many children to stay in their own homes who previously would have had to turn to a local orphan asylum for help. But the limited funds and scope of most mothers' pension programs meant that they helped only a small percentage of the families that needed help.[105] Most poor parents continued to scrape by, receiving occasional help from family and friends and struggling to feed their children and themselves. Those who could not manage to do so, but did not receive mothers' pensions, often turned to orphan asylums, as they always had.

The creation of Aid to Dependent Children and then its broadening availability in the 1940s and 1950s meant that institutions for poor children would no longer have a meaningful role to play in American society. In individual asylums, of course, other factors—such as the growing power of social work, the growing prominence of placing children in foster homes, and the changing preferences of trustees—might have played a more important role than mothers' pensions and ADC in changing an asylum away from institutional care of poor children. But even then, the availability of another means of caring for dependent children, one that did *not* require parents to give up their children, was an overwhelmingly important factor. Ken Cmiel writes that "the changes at Chapin Hall had nothing to do with a New Deal legislation."[106] Yet even at Chapin Hall, ADC probably did have a powerful impact. As was mentioned earlier, Cmiel finds that Chapin Hall changed dramatically starting in the late 1940s and ceased being a real "orphanage." When Illinois finally passed enabling legislation for ADC in 1942, its effect was immediate and overwhelming. In Cook County (Illinois's main population center and the home of Chapin Hall), the number of children receiving ADC in 1943 was *six times higher* than the number who had received mothers' pensions in September 1941.[107] The fact was that orphan asylums had been created to care for children whose parents could not do so, due to illness, death, unemployment, or some other problem. ADC served that same purpose, and it did so without splitting families apart. With their traditional clientele going elsewhere, orphan asylums had no choice but to change.

Table 1.1. Orphan asylums founded from 1727 to 1860, by management type, still extant in 1910.

Period	Catholic	Protestant	Jewish	Public	Unknown	Total
1727–1800	2	0	0	1	2	5
1801–1810	0	2	0	0	5	7
1811–1820	4	4	0	0	1	9
1821–1830	4	0	1	0	7	12
1831–1840	15	9	0	0	19	43
1841–1850	19	8	0	1	14	42
1851–1860	34	20	3	2	18	77

Source: *Benevolent Institutions, 1910.*

Table 1.2. Orphan asylums founded from 1861 to 1890, by management type, still extant in 1910.

Period	Catholic	Protestant	Jewish	Fraternal	County/City	State	Unknown	Total
1861–1870	27	36	2	1	3	5	29	103
1871–1880	41	32	5	2	14	1	30	125
1881–1890	37	39	2	3	46	8	62	197

Source: *Benevolent Institutions, 1910.*

Table 1.3. Total number of orphan asylums, by management type, 1890–1933.

Year	Catholic	Protestant	Jewish	Fraternal	County/City	State	Unknown	Total
1890	175	130	9	4	71	16	158	563
1910	260	263	21	18	97	17	296	972
1923	339	355	40	80	100	24	389	1,327
1933	262	300	38	90	120	26	485	1,321

Source: *Eleventh Census: 1890; Benevolent Institutions, 1910; Children Under Institutional Care, 1923; Children Under Institutional Care, 1933.*

Table 1.4. Mean populations of orphan asylums, by management type, 1890–1933.

Year	Catholic	Protestant	Jewish	Fraternal	County/City	State	Unknown	Total
1890	139.9	54.6	186.6	79.0	37.8	162.6	132.9	84.5
1910	173.0	96.2	224.4	109.7	46.3	277.3	66.2	109.8
1923	142.7	68.9	133.9	114.6	64.9	230.7	54.9	91.0
1933	162.1	83.9	173.9	105.3	183.7	523.8	67.9	115.3

Source: *Eleventh Census: 1890; Benevolent Institutions, 1910; Children Under Institutional Care, 1923; Children Under Institutional Care, 1933.*

2

The Changing Nature of Orphan Asylums

Orphan asylums were just one of the many kinds of institutions that flourished during the nineteenth century. Public schools, hospitals, prisons, poorhouses, reformatories, and mental hospitals also dotted the landscape. While orphan asylums shared traits with each of these institutions, in some crucial ways they were unique. Their most distinctive aspect may have been the relatively favorable attitude orphan asylum managers usually had toward their wards, whom they viewed as innocents to be protected; other institutions, even public schools, usually had a less friendly view of their inmates, even when they were children. And the trajectory orphan asylums followed over time differed markedly from the path followed by most other nineteenth-century institutions. Rather than changing from rehabilitative institutions into custodial warehouses, orphan asylums gradually opened up to the outside world. Starting at some asylums in the last decades of the nineteenth century, and accelerating in the first two decades of the twentieth century, orphan asylums gradually shed many of their harshest practices and became more likely to encourage their children to venture into the broader world on a regular basis than to lock them inside asylum walls.

Antebellum orphan asylums often fulfilled their modest goals: they took in poor children and supplied them with shelter, food, education, and moral and religious guidance. Almost all kept close control over their children's lives, but not all asylums did so for identical reasons. Isolating asylums wanted to break children away from the culture, and often the religion, of their impoverished parents. Protective asylums intended to protect children's religious and/or cultural heritage from a world that asylum managers saw as hostile to it. Until at least the 1870s, virtually all orphan asylums were either isolating or protective in nature and kept close watch over their children at all times.

But between the 1870s and the early twentieth century, the isolating and protective asylums of the antebellum period slowly began to evolve into integrative institutions that encouraged parental visits, gave their children summer vacations in the country, and sent their children to public schools where they mingled with other children daily. The change was slow; before at least 1890, almost all asylums still kept tight control over their children's lives, though usually less so than they had a few decades earlier. By the 1910s, most asylums were in the process of shifting toward a more integrative stance; some did so rapidly and thoroughly between 1900 and 1920, while others moved more haltingly. Throughout this period, the vast majority of orphan asylums in the nation remained community institutions, controlled by local groups and serving local interests. Most notably, far more than most other charitable institutions, orphan asylums helped poor families by caring for their children, for months or years, and then allowing families to reunite.

Three Asylum Types

Probably the most important historical question about orphan asylums concerns their view of, and treatment of, their clientele. Were orphan asylum managers trying to break children away from their parents (if one or both were still alive) and from their religious and ethnic heritages? Or were they trying to raise children in a manner matching their family background? Whether or not orphan asylum managers sought to impose some form of social control on the children within their institutions is, in large part, a matter of semantics. Certainly, asylum managers did want to control many aspects of their children's lives, but then so did parents in intact families. The most useful way to look at the issue is to examine a number of related issues: the intentions of asylum managers, the actual day-to-day working of orphan asylums, and the role asylums played in preserving or splitting apart poor families.

With these issues as the focus, it is clear that over the century when asylums were commonplace, there were three basic types of orphan asylums. *Isolating* orphan asylums fit the social control model in a number of ways. They kept close watch over their children's secular and religious education. Children inside isolating institutions were thoroughly closed off from society, and their daily routines were closely regulated; their contact with their parents was severely limited. Isolating asylums usually sought legal guardianship over children and were likely to place children out in family homes without much, or any, concern for whether the religion of that home fit the child's. They often explicitly sought to break the bonds between parent and child. The managers of isolating orphan asylums were determined to separate children from their heritages, which the managers saw as harmful. In the antebellum era, most Protestant and most nonsectarian asylums were isolating institutions, and in the postbellum era some, though not all, state-managed asylums were as well. The heritages from which isolating asylums hoped to "save" children included, but were not necessarily limited to, Catholicism, poverty, and the presumed moral flaws of their parents.

Protective asylums also effectively removed their children from the outside world. As in isolating asylums, protective institutions provided both secular and religious education to their children. However, in protective asylums, that religious training closely mirrored the children's backgrounds. Furthermore, if a living parent could reclaim his or her child at some point, managers of protective asylums were willing, and sometimes happy, to return children to their own homes. Catholic asylums fit this mold throughout the nineteenth century. Some Protestant and nonsectarian orphan asylums were also basically protective in nature, particularly toward the end of the century. In the case of Catholic asylums, destitute Catholic children were to be protected from a society that was basically Protestant and anti-Catholic in nature, as well as from Protestant charity organizations (including some Protestant asylums) that might deliberately try to break Catholic children away from their backgrounds. It is worth noting that the same institution might be protective for some children and isolating for others. For example, a Protestant asylum might be preserving the faith of a Protestant child at the same time that it was trying to break a Catholic child away from his or her heritage.

It is important to recognize that virtually all orphan asylums, whether isolating or protective, were operating from different motives than other nineteenth-century institutions that separated their inmates from society. Many antebellum institutions, including prisons and mental hospitals, intended to "reform" their inmates. Poorhouses, on the other hand, shut "the old and sick away from their friends and relatives to deter the working class from seeking poor relief." But orphan asylums rarely thought their children needed to be reformed, and the very act of accepting a child also meant that the family was receiving a kind of relief. Few isolating asylums sought to deter poor families from seeking their services; if anything, they hoped the unworthy poor would seek them out, so that families could be broken up and children "saved." Similarly, protective asylums generally assumed that the families coming to them needed help, and they tried to provide it, whatever they may have thought of a particular child's parents or relatives.[1]

Finally, *integrative* orphan asylums tried to help their children experience the outside world even while they ate and slept within the asylum. Children in integrative asylums mixed with neighborhood children in local schools and churches. They also had regular contact with their families and were returned to them once parents were capable of caring for their children. (The majority of children leaving protective asylums also returned to their families.) Integrative asylums were rare—or nonexistent—in the antebellum period. In a sense, they were impossible to create then, because most of the institutions that would eventually be employed by integrative asylums, such as public school systems, Boy Scout and Girl Scout troops, and athletic leagues, were themselves few and far between. However, over the last few decades of the nineteenth century, many older asylums began slowly shifting from an isolating or protective mode toward a more integrative stance, and new asylums sometimes started out with the intention of allowing their children some contact with the outside world. By the 1910s, the majority of orphan asylums were clearly shifting toward an integrative philosophy, though many traits of isolating and protective asylums remained, such as gaining legal control over children or educating them within the asylum itself rather than sending them to public schools. Many asylums retained some protective traits into the 1920s and beyond, especially Catholic asylums, which often continued to educate children within the asylum until they were old enough for high school.

The three categories described above—isolating, protective, and integrative asylums—should not be seen as mutually exclusive. Orphan asylums usually fit one of the basic types reasonably well but also had some aspects of another type. For example, an institution might wish to preserve contacts between parents and children and preserve a child's religious heritage (thus seeming protective), yet at the same time seek legal custody over the child, as isolating asylums did. Perhaps the most important factor in categorizing an asylum is the attitude its managers demonstrated toward surviving parents of institutionalized children and the relationships between parents and their children, which is discussed at length in Chapter 4.

Antebellum Asylums and Their Goals

Orphan asylums flourished from the 1830s onward, at the same time that many other kinds of institutions were spreading across the United States. Many of the institutions of this era had lofty goals; some were so ambitious that they intended to heal society as a whole as well as help their clients. David Rothman has written that "no reformers were more confident of the advantage and success of their program than the philanthropists who founded child-saving institutions."[2] However, Rothman's work on children's institutions focused on evidence for reformatories, not orphan asylums. In fact, few antebellum orphan asylum managers thought they were reforming society, or for that matter even believed that most of their children needed extensive rehabilitation. Most antebellum orphan asylums had a more straightforward, though hardly easy, mission: to serve as surrogate parents, either temporarily or permanently, for destitute children whose own parents were for some reason unable to care for them. This was true across the entire nation, in asylums run by Catholic, Protestant, and nonsectarian groups, as well as for the handful of Jewish and publicly managed orphan asylums. It was true of both isolating and protective asylums. In both cases, asylum managers hoped to be better parents than their children's natural parents had been.

Most asylum managers in this period did not believe they had to rehabilitate children in the way that inmates in prisons or insane asylums needed to be reformed; it was usually the child's environment, not the child, that needed to be changed. For example, in her study of the Boston Female Asylum, Susan Porter argues convincingly that "the founders of the BFA thought of the Asylum as a 'place of refuge' rather than a socialization camp, and worked out a program with the children's welfare at heart." The asylum's managers hoped to create "a class of well-trained, moral, and self-reliant working women, virtuous citizens for the new nation."[3] This was true of many antebellum asylums, which presumed that dependent children needed to be raised properly more than they needed to be reformed.[4]

A central reason for most orphan asylums' existence in the antebellum period, whether isolating or protective, was to provide their children with religious training. This was true for all Catholic asylums, which existed in large part to preserve the religious faith of the children of Irish and German Catholic immigrants. As John O'Grady wrote in 1931, all the Catholic Church's work from 1830 to 1880 was "colored by the outlook and the needs of these two peoples."[5] Children cut off for one reason or another from parents were the most vulnerable members of the Church, both physically and spiritually. Catholic orphan asylums sought to feed and clothe them, place a roof over their heads, educate them, care for their health, and, perhaps most fundamentally, provide them with proper religious training. Most Protestant orphan asylums had similar intentions.

In many ways, the goals of orphan asylums were much like the goals of the parents they had at least temporarily replaced. In the 1840s, the managers of New York's Colored Orphan Asylum wanted to give their children "a good practical education," but they considered "moral and religious culture as the object to which all others should be made subordinate." The Protestant Orphan Asylum of St. Louis, founded in 1834, "saw its function as offering protection and shelter to any child whose situation appeared desperate." But the Protestant Orphan Asylum held an especially dim view of their children's parents. In the 1840s and 1850s, its managers sought to indenture their children, viewing that as preferable to returning children to their own families.[6]

In fact, this was one of the two fundamental differences between protective and isolating asylums in this era: protective asylums eventually returned children to their families in most cases in which a parent still survived, while isolating asylums did not. The other difference, involving religion, was less clear-cut. Isolating asylums often sought to take in children from religious backgrounds different than the asylums' managers, while protective asylums sought children from the same religious background. In both cases, the asylums would then shape children's religious training, but in the case of isolating asylums, this would often be a very different training than the child could otherwise have expected.

Most orphan asylum managers hoped to create a homelike atmosphere for children, at least as much as it was possible to do so within an institutional setting. They hoped that they, along with the children, would be a family. This goal was hardly unique to orphan asylum managers in the antebellum period. Doctors who ran asylums for the mentally ill also hoped to establish "the family home writ large." In both orphan asylums and insane asylums, superintendents and matrons were to serve as parents, while inmates played the role of children regardless of their actual age.[7] This obviously made far more sense in homes for children than in institutions housing adults. The desire to make the institution a "home" tied into powerful beliefs in Jacksonian America. As Barbara Berg writes, "The endowment of home with transcendent attributes was part of an intricate web of ideas which enveloped American women. It reflected the yearning for order in a chaotic society and enabled accommodation to the present without completely relinquishing the past."[8]

But not all asylums considered creating a "home" for their children as a fundamental goal. Some asylum managers focused more on assuring that children would become self-supporting. Priscilla Clement argues that all three of the private orphan asylums founded in Philadelphia in the 1820s sought to care for children temporarily and then indenture them to someone who would provide them with a trade. In practice, this seems similar to the Boston Female Asylum's methods, but Clement interprets it instead as imposing "social control as economically as possible."[9]

Many of the institutions that rose to prominence in American society in the first half of the nineteenth century were deemed failures within a few decades of their appearance. This was at least partially due to their lofty initial claims, which were virtually impossible to fulfill.[10] But orphan asylums were different since they rarely set out with the intent of reforming society, or even of reforming their inmates to any great extent. The Charleston Orphan House's managers insisted that children were innocents who could turn out well if raised properly, no matter how immoral their parents might have been. The taint of one generation, they believed, did not automatically pass to the next. In 1855, New York's Orphans' Home and Asylum stated that its goal was to provide "protection and training" to the children under its care.[11] Four years later the asylum's goals were hardly optimistic; there was no sense of quickly turning poor children into success stories. "It is as much as the nature of the case admits, if, at the end of every year, they who have it in charge can say that it has met with no disaster, that it has been favored with its usual helps and advantages, and that it keeps its course of sure and steady progress."[12]

Children in orphan asylums were not flawed; they were in need of a home, and that was what orphan asylum managers tried to provide. In other charity institutions, such as poorhouses, the desire to deter the poor from asking for aid often led to particularly harsh policies within institutions and to tightly limited admission policies. Keeping the unworthy poor from receiving aid was also a factor in some orphan asylums' policies. Those asylum managers determined to punish the unworthy poor were likely to do so by blocking off all contact between children and their parents, but this attitude did less harm to asylum inhabitants than to the inmates of poorhouses, who lived in conditions far worse than even the worst orphan asylums presented.[13]

Asylum Philosophies in the Late Nineteenth Century

The relatively benign view of the poor held by managers of protective asylums was not shared by most child welfare activists, such as state charity board members and advocates of placing dependent children in families. In the last two decades of the nineteenth century, views of the poor became even harsher as the belief in hereditarian explanations of individual flaws became more prominent. By the 1890s, many of the speakers at the annual meetings of the National Conference of Charities and Correction who were concerned with the problem of dependent children were placing-out advocates who took a harsh view of the characters of poor adults, and often opposed institutions that allowed children to return to their parents. Orphans, and perhaps even children with living parents, might be deserving of aid, but in the eyes of many placing-out advocates, poor parents were not, virtually by definition. Children were not only orphaned by death in their view; some children became "virtual orphans" when their parents became "morally dead" due to "drink, licentiousness, crime," and other causes.[14]

This harsh attitude toward poor parents held important consequences. For one thing, it encouraged the institutionalization of children by promoting the breakup of poor families with "morally dead" parents.

This harsh view also argued against returning children to their parents, even if the parents' economic situation improved, since poor parents were seen as immoral and unfit. Throughout the nineteenth century, poverty was seen by many reformers as "a personal responsibility, a fault of the individual more than the social system."[15]

Some asylum managers shared these harsh attitudes toward poor parents, especially in the early years of an asylum's existence. The Brooklyn Industrial School Association was founded in 1854 to provide education and clothes to poor children. Within a few years its mission expanded to include a "Home for destitute children." In the early 1860s, the Industrial School Association viewed reforming "debased" adults as almost impossible, so, like many reform organizations in the middle of the nineteenth century, it focused on children. The home's managers hoped to "stem the tide of youthful depravity and crime, by teaching these children industry and habits of application, by inculcating refinement, purity, self-sacrifice and Christian obligation."[16]

Many asylum managers disagreed with this harsh view and saw poor parents as unfortunate rather than depraved. Managers' conceptions about the types of children who deserved aid, and the reasons parents were unable to care for their children, sometimes changed once they became regularly involved with poor children and their families. After the Brooklyn Industrial School's Home had been in operation for a few years, its managers' views began to shift away from an emphasis on preventing crime and depravity and toward aiding the poor simply because they needed help. In 1867, the home's managers still felt that children's poverty was sometimes "partly caused by the intemperance of their parents," but they also believed that unemployment or a death in the family was the problem more often than a flawed character or lack of parental love. Some families that had been prosperous were now "through loss of health" unable to provide properly for their children. The home's view of poor parents (and therefore its purpose) gradually shifted, and by the 1870s it hoped to help poor families survive in the long term by providing short-term care for their children. If a parent's health improved, or the family's fortunes otherwise rose, their children would be returned to them.[17] This kind of change in asylum managers' thinking occurred again and again in the late nineteenth century.

Not all asylum managers decided that poor parents were innocent of blame. Throughout the late nineteenth century, some asylums continued to turn away children who had living parents. But this policy was not always the result of the belief that parents were unworthy. The Orphans' Home and Asylum of New York City felt the need to remind its supporters that it was "a home for parentless children; that is, children deprived by death of one or both of their natural protectors." While the home's managers had sympathy for applicants who were sometimes in a condition "worse than orphanage," children who had two living parents were not accepted. New York's Roman Catholic Orphan Asylum also refused children with two living parents in the 1870s on the grounds that other institutions existed to aid them.[18]

Nevertheless, this stand became increasingly rare in the postbellum period. Many orphan asylums were specifically established to care for destitute children regardless of their parental status. The Chicago Orphan Asylum, founded in 1849, continued throughout the second half of the century in its mission: "the protecting, relieving, educating of, and providing means of support and maintenance for orphan and destitute children." The Maria Kip Orphanage, which opened in San Francisco four decades after the Chicago Orphan Asylum was founded, had a virtually identical avowed purpose: "to take under its care and charge orphans, half-orphans, destitute and friendless children, and provide them with a home, sustenance and education during the period of their dependence." The same basic purpose was held by many asylums, including most Catholic orphan asylums. St. Ann's Home for Destitute Children, a Catholic asylum in New York State, accepted destitute and orphan girls, as did St. Joseph's Asylum in Yorkville and St. Stephen's Home for Children in New York City. Similarly, eleven of the fourteen Jewish orphan asylums in existence at the turn of the century accepted orphans, half-orphans, and dependent children with both parents living.[19] (For more on admission policies, see Chapter 4.)

The fact that an asylum accepted "destitute" children with living parents did not necessarily mean that that asylum wanted to help families reunite. For many asylum managers, as well as for other reformers who were opposed to institutions, children with living parents were to be cared for until a new home could be found for them or until they were old enough to care for themselves. But some asylums embraced the idea of giving temporary care to dependent children until their family's fortunes improved. For example, the Brooklyn School Industrial Association's Home specifically gave "temporary care and protection in the 'Home' to children whose parents need this relief," as well as to neglected or abandoned children.[20] Again, it was the asylum managers' view of poor parents that determined whether or not an asylum willingly served this function. When poor parents were still seen as automatically unworthy, asylums tried to break ties between children and their parents and find them a new home.

During the Civil War, some northern asylums were flooded with the children of Union soldiers whose widows could not afford to care for their children by themselves. They were the most obvious example of children with living parents who were clearly deserving of temporary care. As the Orphans' Home and Asylum wrote, "How can we refuse them admittance?"[21] At the same time, many asylum managers extended this benevolent view toward other families. This attitude often led to debates, with placing-out advocates and among orphan asylum managers themselves, over whether children with living parents should be cared for temporarily, placed out in other families, or not helped at all. These debates would continue to rage into the twentieth century. Some asylum managers were among the strongest advocates of returning children to their own homes, but the eventual triumph of this viewpoint would come, not through greater use of asylums, but instead with the spread of mothers' pension laws in the 1910s, which obviated the need for an asylum, and the eventual creation of Aid to Dependent Children in 1935.

Between 1870 and 1890, religion, which had been so important in the creation of antebellum orphan asylums, gradually gave way to scientific philanthropy, a more secular philosophy that placed considerable emphasis on using organization and administration, rather than charitable giving, as the way to address poverty. Despite this change, which may be seen as a first major step on the road to the creation of social work as a discipline, religion continued to be a central factor in the founding and management of many asylums after the Civil War. The Maria Kip's secretary's optimistic message of 1895 was typical. Though the asylum's work had just begun, she felt that "surely the loving Christian training which these children are now receiving must leave its imprints upon their trusting, susceptible natures, and though temptations may assail them on life's journey, we are full of hope that they may be given grace to withstand them, and to continue Christ's faithful soldiers and servants, until their life's end."²²

The protection of a child's religious heritage remained crucial to Jewish, Catholic, and sectarian Protestant asylums. Often, the desire to protect a heritage was ethnic as well as religious; Germans, Italians, and other ethnic groups built Catholic and Protestant homes specifically for their community's destitute children. It could also be a matter of racial pride to take care of one's own, as in New Orleans' black community after the Civil War. Strong religious impulses played an important part in asylum managers' compassion toward poor families, and in managers' growing willingness to help poor children temporarily, just as they had in the original founding of many asylums. Catholic asylums may have been especially willing to help families reunite; Catholic charity was generally "less judgmental, more ready to help, less quick to condemn" than Protestant charity throughout the nineteenth century. But it is important to recognize that religious motivation could be opposed to children's cultural background as well, as it was in many isolating asylums. The classic example is Protestant proselytization of Catholic children, but that was hardly the only such dynamic. In this period, German Jews ran asylums that were clearly hostile to the cultural background of east European Jews, who increasingly filled Jewish asylums at the end of the century. And the Catholic Church in New York City was dominated by an Irish hierarchy that "doubted whether Italian immigrants understood Catholicism at all."²³

Orphan asylum managers viewed their institutions as homes, just as they had before the Civil War. The most commonly used phrase in orphan asylums' annual reports was the "homelike" quality of their institutions. Though it was undoubtedly overstated in many cases, this was not just talk. Managers tried to make their institutions as homelike as possible, though they knew that this was as difficult as it was important. It was crucial to their existence that asylums be a substitute, at least in part, for a family home that had been lost through illness, unemployment, or death. The Orphans' Home and Asylum of the Protestant Episcopal Church in New York City stated that

> [I]t has been our aim, as managers of the Orphans' Home, to make it as little as possible like an institution, and to promote, by every means in our power, the *home-feeling* among its inmates, and our efforts have

not been altogether in vain. But, after all, no institution can ever be to the fatherless and motherless like that place which God intended should be to them, of all others, the dearest—*their own home*.[24]

This emphasis on a homelike atmosphere existed partly because environment was seen as a crucial element in a child's chances for the future. Asylum managers, placing-out advocates, and state charity board officials all tended to see heredity and environment as things that worked together in forming a child's character and abilities.[25] Neither asylum managers nor placing-out advocates saw heredity as destiny. Most reformers concerned with children's welfare believed that a good environment could help the child of even the worst parents to turn out reasonably well. This was partly why organizations favoring placing out, such as the Children's Aid Society and Michigan's State Public School, wanted children placed in families quickly. They fervently believed that a good home could save a child, and they did not believe that an institution could ever really be a home. Conversely, asylum managers realized that orphan asylums had to be homes, or there was no real justification for their existence. But not all asylums viewed themselves as "homes" in this period. Ken Cmiel writes that the managers of the Chicago Nursery and Half-Orphan Asylum believed "that the institution was *not* a home; it was something else, an 'asylum,' a temporary home for families in distress."[26]

Children in poor families lived in the world in a way that many asylum children did not before the turn of the century. For example, poor children living with their families attended community institutions such as schools and churches, where they interacted with other children as well as a variety of adults.[27] Asylum children rarely enjoyed such simple activities. Just as they had before the war, orphan asylums in the 1870s and 1880s were still likely to keep their children within asylum walls. Children might venture outside the asylum once a week for church, but they usually attended school, and often even church services, within the asylum itself. Different asylums had different reasons for this isolation. Sometimes a lack of available schooling or appropriate religious training in the outside community forced asylums to provide their own education and church services. For many Catholic asylums, isolation was a way of protecting the religious, and often ethnic, heritages of their children. For some Protestant and nonsectarian asylums, it was a way of breaking poor children away from an impoverished heritage that was seen as flawed. According to Reena Sigman Friedman, this was also true of Jewish asylums in this period, whose directors tried "to create 'total institutions' that severely limited youngsters' contact with the outside world." They saw this as the best way to shape children's characters properly.[28] In the 1870s, most orphan asylums remained either isolating asylums, seeking to block children off from "evil" influences (including their own families), or protective asylums determined to see that children received a religious and cultural upbringing such as their parents presumably would have wanted them to have.

In the 1880s and 1890s, many asylum managers began to increase the interaction between their children and the outside world. (These changes are detailed in Chapters 6 and 7.) However, for most asylum children, such contact was less extensive than it would become after the turn of the century. The asylum was for many children not just a home but a cocoon that enveloped their entire lives for however long they were inside. The superintendent of the Franklin County Children's Home of Ohio wrote in 1887 that the asylum should be "made a home, a school, a chapel,—a kind of workshop, where all the faculties are developed," after which the children might be placed out for adoption.[29] Though not the child's natural home, orphan asylums had to try to fill that role as completely as possible. Unfortunately, in many cases this meant that the natural ties that families maintained with the community were replaced by the asylum itself. But the general trend was clearly toward more interaction with the world outside asylum walls.[30]

Unlike other institutions in the late nineteenth century, orphan asylum goals did not deteriorate from seeking rehabilitation to "rigid training and custodial care."[31] The "shift from reform to custody characterized the history of reformatories, mental hospitals, prisons, and school systems in the first two or three decades of their existence."[32] This shift did not, however, happen with orphan asylums. One reason they never became too custodial was that they only rarely thought their children needed reform. And they became more open over time at least in part because most asylums were privately managed, community institutions rather than government entities. In any event, as orphan asylums became more integrative and allowed their children more time outside asylum walls, they were headed in the opposite direction from most other social welfare institutions. By and large, their mission remained what it had been since early in the century: to protect and raise children as best they could.

Asylum Philosophies in the Progressive Era

Over the first two decades of the twentieth century, many orphan asylums shifted toward an integrative framework, sending their children to public schools, letting them visit much more often with family members, and allowing them to play sports and join groups where they mixed with other children from the community. The greater availability of public schools and groups such as the Boy Scouts and Girl Scouts made such increased interactions possible. Many asylum managers made use of these options, and they had more than one good reason to do so. For one thing, opening up was an effective response to the criticisms orphan asylums had long undergone as impersonal, rigid, dehumanizing places. The progressive focus on children's individual psychological and emotional needs, central to the growing professions of psychiatry and social work, was also crucial in opening asylums up to the outside world.[33] As the president of the Carson College for Orphan Girls put it at a national gathering in 1924,

> [T]he third fundamental need or right of children, is for a measure of experience in the world as it is. Children need experience with money, real money; with neighbors, friends, community life. Orphanage or dependency in itself is sufficiently abnormal. Children with this background, all the more need normal activities, normal interests, normal experiences, in the world as it is. Children learn by living, and by living today.[34]

Not all asylums opened up to the outside world so easily during this period. As Chapter 6 discusses, Catholic asylums were reluctant to send their children to public schools. And Ken Cmiel found that the Chicago Nursery and Half-Orphan Asylum actually developed tighter control over its children immediately after 1900.[35] Nonetheless, in most asylums, including Catholic ones such as the Angel Guardian Orphanage, the trend during the Progressive Era was clearly toward more contact between asylum children and the broader society.

The desire to make the asylum like a home, a goal that many asylum managers had held during the nineteenth century, continued to be widespread and became more easily attainable in the early twentieth century, especially in small and midsized institutions. Asylum managers hoped, as always, "to make the [asylum] family life as much like individual home life as possible," by treating the children as individuals, giving them love, and teaching them to be self-supporting. Discipline was to be "as nearly as can be parental," and children were to be surrounded by "the genial warmth of family affections." Like private institutions, most publicly run asylums held these goals. Montana's State Orphans' Home stated in 1904 that it aimed "to make the institution as much like a family home as possible" by treating the children with "kindness, reason and persuasion." Asylum children were to be raised, in other words, as asylum managers assumed good parents would have raised them.[36]

Even more than in the late nineteenth century, many orphan asylums in the Progressive Era consciously functioned as aids to working-class family life, rather than attempting to supplant that life. St. Mary's Home for Children opened in Chicago in 1895 "primarily in an effort to assist overweighted parents, unable to provide a proper home for their children, yet unwilling, as every parent ought to be, to give up entirely the responsibility and control of their children." A speaker at the National Conference of Charities and Correction in 1900 stated that the "natural and proper function" of private orphan asylums was "to receive the children of unfortunate parents with the view of returning them to assist, perhaps, in reuniting the family." The State Orphans' Home of Montana did place children out, but its superintendent was pleased that three-fourths of the children the home had cared for by 1908 had been returned to parents or relatives. This goal was widespread during the Progressive Era, marking the middle ground between those opposed to institutions under any circumstances and the occasional asylum manager who still considered lengthy asylum stays to be in a poor child's best interest.[37]

Perhaps even more strongly than most Protestant and public asylums, Jewish and Catholic asylums hoped to send children back to their own parents, though in fact they often kept their charges for lengthy periods. The report of the committee on dependent children at the National Conference of Jewish Charities in 1902 stated that orphan asylums "must ever keep in sight the possibility of reuniting the family when the destitution which has occasioned the breaking-up has disappeared or been overcome." Two years later an official of a New York asylum announced at the same conference that orphan asylums "were really excellent boarding homes, and as such they are useful especially for poor mothers and poor fathers who are unable to maintain their children." The Marks Nathan Jewish Orphan Home of Chicago encouraged frequent parental visits to its children partly in the hopes that such visits would increase parenting skills, as parents would see how asylum workers and children interacted. In 1912, one Catholic reformer from Chicago announced that Catholics had always hoped to return children to their own homes because "the Church has ever taken not the individual but the family as the unit in society and in the State." The Program for Catholic Child-Caring Homes, an influential statement of goals for Catholic asylums in the 1920s, stressed that every effort should be made to help children and families reunite as soon as possible. To Catholic charity workers, poor Catholic children were fundamentally *poor*, while, at least in the nineteenth century, many Protestant placing-out agencies and institutions saw poor Catholic children as *Catholic*.[38]

Returning institutionalized children to their own homes was a central goal for most asylum managers by the early twentieth century. Even so, for asylums that aspired to be homes to their children, where managers and children formed a large "family," it was not without regrets that asylum managers watched their children leave. As the San Francisco Presbyterian Orphanage and Farm's annual report for 1900 stated,

> [O]ne of the saddest things in an Orphanage is the partings that must come. These children grow up together, become fond of one another and then, when some must go away it seems like the breaking up of a large family. We aim as much as possible to keep up the love for their own parents, that they may some time return to them. Thus, while helping the parent and child in their hour of distress, we still lead parents to feel the children are theirs, to be returned to them, whenever they can make a good home for them.[39]

While this statement may have reflected wishful thinking as well as reality, children who spent years together in an asylum undoubtedly were emotionally connected to one another, and in some cases to adult staff members as well. At the same time asylum managers were praising the bonding of children to one another, many also admitted that encouraging children as individuals was a fundamental problem for any large institution.[40] The recognition that children needed to be treated as individuals was at the heart of many of the advances in asylum life in the early twentieth century. The goals of building character, teaching responsibility, and in general preparing children for adult life continued to be central to all asylums, but many asylum managers had come to believe that this should be done through individualized treatment of each child[41] (see Chapters 5, 6, and 7).

Catholic asylum managers were also determined to build character in their children, though for them this was often less an issue of developing an individual's unique traits than it was of inculcating a specific moral and religious worldview. Some Catholic welfare reformers agreed with the oft-repeated criticism of large institutions that reared children by marching them from place to place. Instead, they argued, children needed to be given individual attention, as was increasingly being done in smaller asylums. If Catholic institutions were to "diminish the number of dependents" leaving their institutions, they needed to adopt the improvements in asylum management that had occurred since the 1890s.[42]

Religion continued to be an important part of many asylums' programs. Catholic, Protestant, and Jewish asylums all accepted children chiefly of their own faith, with the express intent of preserving that faith. Some Catholic child welfare activists still feared in 1912 that many Catholic children were being raised in public or "non-Catholic" institutions. Sectarian orphan asylums, which still made up the majority of institutions for children in the 1920s, "retained their religious impetus and character, for they had vital spiritual and financial ties to their particular denominations."[43]

A central question about attempts to "build character" and "instill values" is, What kind of character and what specific values were to be instilled? Jeanne Abrams argues in her study of the Denver Sheltering Home for Jewish Children that while the home sought to "provide a Jewish environment and education," its founders were also, in good progressive fashion, hoping to lead the children to adopt "acceptable middle-class behavior." Orphan asylums tried to instill specific cultural and religious values in tandem with respect for authority, a strong work ethic, and a sense of proper gender roles. In fact, there was a dilemma at the core of orphan asylum managers' goals for a century or more: the children were to be turned into good, working-class adults and solid church members, but they were also expected to hold essentially middle-class values similar to those held by asylum managers themselves.[44]

The Chicago Orphan Asylum's annual report for 1933 ended with a statement that reflected the aspirations that most orphan asylum managers had held since asylums first appeared. After an extended discussion of two children the asylum had cared for, one of whom had just been sent to a state hospital for the insane and one who had been returned to his father and stepmother, the report ended: "We know of no 'formula' which will assure a good future for children like Sarah and Leland, but we can marshall all the available skill and understanding to their aid and honestly say of each who comes to us, 'We have done for him all that we can'."[45]

Conclusion

Orphan asylums were far more likely to be all-embracing institutions in the antebellum period than in the late nineteenth and early twentieth centuries, by which time asylum children might attend public schools, be members of scout troops, and spend time with their families while still residing within the asylum. While the limited evidence that survives about orphan asylums prior to the 1850s makes any definitive claims about what constituted a "typical" orphan asylum—if there was ever such a thing—difficult, it does appear that most kept close control over their children, whether for protective or isolating reasons. They did so while providing a home and some education and training. As Susan Lynne Porter writes of the Boston Female Asylum, "the physical security of a home, clean clothes, and three meals daily gave the child the luxury of concentrating her energies on education rather than survival, with long-term positive effects."[46]

There was considerable truth to some of the criticisms regularly leveled at nineteenth-century asylums. Even many asylum managers agreed that large institutions failed to develop children as individuals. The managers of the Brooklyn Industrial School Association's Home maintained "that years of institution life unfit the child for the place it should occupy in the family."[47] Asylums' constant attempts to become more homelike were, in large part, an attempt to meet this criticism.

There is no question that the monotony and discipline of life in asylums was often their greatest flaw, particularly in large institutions. Partly as a response to this problem, between the 1870s and 1900s asylum managers across the nation softened their disciplinary methods, and allowed boys and girls to interact with one another, and with people outside the asylum, more often.[48]

Orphan asylums were spreading rapidly even as many placing-out advocates and state charity board members were arguing at national and state charity conferences that the asylum's only proper role was as a temporary stop until children could be placed with families. Many asylum managers agreed, but with the crucial difference that they believed the ideal family for children to enter was their own. The rapid increase in the number of orphan asylums throughout the nation, and most asylums' willingness to aid families by caring for their children, clearly show the disparity between what reformers at charity conferences saw as the ideal way to care for dependent children and how local communities actually chose to deal with the problem.

In the late nineteenth century, orphan asylums came into their own. Unlike prisons and poorhouses, they had not failed in their mission. This was partly because trying to care for a child by supplying food, education, and a bed to sleep in was a more reasonable goal than that held by prisons, poorhouses, and insane asylums, which initially hoped to "reform" their inmates through routine and discipline. And almost all asylums were community institutions, usually managed by religious or charitable leaders, not state-run institutions governed by patronage appointees. Their nature as community-based institutions played an important role in the gradual opening of asylums to the broader world.

As the turn of the century approached, dozens of new orphan asylums opened almost every year, and existing asylums upgraded their buildings and educational and recreational facilities, and expanded to fit the growing needs of an urbanizing society. The shift toward an integrative philosophy made asylums more like actual homes, in that their children now spent a meaningful amount of time outside the asylum, interacting with children from other homes and adults from other families.

In 1923, the same gathering of Catholic nuns that developed the "small group system" (described in Chapter 5) argued that the best place for children was in their own homes. Every effort should be made to maintain homes intact, but if that was not possible, asylums should try to return children to their own homes as soon as conditions had improved. The emphasis on maintaining homes was much stronger than before, but the goal of eventually returning institutionalized children to their own families was precisely the function many Catholic and other asylums had followed since before the Civil War. Not surprisingly, many Catholics concerned with child welfare were slow to accept that foster care, which was usually managed by Protestant groups or government agencies, was superior to institutional care for Catholic children. Indeed, many Catholic orphanages lasted well into the age of Aid to Dependent Children and continued to function in the 1940s and 1950s. As most asylums shut down or changed their purpose, some Catholic asylums continued on, caring for their own.[49]

No one represents the change in thinking about child welfare that occurred in the early twentieth century better than Homer Folks. In 1900, he had been a devout advocate of breaking up poor families that did not seem able to properly care for their children. Two decades later, he publicly retracted his earlier views at the National Conference of Social Work. Folks announced that it had become "perfectly evident that many of the forces which tend toward poverty, neglect, and crime are, to a substantial degree, within our control." Folks argued that the line of demarcation in child welfare was not between placing-out advocates and institutions, but instead between those "who readily, or even lightly, remove a child from its own home and those, on the other hand, who do so with the utmost reluctance and only after all other efforts have failed." Poor children's mothers were not dangers to their children; instead, they could and should be seen as child welfare advocates' greatest ally.[50] In practice, many orphan asylum managers had recognized this fact since the 1860s or even earlier.

3

Managers and Funding

Most private orphan asylums were begun and managed by groups of women. As asylums became more common in the middle and late nineteenth century, men played an increasingly important role, but women continued to manage the daily operations of most children's institutions and usually had at least some say in making major policy decisions. The nature of male and female roles depended in part on the religious nature of the asylum. Catholic asylums were almost always run by nuns, but there were male authority figures with at least some control over broad issues concerning the asylum, including financial ones. Protestant asylums also tended to be run by women and also had male overseers; in the South, asylums had male superintendents fairly often as well. Jewish asylums, on the other hand, were almost completely dominated by male managers, as were most publicly managed asylums. Whether their daily affairs were controlled by women or men, almost all orphan asylums had male boards of advisers and male consultants such as doctors and lawyers.

Though no real government supervision of orphan asylums existed until the late nineteenth century (and then only very limited supervision, in a few states), institutions for dependent children often received grants of land or money from city, and occasionally state, governments to help them start out or expand. These grants supplemented the private donations that were the main source of asylum funding in most states. Asylum managers dependent in whole or in part on private funds developed a wide range of fund-raising methods, from door-to-door solicitations to theatrical or musical performances whose proceeds went to the asylum.

After the Civil War, government involvement in providing funding for asylums developed in a handful of states, while remaining very limited or nonexistent in most states. California and New York paid private asylums to care for children on a per capita basis, while Ohio, Indiana, and Connecticut supported county-managed asylums. Michigan founded a large state-run asylum that broke all ties between parents and children before placing children in homes; a number of other states followed suit. As noted in Chapter 1, a number of states also opened soldiers' orphans' homes after the war. Private asylums continued to flourish everywhere, caring for thousands of children whose parents retained legal guardianship. Regardless of their funding sources, the vast majority of orphan asylums remained community institutions, controlled by local groups and serving local interests.

Asylum Management in the Antebellum Period

Orphan asylums were just one of many social institutions that became widespread during the antebellum period. Like most of these institutions, orphan asylums were usually the creation of private, benevolent societies. In many ways, the first half of the nineteenth century was the heyday of charity in the United States. City governments provided outdoor relief as well as indoor relief in almshouses and probably helped more people by these means than were helped by private charities. Nonetheless, private charities proliferated in this era, addressing a wide variety of problems. As Kathleen McCarthy writes, "Voluntarism was the social currency which bound antebellum communities together, nurturing a sense of communal spirit and constantly renewing public commitment to community well-being."[1] This surge of charitable activity was a response, in large part, to the increasingly visible poverty and crime that seemed to accompany rapid urbanization and the growing prevalence of wage labor in the northeastern United States in the decades prior to the Civil War.[2]

Many early Protestant orphan asylums were created by groups of middle-class women. Membership in the New York Orphan Asylum Society, founded in 1806, was limited to women. Petersburg, Virginia's Female Orphan Asylum was opened in 1813 by women determined to aid orphan and half-orphan girls. When women founded private associations such as orphan asylums, they often did so with considerable knowledge of what was happening elsewhere, through contacts with friends in other cities involved in similar activities.³ But societies and institutions were not founded solely for the sake of their clients. Suzanne Lebsock has described what creating and managing one asylum meant to its founders.

> For the upper-middle-class women of Petersburg, there was nothing quite comparable to the asylum to give focus to that special combination of sisterhood and ambition, and that helps explain why the women launched the institution so rapidly, took it so seriously, and sustained it so loyally through the decades.⁴

Not all women who formed organizations and founded institutions did so for identical reasons. Nancy Hewitt has found in her study of women activists in Rochester that three distinct types of women organized and managed various types of institutions and societies. Elite, benevolent women became active in the 1820s and gave Rochester "its major social welfare institutions for half a century." Evangelical perfectionists became active in the 1830s, inspired by revivals and determined to "eradicate rather than ameliorate social ills." In the 1840s, radical, or ultraist, women became active, seeking "complete legal, social, and economic equality for blacks and women." They were from families that were new to the area or that were "socially marginal" compared to the families of women in the first two groups.⁵

In 1837, members of Rochester's Female Charitable Society, a benevolent organization, founded the Orphan Asylum Association (O.A.A.) to care for "Orphan and Destitute Children." Hewitt argues that in the O.A.A., benevolent and evangelical women worked together. At least half of the first eighteen managers of the O.A.A. were members of churches that had been deeply affected by recent revivals in the city, and Hewitt argues that "the O.A.A. was clearly evangelical in style in its early years." The asylum's goals for children were not completely clear, as half of the board's leadership sought evangelical, perfectionist salvation of the children while the other half simply hoped to save children from a life of poverty. The O.A.A. was also the closest thing to a nonsectarian organization in the city, though like most other such groups, it was fundamentally Protestant in nature and management. No Catholics, Quakers, German Lutherans, or African Methodists sat on its executive board.⁶

Most Protestant orphan asylums were founded by the type of women

Hewitt calls benevolent. Even though the women she calls evangelicals were not predominant in founding and managing most orphan asylums, religion was important, often even central, to asylums' missions. The central role women played in creating benevolent organizations and institutions, including orphan asylums, in the first half of the nineteenth century was tied to the importance of religion in these organizations. Churches were at the center of many charitable endeavors, and in most churches women made up a large portion of active members and were heavily involved in church work. Ministers and priests often encouraged women's role in benevolent work. Lori Ginzberg argues that "middle- and upper-middle-class women of the antebellum era shared a language that described their benevolent work as Christian, their means as fundamentally moral, and their mandate as uniquely female." Just as important as religion, Lebsock argues, was the fact that charitable associations such as orphan asylums were a way for middle-class women to extend themselves and their roles in the home into the broader world. Some ventures by women into the public sphere drew tremendous criticism, but orphan asylums were a relatively safe haven for middle-class women seeking a place in the world beyond their homes, chiefly because orphan asylums were themselves supposed to be homes.[7]

By the 1830s, an ideology had developed that envisioned women as the special guardians of the home and, through their unique role in raising children, "of democracy itself."[8] Women and men were both heavily involved in creating private associations during this period, but building and running orphan asylums seemed especially appropriate for women. The fact that women were usually managing these institutions was central to the asylums' relations with the poor. Charity workers who came into close contact with the poor often abandoned their early, judgmental attitudes and responded more to the intense need for aid that they encountered. This was particularly true of many women who worked with the poor,[9] though some women involved in charity retained harsh views of the poor, and some men developed sympathetic views of the poor. While not a universal difference, in some places it does seem to have mattered whether men or women were running an orphan asylum. In her study of antebellum southern charity, Gail Murray has found that women running orphan asylums did so differently than men in the same position.[10]

Protestant institutions were not the only ones run predominantly by women. Catholic orphan asylums prior to the Civil War were often founded by a bishop or priest, but they were almost always managed by nuns. They also usually had an all-male board of trustees that was in charge of financial matters, while women were in charge of daily affairs within the asylum. When the Sisters of Charity came to New York in 1817 at the request of Bishop John Connolly, it was established that "the trustees were to have entire charge of the financial affairs of the orphan asylum, and the sisters were to be left free to manage the internal affairs of the institution according to their own rules." Of course, the daily management of an institution cannot be completely separated from its funding. Any plans the sisters might make were constrained by financial limits, and the trustees probably paid considerable attention to requests the sisters made that involved additional funding. This arrangement, with a male board of trustees or managers deciding on new buildings and controlling funding, remained common in Catholic asylums throughout the antebellum period.[11]

Particular Catholic orders quickly became known for their charity work with children and were asked by various bishops and laypeople to come to a given city and open or assume the management of an orphan asylum. The Sisters of Charity of Emmitsburg, "the great pioneering community in Catholic charities," are the most obvious example, but they were hardly alone. Mother Seton's Sisters founded at least seven orphan asylums between 1828 and 1835, from Albany to Pittsburgh to New Orleans, and the School Sisters of Notre Dame from Munich were in charge of many of the German Catholic orphan asylums opened between 1840 and 1860.[12]

Some Protestant asylums also had management structures in which men controlled monetary decisions and women ran the asylum on a daily basis. The Cincinnati Orphan Asylum's state charter gave the male township trustees of Cincinnati control over the asylum's income, while women ran the asylum's "interior concerns." In 1841, New York's Colored Orphan Asylum had an advisory board of men, but the officers and managers were women; they probably made most of the important decisions about the asylum. By 1849, however, a male superintendent was in charge of the asylum's day-to-day life. The Orphans' Home and Asylum of New York City, founded in 1851, had a board of managers dominated by Episcopal ministers. Day-to-day management of the home was left to the Ladies' Committee, which was evenly divided between married women and single women.¹³ The home's founders recognized that it would benefit by mixing religious leaders with laypeople, and women with men, in its management:

> The Constitution of our Society attempts to combine the influence which persons of both sexes are capable of exercising in their very different spheres. At the outset of our undertaking, it was borne in mind that almost every similar institution in this city owed its prosperity, under God, to the zeal of charitable women, who, by natural temperament, appreciate the importance and feel the interest of the minute details which make up so much of the daily course of such a work, more than men in any condition—far more than men immersed in business. At the same time, it was seen that the co-operation of business-men, as well as clergymen, would in many respects be serviceable; while on certain occasions their names, especially if well known in the community, would have peculiar weight, and come with peculiar propriety before the public.¹⁴

Similarly, Boston's Church Home for Orphan and Destitute Children, founded in the late 1850s, had a board of trustees made up mostly of laymen, but the board's president and all three vice-presidents were ministers. The board of managers, like the Orphans' Home's Ladies' Committee, was composed of married and single women and ran the Church Home's daily operations. These asylums had management structures typical of Protestant asylums in the decade before the Civil War. Women ran the daily operations, and religious and business leaders of the community provided prestige and increased access to funding sources for the asylum. In many cases, virtually all of the women on a board of managers were likely to be married, though in some asylums single women did play important roles. It is important to note that not all asylums run by women gave men power over their monetary decisions. The women who managed the Boston Female Asylum at the start of the nineteenth century retained control over everything concerning their institution, including money, despite considerable criticism for doing so.¹⁵

In Catholic asylums, men played an important, if sometimes remote, role in asylum management from the early part of the century onward. However, in Protestant orphan asylums, men's heavy involvement in financial matters may have been a new matter in the 1840s and 1850s. Suzanne Lebsock's study of women in Petersburg, Virginia, found that "after several decades in which single-sex societies were the rule, the 1850s witnessed the rise of mixed associations in which the women usually assumed auxiliary roles."[16]

Rachel Marks has argued that in early orphan asylums, superintendents and matrons were treated as staff members while the board of trustees or the board of managers (whether male or female) actually managed the asylum, holding weekly meetings and making most administrative decisions. Kathleen McCarthy has found a similar pattern in Chicago's first orphan asylums.[17] In many asylums, however, superintendents and matrons clearly were more than just employees. Who made most important decisions probably varied from asylum to asylum and was likely more dependent on the individual personalities involved than whether the asylum was Catholic or Protestant, or northern or southern.

When asylums hired a superintendent or matron, they often hired that person's family as well. In the 1850s, the Orphans' Home and Asylum of New York was "conducted by a very efficient Matron, resident in the House, whose daughter instructs the children." This was not unusual. When the matron or superintendent had teenage or adult children, they often taught in the asylum school. If a married couple was hired, the superintendent's wife usually functioned as an unpaid matron. When an asylum's trustees found a superintendent or matron they liked, that person might stay for decades. The longer a person stayed on the job, the more likely that person was to have considerable power in how an asylum functioned. Asylums were not always able to find employees they were happy with, however. In its first twelve years of existence, from 1833 to 1845, the Cincinnati Orphan Asylum had three single women as matrons followed by three married couples as superintendents and matrons, without finding anyone that seemed to work out well.[18] Partly in response to this problem, and also as a means of finding employment for their wards, some asylums hired their own "graduates." At the Charleston Orphan House in the 1850s, "the most accomplished girls tended to remain in the institution past their eighteenth birthdays," working as teaching assistants or sewing instructors.[19]

Staffing the Asylum After the Civil War

After the Civil War, small asylums were often managed by their founders, just as they had been earlier in the century. Aside from a board of trustees or female managers, an entire staff might consist of a matron or superintendent and just one or two other workers. Women board members often spent large amounts of time in these asylums, making decisions, supervising staff members, and caring for children. In some asylums, this pattern held true to the end of the nineteenth century and beyond. At St. Mary's Orphanage of Providence in 1897, members of the board of managers took turns "identifying themselves with every interest of the Orphanage." Similarly, Ken Cmiel found that at the Chicago Nursery and Half-Orphan Asylum in the late nineteenth century, it was "the women volunteers of the managers board," not male trustees or the asylum's matron, who made daily decisions about children as well as basic policy decisions about admission, staff, and money.[20]

Large asylums were a more complex matter. Whether managed by male trustees or female managers, or by a superintendent or matron, they required large staffs to function smoothly. By the 1860s, large asylums were becoming more common and probably already housed the majority of institutionalized dependent children. The management structure of the Chicago Orphan Asylum was fairly typical for large Protestant and nonsectarian institutions. A board of trustees consisting of a president, vice-president, secretary, treasurer, and eleven other male trustees controlled all major decisions about the asylum's overall structure, funding, and goals. The trustees appointed a board of directresses "for the supervision, direction and management of the internal concerns of the Asylum, to consist of forty ladies." Because the asylum was nonsectarian, no more than five directresses could come from any one religious denomination, though all were Protestant. The directresses would in turn appoint a matron and a teacher for the asylum's school. The directresses determined the salaries of these two women, a power that other asylums often reserved to men; given that they had at least some power over the purse strings, it seems likely the directresses were running the asylum. The directresses were almost all married women, though a few were single. Matrons were also almost certain to be married (or widowed), though teachers were likely to be young and single.[21]

Some Catholic asylums also had management structures in which men made most long-term decisions, particularly financial ones, and women ran the asylum from day to day. Philadelphia's St. Vincent's Orphan Asylum was run by a board of managers composed of four priests and twelve laymen that controlled funding, provided food and clothing to the children, and even controlled admissions. But the Sisters of Notre

Dame were in charge of the children's actual lives and undoubtedly had considerable input into the decisions made by the board. Other Catholic asylums were run by a single group of women such as the Sisters of Charity, with relatively little male oversight or interference. In many asylums, Catholic and otherwise, male fund-raisers and asylum founders were reluctant to place women in charge without a man looking over their shoulders. At the Roman Catholic Orphan Asylums of New York City in the 1870s, all of the committees making decisions about entry, discharge, funding, and other central issues consisted solely of men. Similarly, the Lutheran Children's Home of the South was founded by a man, who served as its first superintendent. When he suggested to the board of trustees in 1893 that the home would be better served with a woman who could serve as a "mother" to the children, a matron was found. But the trustees insisted that the founder remain involved, naming him "non-resident superintendent."[22]

Jewish orphan asylums were strikingly male-dominated in their management. The Hebrew Orphan Asylum Society of Brooklyn was typical. As with most Protestant orphan asylums, the Hebrew Orphan Asylum's trustees were all male. But women did not play the same crucial role for the Brooklyn Hebrew Orphan Asylum that they so often played in Protestant and Catholic institutions. The all-male board of governors closely controlled the asylum, its board of education was completely male, and the asylum was run by a male superintendent.[23] Similarly, Nurith Zmora found that the German Jewish board that ran Baltimore's Hebrew Orphan Asylum either made, or had to approve, all important decisions concerning the asylum.[24] Women did have a role in Jewish orphan asylums, but it was quite limited. A Ladies' Sewing Society helped raise money for the Brooklyn Hebrew Orphan Asylum, sewed clothes for the children, and taught sewing in the asylum. They would be found there every Wednesday "actively engaged in women's work, cutting, sewing, and inspecting, speaking words of cheer to the little children." The Hebrew Orphan Asylum's president wrote that "the prosperity of this Society is largely dependent upon the efforts and labors" of the Ladies' Sewing Society's members, but in reality they brought in only a tiny portion of the asylum's funding and apparently had little influence. Women were clearly subordinate in the running of the asylum. The one woman who did carry some power was the matron, who had been hired along with the superintendent, her husband.[25] Philadelphia's Jewish Foster Home was managed by women from its founding in 1855, but in 1874 power shifted to men.[26]

Probably the most important decision made by an orphan asylum's managers was whom to put in charge of day-to-day operations as matron or superintendent. Some asylums hired married couples to share this duty, though, not surprisingly, the man usually seems to have been in charge. Trustees and asylum management boards hoped to find someone who would stay for a long period of time as well as be good at the job and were reluctant to give up a good manager once one had been found. The Chicago Orphan Asylum's matron resigned in 1893, after two decades' service. The trustees tried to refuse her resignation, but she insisted. Her replacement lasted only six weeks, leaving "on account of failing health." The asylum's trustees had greater hopes for the next woman hired, as she had "some experience in similar lines of work and good executive ability." In 1896, St. Vincent's Orphan Asylum in Philadelphia regretted the departure of a nun who had "been a faithful mother to the orphans" for thirty-three years.[27]

If a superintendent or matron failed to meet expectations, it was usually quickly evident, as in the Chicago Orphan Asylum's case, and the failure was often blamed on poor health in annual reports. If a superintendent or matron succeeded, however, he or she was likely to have long job tenure. Once they had made it through their first year, asylum managers usually stayed on for many years. Of course, the more involved in daily affairs board members were, the less authority the superintendent or matron actually wielded. At Baltimore's Hebrew Orphan Asylum, as at many asylums in the late nineteenth century, the superintendent made few major decisions on his own. Superintendents at state-managed asylums, such as the Illinois's Soldiers' Orphans' Home, may have had more leeway than most superintendents of private asylums. This is ironic, given that many of these men were political appointees who may not have had any affinity for their work.[28]

While some asylums operated with a matron or superintendent, and perhaps a teacher and cook, large asylums had suitably large staffs. In the 1890s, Brooklyn's Hebrew Orphan Asylum employed a cook, three laundresses, two seamstresses (despite its Ladies' Sewing Society), two baby nurses, one hospital nurse, two "kitchen help," five chambermaids, and several others in addition to a superintendent, matron, and primary school teacher.[29] Asylums hoped for continuity within their staffs. Keeping a matron or superintendent for many years was just one part of having a happy, successful home. Hiring good staff members was another important factor. All nineteenth-century institutions struggled to find good staff members for the low pay they offered, and orphan asylums were no different.[30] As had sometimes happened in the antebellum era, some asylums sought to hire former inmates, either as they became old enough to leave the asylum, or later, after they had been away from the asylum for a few years. In 1874, the Chicago Orphan Asylum tried the "experiment" of hiring several of its older girls (ages fifteen to seventeen) to attend to dormitories, the dining room, and other aspects of the asylum, "with a good degree of success." In 1878, the Orphans' Home and Asylum of New York's annual report stated that "It has long been our wish, as some of our friends know, to train up our own beneficiaries for domestic service in the Home, and this wish has been so far accomplished, that we have at present five of our own girls filling various situations there, according to their age and ability, and receiving the same compensation for their services that they would obtain outside of the institution."[31]

Hiring former inmates made for continuity. It not only gave managers a staff that knew the asylum's rules but also proved the asylum's success in preparing their children to hold the jobs for which they had been trained. In addition, it often meant that at least a few staff members would share the ethnic background of some, and perhaps many, asylum children. Of course, this was often not the case. For example, late-nineteenth-century Catholic asylums might be staffed by Irish women whether or not most of the children were Irish. Jewish asylums in the same period were run by German Jews, but by 1900 many contained a majority of Russian Jewish children. Similarly, some asylums for black children, such as the Colored Orphan Asylum in New York City, had all-white staffs.[32]

Asylum Management in the Progressive Era

Just as they had been in the nineteenth century, after the beginning of the twentieth century most orphan asylums continued to be run by women. While most asylums continued to have men in advisory positions, it was women who ran daily operations and did all the work involved in actually caring for children. For example, in 1908 the

Chicago Orphan Asylum's board of trustees were all men, as was its advisory board. But there was a large board of managers, consisting almost completely of women, that, along with the asylum's matron, seems to have actually run the asylum. Similarly, a few years later the Brooklyn Home for Children was run by women; both the matron and the superintendent were women. The only men involved in the home's management were a variety of doctors, one lawyer, and a twenty-man advisory board that had little or nothing to do with day-to-day operations.[33]

The management of St. Francis' Orphan Asylum of New Haven, Connecticut, in 1904 seems fairly representative of Catholic asylums at the turn of the century. Its board of trustees was composed of parish priests and lay members of New Haven's Catholic parishes. The trustees were relatively remote from the asylum's daily operations, but they chose a board of managers (apparently male) to handle "the financial and secular affairs of the orphanage." The Sisters of Mercy controlled "the internal management" of the asylum, devoting their lives to their charges without pay.[34] Some Catholic asylums were managed by priests. The Angel Guardian Orphanage, which was technically separated into male and female institutions, was run by a priest. The directors for the boys' industrial school half of the orphanage were male, while those for the girls' school included four men, four married women, and one nun. But nuns ran the daily operations of the orphanage, working under a superioress.[35]

No single management structure describes all orphan asylums in the Progressive Era. One San Francisco Protestant asylum had an eighteen-woman board of managers that seems to have made all major decisions regarding the institution. There were five male trustees whose only role was to "advise the Board of Managers on the financial matters of the Society." But despite the fact that women were clearly running the asylum, the person in charge of day-to-day issues was a male superintendent. Another asylum was completely run by women in 1905 but was not willing to totally forgo the respectability and social contacts that prominent men might provide: while it did not have a board of trustees, its annual report listed nine "references," all male, five of whom were married to the "Lady Associates" who in fact served as the asylum's trustees. A few orphan asylums remained male domains. This was particularly, but not solely, true of Jewish institutions. The Colored Orphan Asylum of North Carolina also had an all-male board of trustees, one of whom was the superintendent, in the early 1930s.[36]

Between 1890 and 1910, social work began to take shape as a discipline. The number of paid workers in charitable agencies grew, and by 1910 schools of social work were beginning to appear. In the 1910s, some charitable agencies began having difficulty attracting volunteers.[37] During the 1920s and early 1930s, increasing numbers of orphan asylums hired social workers to help them develop better methods of rearing their children. The social workers filled a variety of roles that had previously been handled by a matron, superintendent, or committee. One California asylum that hired a social worker in 1930 stated that "Never before has it been possible to give such careful and well-directed attention to all applications for admission and requests for discharge." The social worker also proved important in achieving another asylum goal: "establishing and maintaining contacts with parents, relatives and friends of children." The Chicago Nursery and Half-Orphan Asylum hired a superintendent with some social work training for the first time in 1932. Social workers began to work at other asylums, though many asylums had not yet hired full-time, trained social workers before the depression. A study conducted in the early 1930s of North Carolina's asylums for African-American children recommended that social workers be hired on a full-time basis. The arrival of social work sometimes changed an asylum's function fairly directly. When a new generation of women gained control of the Chicago Orphan Asylum in 1926, they placed social workers in charge; the social workers then led the asylum in a shift toward boarding children out, as described in Chapter 1. Some asylums had hired more than one person trained to work with children by the 1930s. One California asylum had a staff of "eight recent college graduates with advanced degrees" who had "been trained for their special work with children," along with "eight older men and women who have been teachers and are parents with a sympathetic understanding of child nature and nurture." Scientific expertise and training were important but so was the idea of having caretakers who loved their children.[38]

By the early twentieth century, the child-staff ratio seems to have become relatively low in most orphan asylums. The 1910 census of benevolent institutions collected data on the number of "paid employees at close of year" for each institution it listed, along with the number of children in the asylum at year's end, thus revealing the ratio of workers to children. There were notable differences among the child-staff ratios for Catholic, Protestant, Jewish, fraternal, and publicly managed orphan asylums. Not surprisingly, smaller, cottage-based institutions had better child-staff ratios than did older, large congregate asylums. On average, cottage asylums had one paid employee for every ten children, while congregate institutions had one paid employee for every sixteen children. Overall, Protestant asylums had one paid employee for every twelve children they cared for, while public and Jewish asylums averaged between six and eight children for each paid employee (see Table 3.1). Of course, poorer asylums had more children per worker than better-funded institutions. Asylums for minorities in particular sometimes suffered from poor staff-child ratios. In 1928, North Carolina's Colored Orphan Asylum had an appalling ratio of eighty-six children per "cottage matron."[39]

Although these numbers are generally trustworthy, the findings from the 1910 census are meaningless regarding Catholic asylums. Catholic orphan asylums were almost always run by Catholic religious personnel who were not paid and would not have shown up in the census. Catholic asylums may indeed have had a worse child-staff ratio than other asylums, but it was almost certainly far better than thirty children per worker. Another important problem with the census information is that it does not distinguish between full-time workers and part-time workers; teachers who were with the children constantly and gardeners who came to the asylum twice a week were probably treated the same in most institutions' responses to the 1910 census.

Catholic asylums were not the only institutions to benefit from unpaid work. Board members at virtually all asylums were probably unpaid—in fact, since many board members were also donors, they in a sense actually paid for the right to help—and many doctors and dentists donated their time as well. In at least one case, the Mennonite Children's Home, the entire staff, including the supervisor and matron, worked without pay (presumably except for room and board) from the home's founding in 1911 until 1950.[40]

Quality of staff mattered as much as, or more than, the quantity. Finding and keeping quality staff members had been a problem for all types of institutions throughout the nineteenth century, and orphan asylums faced the same dilemma. In the early twentieth century, workers in North Carolina's orphan asylums were still poorly paid.[41] The increased availability of staff members with training in social work probably raised the quality of staff members somewhat. Nonetheless, for most asylums finding (and affording) quality staff members was still a problem in the 1920s, just as it had been a century before. As in other areas of welfare, limited funds and overburdened staffs were commonplace problems in many orphan asylums. And while the rise of social work played a role in asylums during this period, some asylum managers turned authority over to professionally trained staff slowly and reluctantly. Ken Cmiel found that "the move from volunteer to professional was still incomplete as late as 1945" at the Chicago Nursery and Half-Orphan Asylum.[42]

Antebellum Funding

Prior to the Civil War, orphan asylums throughout the nation depended heavily on private donations for survival and expansion. Asylum managers actively sought out individual subscribers, who gave a specific amount every month or year. Small asylums could start with relatively little funding, as could Catholic asylums managed by an order of nuns. For example, in 1829 the pastor of St. John's Church in Philadelphia helped organize subscribers to provide care for poor Catholic children. A house was rented, and "Furniture was provided by a few charitably inclined women." With that, and with a staff that worked long hours for no pay other than minimal room and board, St John's Orphan Asylum was established. A subscription list could go a long way toward maintaining an asylum once a permanent building had been constructed. In its first year of existence, 1833–1834, more than one-third of the Cincinnati Orphan Asylum's $1,868 income was from subscriptions. Rochester's Orphan Asylum Association, founded in 1837, relied heavily on door-to-door canvassing for donations in its first few years. By the mid-1840s, however, it had "developed more regularized forms of fund raising, including annual sermons in selected churches, exhibitions at the asylum, and public performances by orphans."[43]

Prominent church or community leaders were often willing to help an asylum, especially for a specific purpose such as a new building. Donations of all sizes were publicly acknowledged in annual reports, which often listed donors by name along with the amount they had given, to thank and encourage them as well as to spur others in the community. During the first sixteen months of its existence, the annual report of the Orphans' Home and Asylum of New York listed fifty donors who had given less than $10 each. Ten donors had given between $10 and $37, and an additional five had given between $50 and $100.[44]

Giving was often prompted by a combination of ethnic and racial pride and a powerful awareness that it was desperately needed for the survival of the community's poorest members. Nowhere was this more true than in African-American communities, which often marshaled limited resources to protect their children. John Blassingame found that during the Civil War era, New Orleans's black community did all it could to support a variety of charities, with orphanages perhaps the most important. Black churches and newspapers sought funds for these asylums, and the wealthier members of the community often contributed heavily.[45]

Like so much else about charity work in the antebellum period, asylum funding was a local affair. By the mid-1830s, there were two Catholic orphan asylums for girls in Philadelphia, St. Joseph's and St. John's.[46] Their sources of support were local and heavily dependent on nearby Catholic churches and organizations of Catholic laypeople:

> The main sources of revenue for both institutions were the yearly contributions of the Orphan Societies connected with the Homes. The yearly "Charity Sermons" preached in the different churches of the city were also of great importance. Fairs were held only on a few occasions. Diocesan support was lacking at this time. The upkeep of the asylums throughout the United States was distinctly a matter of the parishes that founded them.[47]

Catholic institutions had one advantage and one disadvantage in seeking funds to care for children. Their disadvantage was tied to the reason that so many Catholic children were destitute: in the antebellum period, Catholic communities were usually made up largely of recent immigrants with few resources. Their advantage was, of course, that they had trained, willing workers to run and staff their orphan asylums for little or no pay.

Since they were regularly inundated with far more applicants than they could accept, many orphan asylums solicited money for building funds as they outgrew their current home and felt the need for either additional buildings or a new, larger institution. When this happened, wealthy community members were approached for help, often successfully. Asylum founders and managers also had considerable success in obtaining public money when they were trying to afford a new building. City governments often provided either a plot of land or money, and state governments also occasionally provided funds for new buildings. Just nine years after its opening, the Orphans' Home and Asylum of New York City, which had already established a building fund of $18,500 through private donations, began work on a new, larger institution on a plot of land provided by the city.[48] Though city and state government involvement in orphan asylums was usually limited in the antebellum period to providing land or money for new buildings, public and private funding and management did mix on occasion. The Charleston Orphan House, managed by the city, also received private donations and bequests over the years that amounted to a large part of its funding.[49]

Substantial public funding of orphan asylums' day-to-day operations was limited in the antebellum period, but some towns and cities were already paying for private asylums to care for dependent children. The majority of the children in the Cincinnati Orphan Asylum, which opened in 1833, were placed there by the township trustees, who paid for their care. In fact, more than half of the asylum's income in its first year came from the city, and the state legislature also provided funding until the early 1850s. From 1833 to 1852, nearly two-thirds of the money the Cincinnati Orphan Asylum received came from public sources. In the early 1850s, public funding for private charity organizations came under attack in Ohio, as it often would in other states for the rest of the century. A new Ohio constitution ended state funding in 1851, and the next year the township trustees of Cincinnati, who had long supplied the Cincinnati Orphan Asylum with both inmates and income, were disbanded.[50]

Public funding for orphan asylums in New Orleans followed a pattern similar to Ohio's. Beginning in 1816, the Louisiana state government gave lump sums of money to a number of asylums. Although the amounts received by individual asylums were small, as the number of institutions grew so did the total amount of state funding. The city of New Orleans also provided money to some of its institutions, beginning with a "city alimony" paid to the Poydras Female Asylum when children were transferred to it from the Ursuline Convent. By 1870, the state government was refusing to make any more grants, and in 1879 state aid to private institutions such as orphan asylums became unconstitutional.[51]

In the late nineteenth century, New York and California provided far more funds for their private orphan asylums than any other state, for which they were regularly criticized at charity conferences. Though California's first orphan asylums appeared only in the 1850s, New York's asylums for dependent children, and public funding of them, had a long past. In 1811, New York State provided what became an annual appropriation to the New York Orphan Asylum. In subsequent years, other asylums also began to receive lump sums of money from the state. Cities also provided money or land, especially to help an asylum erect a building. In 1851, New York City was required to appropriate $40 per child per year to asylums, an amount that rose several times over the course of the century. New York State began distributing money to asylums on a per capita basis in 1855. It appropriated a sum of $35,000 that year, which was given to county officials, who in turn passed it on to asylums. In 1857, "it was estimated that there were twenty-six orphan asylums maintaining a total of 2,816 children, which were receiving state support."[52]

If these numbers are accurate, then fairly large orphan asylums must have existed in New York before state per capita money became available. Just two years after such payments began, the average asylum receiving the payments held more than one hundred children and must have had the capacity to do so before the per capita payments began, since it is highly unlikely that many of them moved to new, larger buildings in the period from 1855 to 1857. The asylums were large, but not because state money was available. It is more likely that their size, and the obvious need of thousands of children, made it easier to persuade the legislature to help. Over the next few decades, however, the availability of public money would help spur the expansion of New York's asylums into huge congregate institutions.

The Search for Funding After the Civil War

The managers of orphan asylums were always actively raising funds. Poorer asylums had to find money just to feed their children, while better-funded asylums tried to raise money for long-term endowments, larger and better buildings, or summer homes. In California and New York, public funding gave asylums some measure of security. In most other states, there was no government funding available and little county or city money for orphan asylums. Asylums throughout the nation tried a wide variety of methods to raise funds, and an asylum's success or failure depended on both its location and its religious and societal connections.[53]

Asylums in California and New York, which received per capita payments to support children from either the state or the county, had advantages that private asylums in other states lacked. Though state money was not enough to support children fully, it allowed asylums to channel much of their fund raising into building funds or endowments for the future. Public funding also allowed these asylums to survive depressions more easily than asylums elsewhere. Most importantly, it allowed asylums in California and New York to expand in response to growing needs. They could care for more children because each new child meant an increase in their payments from the government. Critics at the National Conference of Charities and Correction often complained that per capita payments led to large asylums that took in anyone who applied. Without accepting the claim that some of the children being helped were "undeserving," it is quite clear that these critics were right in one respect: asylums in California and New York did tend to be larger than those in other states.

The Maria Kip Orphanage of San Francisco, California, opened in 1890 for the care of orphan, half-orphan, and abandoned girls. State funding was crucial to the Maria Kip during the 1890s. Public money made up 45 percent of the Maria Kip's annual expenses in 1891, and 55 percent in 1892. Because of this aid, during that same period it was able to develop a separate building fund, which raised $7,600 from private donations in 1891 and 1892.[54] This was a reversal of the typical form of antebellum public funding, in which city or state money was often available to help asylums afford new buildings but was not available for daily expenses. By 1896, a new building had been completed, and the continued availability of state money allowed the Maria Kip to have a sizable surplus at the end of the year, a luxury orphan asylums in other states rarely enjoyed.

Orphan asylums in New York also benefited from regular public funding. As in California, public funding in New York made up a large portion of the money raised by orphan asylums. In 1876, the Roman Catholic Orphan Asylums of New York City received over $19,000 from the Board of Education, which was roughly 15 percent of their total receipts for the year. In 1893–1894, public money made up 32 percent of the Brooklyn Hebrew Orphan Asylum's income; in 1899, it rose to 53 percent.[55] The difference between California's provision of direct state funds and New York's more local county-based system was unimportant to orphan asylums. For them, what mattered was that they could count on receiving thousands of dollars in public money every year. If private fund raising was even moderately successful, asylums in these states could apply some of it to a new building, an endowment fund, a summer home, industrial training, or other advances that many private asylums in other states might not be able to provide their children. If fund raising was poor, asylums could still continue to function, whereas in other states they might have to close, or skimp on basic care of their children. Even when public funding was available elsewhere, it was often quite limited. In 1896, the Colored Orphan Industrial Home of Lexington received $50 per month from the city and an additional $1,000 for the year from the county.[56]

Other sources of funding—such as board money from parents, donations, and dues from members and patrons—were crucial to asylums in most states, where public money was much less readily available. In the antebellum period, many asylums had cared largely for orphans, so there had rarely been parents for asylums to ask for board payments. By the 1870s and 1880s, however, the vast majority of asylum children had at least one living parent, and many had two living parents. Many asylums urged surviving parents to pay at least small amounts toward their children's board. For example, in 1891 the Maria Kip Orphanage received $943 from parents, which amounted to more than 17 percent of its receipts that year. The Chicago Nursery and Half-Orphan Asylum requested board payments that were "usually someplace between 25 and 40 percent of a parents' income" in the late nineteenth century.[57]

Asylum managers saw board payments made by parents as more than mere financial help for the asylum. They also served to strengthen bonds between children and their families. Since many asylums in the postbellum era intended to return children to their parents, this was an important issue. In the 1870s, the Brooklyn Industrial School Association's Home asked for $4 a month from all parents able to work. Along with helping the home function, this allowed working fathers and mothers to "have the children comfortably provided for without resting under the imputation of begging or asking for charity." The Orphans' Home and Asylum of New York City expected seventy-five cents a week from the relatives or friends of its children whenever they could afford it. Though this money was hardly enough to fully support a child, it did help, and "to the contributors it is of importance as a means of keeping up their interest in their young relatives, and their own self-respect." Some Catholic asylums also counted on board money from parents.[58]

Regular donors also helped on a monthly or annual basis, just as they had always done. For 1887, the Chicago Orphan Asylum's solicitor reported ten $50 and forty-five $25 donations, from individuals, couples, and small businesses.[59] Donors also gave goods such as clothing, furniture, coal, books, and toys. The Chicago Orphan Asylum took in "lumber, provisions, and other articles" valued at more than $2,300 in 1881, and many asylums' annual reports contained lengthy lists of donated goods as well as cash donations.[60]

The death of a patron did not necessarily mean an end to giving. Some asylums received large bequests in the wills of wealthy patrons. Jewish and Episcopal asylums seem to have particularly benefited from this type of help, though other Protestant asylums and Catholic asylums also received legacies. California's Maria Kip Orphanage received more than $12,000 in legacies in 1896, most of which went to its building fund. Another Episcopal orphanage, the Orphans' Home and Asylum of New York, received two legacies in 1871, one for more than $10,000 and the other for almost $18,000.[61] Most large asylums and some small ones received bequests at one time or another. Poor asylums used them to survive, while richer ones used them to improve their facilities, as in the Maria Kip's case. For the Chicago Nursery and Half-Orphan Asylum, legacies in the late 1880s and early 1890s dramatically improved its finances. Between 1888 and 1895, the amount of the asylum's total income derived from interest on its endowment rose from 16 percent to 50 percent.[62]

Donations, dues, and bequests were sources of income for many orphan asylums, but church fund raising was the single most important source of income for most asylums. Some asylums, especially broadly Protestant "nonsectarian" ones, received money from an astounding variety of churches. In 1892, the Brooklyn Industrial School Association collected from forty-seven different churches, including Presbyterian, Episcopal, Methodist, and Baptist churches. Catholic asylums also tended to take in money from more than one church. St. Vincent's Orphan Asylum of Philadelphia received money from a variety of Catholic churches inside and outside the city in the 1860s. In 1876, New York's Roman Catholic Orphan Asylums received $37,000 from church collections on Christmas and Easter Sunday, which was more than one-fourth of the asylums' total income for that year. Catholic asylums also hoped for, and occasionally received, the religious equivalent of city support: regular aid from the diocese.[63]

Concerts, performances, and fairs that gave their profits to asylums were common by the 1870s. Some were amateur events, such as the Chicago Orphan Asylum's "Old Folks Concerts" of April 1874, featuring performances by male trustees and female directresses. Other fund-raising performances featured outside groups, probably ones a trustee or directress had strong connections with, such as the Dramatic Club's entertainments for the same asylum seven months later.[64] Some fund-raising events could be enormously profitable, even in depression years. In 1894, a charity ball netted more than $7,000 for the Hebrew Orphan Asylum Society of Brooklyn, and the next year it made more than $8,600.[65] Asylums benefited from an astounding variety of other fund-raising events, such as the charity baseball game held by the Pacific Union Club and the Bohemian Club, which donated $581 to the Maria Kip in 1892.[66]

When asylums found solid fund-raising events, they tried to make them into annual affairs. The Brooklyn Hebrew Orphan Asylum's annual New Year's reception brought in more than $1,200 in 1897. In the same year, the asylum's annual "Children's Day," featuring entertainments by the asylum children for other children, made $381. Catholic and Protestant asylums dominated by a single ethnic group relied heavily on annual festivals, where ethnic pride in the asylum translated into dollars. In Nashville, St. Mary's Orphanage held an annual Fourth of July picnic that was a fund-raiser as well as "a major social event" for the city's Catholic community. In some cases, events could bring in support from the broader community as well. Beginning in the late 1850s, the Sisters of Charity in Los Angeles held an annual fair that raised funds for their orphan asylum from across both denominational and ethnic boundaries.[67]

Orphan asylums sought funds in a number of other ways. One successful method was to ask for funds in connection with specific needs. The closer these needs were to the children, the better. For example, in 1891 the Maria Kip Orphanage had four "donor" bedrooms, each of which housed between four and seven girls who had been clothed by a donor or group of donors. In two of these four rooms, furnishings had also been supplied by the donor. This appealed to a variety of potential benefactors; one of the rooms was supplied by a church, two by groups of women, and one by a single donor. During the 1870s and 1880s, the Chicago Orphan Asylum had a "Shoe Day" on October 12, when a donor paid tribute to the memory of her husband by giving a pair of new shoes to every child. After her death, the asylum continued the tradition, probably aided by a bequest in her will.[68]

Some asylums found particularly innovative methods of fund raising, especially when trying to establish or increase a building fund or endowment fund. These often relied heavily on the social connections enjoyed by the asylum's trustees or managers. One of the more unusual examples comes from the Maria Kip. "Through the kindness of a number of prominent ladies and gentlemen, in loaning for public exhibition gems from their art galleries, and the generosity of Geo. C. Shreve & Co., in allowing their art room to be used for the occasion," the Maria Kip Orphanage made a "substantial addition" of $1,333 to its building fund in 1891.[69] Even in states where considerable public money was available, fund raising from private sources was a continual process. The Maria Kip Orphanage received $553 from a "Charity Fete" in 1890, its first full year of existence. It also received aid from "various city churches" as well as children's societies. In that year, it received $1,240 from the state but took in a larger sum, $1,661, from entertainments.[70]

Asylum funding problems increased during depressions, as the number of children needing aid rose and the number of able donors decreased. (Other charity institutions, such as hospitals, also struggled during depressions.) Some asylums weathered economic downturns better than others. In 1894, the Maria Kip's annual report noted that "The cry of hard times has been constant," but even so the orphanage purchased a half block of land in San Francisco as a site for a new, larger building. By 1896, the orphanage was in a newly built home and had even begun an endowment fund.[71]

Through all these means, asylums in the 1870s and 1880s managed to feed, clothe, and house children in increasing numbers. Churches, wealthy individuals, asylum trustees, business groups, and middle-class donors all contributed to the ability of orphan asylums to fulfill their mission. But only in California and New York were all asylums virtually assured of continued existence. Elsewhere, Jewish asylums and Episcopal asylums were generally well funded, while other Protestant and nonsectarian asylums were continually seeking funding to survive. Catholic asylums, aided by unpaid staffs but pressed by the poverty of their constituents, also struggled to continue fulfilling their mission.

Funding and State Involvement

After the turn of the century, asylum needs remained much as they had been a century earlier. One asylum's annual report stated in 1900 that its primary need was cash, and that "Next to coin we need food, and any gift that will fill our larder or pantry" would be gratefully received. St. Mary's Home for Children of Chicago, an Episcopal asylum that was quite well funded, nonetheless still received "donations in kind" in the 1920s. Its 1923 annual report listed six pages of donations such as "worn clothing," "ice cream," "95 plants," "books," "candy," and "toys."[72]

Orphan asylums continued to seek funds through many of the methods that had worked in the nineteenth century. Payments from parents for their children's board were still expected when possible. Some superintendents of religious asylums still contacted congregations throughout their states in hopes that they would "please remember the Orphanage." In the 1920s, the Angel Guardian Orphanage apparently received 80 percent of the money collected by the archdiocese for all its charities. Fund-raising drives for specific goals, such as a summer home, continued to be important to an asylum's ability to improve its facilities. Bequests to institutions were still sought after; one annual report in 1928 encouraged lawyers to "consider this Home when engaged in preparing wills for any of their clients who are inclined to make bequests for the benefit of charitable institutions."[73]

By the 1920s, some orphan asylums had stopped seeking contributions directly after joining city-wide fund-raising groups. For example, by World War I, Baltimore's Hebrew Orphan Asylum had joined an organization supporting a wide variety of German Jewish charity causes in the city.[74] By the early 1920s, community chests and social service agencies that served as central funding sources for a variety of charities were becoming common.[75] Some asylums rejected membership in such organizations; though they provided some measure of financial security, they also limited an asylum's ability to make decisions for itself. The managers of the Cincinnati Orphan Asylum turned down several offers to join the Council of Social Agencies in the 1910s out of a determination to maintain "their prized autonomy."[76]

In 1910, the single largest source of asylum funding remained private donations. For religious institutions, a large portion of private donations came through churches. For example, in 1925 almost half of the funding for all orphan asylums in North and South Carolina came from churches.[77] In 1910, for the nation as a whole, one-quarter of asylum funding came from private donations by individuals and groups, almost one-quarter came from appropriations of public money, while just one-eighth came from parents' board payments for their children. The funding an asylum received depended on what group was running it (and thus what types of contacts it had in society) and on where it was located. Catholic asylums received funds from all sources in a fairly even mix, and as a group were the only asylums to successfully depend on board payments as a large part of their income. Protestant asylums, on the other hand, received more than half their funding from private donations and nearly a third from "other" sources. These presumably included money raised at entertainments, bequests in wills, profit from sales of land or other goods, and interest on savings funds. Jewish asylums depended on the same mix of donations and other sources, and took in almost no board money. Not surprisingly, publicly managed asylums depended almost completely on tax money that came from state, county, and city governments. Like Protestant and Jewish asylums, institutions run by fraternal groups such as the Masons and Odd Fellows relied heavily on donations, taking in relatively little in board money and appropriations (see Table 3.2). Increases in one kind of funding could lead to a decreased emphasis on other sources. Just as critics of public funding had feared, the increased availability of public funding led some private asylums to lessen their private fund-raising efforts. When a trustee of Catholic St. Vincent's of Philadelphia, who also happened to be in the state legislature, managed to gain annual state grants for the asylum in 1909, it stopped holding its "city-wide orphan festivals."[78]

At the turn of the century, most heavily populated states that had dozens of orphan asylums also had some sort of regulatory body, usually a state board of charities, that inspected, and often licensed, children's institutions. In most states, however, no such public body existed. By 1901, only thirteen states had state boards that supervised their orphan asylums. California, where state funding of private asylums had been available for decades, waited until 1903 to create a State Board of Charities and Correction, which, like most state boards at their beginning, only had authority over public institutions. In 1911, the board was granted limited powers over private asylums as well.[79]

State involvement in inspecting and licensing, if not funding, orphan asylums also grew in the South in the 1910s. North Carolina's General Assembly established a state system of public welfare in 1917 and revised it in 1919. The State Board of Public Welfare was empowered to inspect and license all orphanages, and it became illegal to conduct an orphanage without the board's approval. The board was also to be a cheerleader, promoting the care of delinquent and dependent children, and could gain guardianship of children through the juvenile court system, which was established in 1919. County superintendents of public welfare were responsible for all dependent children placed by the board within their counties. Between 1915 and 1921, state boards were also created in Tennessee, Kentucky, Delaware, Virginia, South Carolina, and Georgia. In addition to these groups, many of which had at least some responsibility for overlooking orphan asylums and dependent children in homes, a State Child Welfare Department was created in Alabama and a State Board of Children's Guardians in West Virginia. As in the North decades earlier, the appearance of state boards did not automatically mean a shift away from orphan asylums to other forms of care.[80] Its first impact was usually to improve the quality of care offered in poorer and less well-managed asylums.

In California, the creation of mothers' pensions led to an almost complete end to state money for orphan asylums. As the state took responsibility for children within their own homes, it nearly halted its per capita payments to asylums. In 1928, the San Francisco Presbyterian Orphanage and Farm received $52,000, $11,000 of which came from county treasuries, but only $750 of which was state money. The orphanage's largest single source of money by 1928 was the Community Chest of San Francisco, which provided $13,000.[81]

In the Progressive Era, many private charities "fought to sharpen the lines between themselves and public agencies." Most orphan asylum managers, however, actively sought at least some government involvement in their operation, though the type of involvement sought varied from group to group. For example, many Protestant child welfare workers had opposed state funding of private institutions because such funding went largely to Catholic asylums, especially in New York. However, they favored inspection of asylums, particularly when they might well be on the state boards performing the inspections. Catholic orphan asylum managers, on the other hand, had always sought out public money but were otherwise opposed to government interference in poor children's lives. This opposition came out particularly on issues of education. By the 1910s, most asylum managers and other child welfare advocates seem to have supported state inspection and licensing of orphan asylums, though advocates of other forms of child care (such as placing out and mothers' pensions) were probably the strongest champions of state involvement, which they hoped—with good reason, as it turned out—would lead to a movement away from institutional care.[82]

Conclusion

One speaker at the 1890 National Conference of Charities and Correction praised orphan asylums and their generally "wise and competent matrons and superintendents" for their "good work in the care bestowed upon the little ones."[83] In practice, asylum managers and superintendents ran the gamut from wise to foolish, from loving to harsh, from attentive to distant—as do parents. Aside from some of the political appointees who ran publicly managed asylums, virtually all asylum managers, male and female, were genuinely concerned for their children's welfare. Toward the end of the nineteenth century, asylums shifted from being institutions that controlled virtually all aspects of their children's lives, whether for isolating or protective reasons, toward being more integrative. Some female managers embraced this change, while others opposed it; the same was true of male orphan asylum managers.

No matter how good their intentions, asylum managers often lacked the money, knowledge, or other resources necessary to provide well for their children. In particular, the problem of finding, hiring, and keeping quality staff members was very difficult on the limited funds most asylums enjoyed. Prior to the 1920s, orphan asylums had been managed by people who viewed themselves as charitable workers and who often saw themselves as doing "God's work." They were not "professionals" in the same sense as the people who ran schools and hospitals. The rise of social work and its entrance into asylums between the 1910s and the 1930s helped improve the quality of staffing somewhat, but it also sometimes encouraged asylums to shift away from a clientele that was *poor* to one that was *troubled,* as described in Chapter 1. As with all institutions dealing chiefly with poor people (today's prisons and, in many cases, old-age homes come to mind), most staff members were unprepared to perform their jobs in anything beyond a perfunctory way. This had a great deal to do with the problems of regimentation, harsh discipline, and lack of individual attention that asylum children often faced within institutions, as will be discussed in Chapter 5.

Asylum managers used numerous inventive methods of raising funds for their children. Door-to-door subscriptions, parental board payments, and money raised in affiliated churches were just some of the most important ways that allowed asylum children to be clothed, fed, and housed. In some parts of the country, public money for asylums played a crucial role, while in others it was virtually nonexistent. Where it did exist, public funding of private orphan asylums was heavily criticized. In New York in the 1880s and 1890s, such funding provoked attacks on two fronts. On one hand, reformers who accepted the idea of public responsibility for dependent children felt that asylums should be more closely regulated by the state, since they were fulfilling a public duty with public money. On the other hand, some reformers argued against public funding of institutions that were, in many cases, clearly sectarian in nature.[84] The idea that children were a public responsibility made some headway but was usually far outweighed by politicians'—and the public's—distrust of the poor. Because of this, virtually all orphan asylums were regularly short of funds. But the lack of government involvement allowed asylums to remain local institutions that served local needs as best they could.

Table 3.1. Ratio of children to paid employees, in cottage and congregate asylums, by management type, in 1910.

Management	Cottage asylums	Congregate asylums	All asylums
Catholic	11.5	30.6	30.1
Protestant	8.2	13.2	12.1
Jewish	—	6.5	6.5
Public	4.8	7.6	6.9
Fraterna	9.8	7.6	8.1
Unknown	6.1	8.3	8.0
All asylums	9.8	15.7	14.4

Source: *Benevolent Institutions, 1910.*

Table 3.2. Asylum funding sources, by management type, in 1910.

Management	Appropriations	Donations	Board payments	Other
Catholic	21.7%	28.7%	21.3%	28.3%
Protestant	4.8	53.6	9.9	31.7
Jewish	11.1	55.6	1.6	31.7
Fraternal	6.2	74.3	3.6	15.9
Public	91.3	0.5	3.2	5.0
Unknown	16.6	32.2	13.1	38.1
All asylums	24.2%	33.4%	12.6%	29.8%

Source: *Benevolent Institutions, 1910.*

4

Through the Asylum Doors

Between the antebellum decades and the Progressive Era, the ways children entered and left orphan asylums—and the kinds of children entering and leaving—changed in several fundamental ways. Perhaps most important, between the 1830s and the postbellum era, most asylums gradually came to accept dependent children from a wider variety of family situations. By the middle of the nineteenth century, many asylums had begun accepting half-orphans with one living parent, as well as full orphans. By the end of the century, most orphan asylums also accepted at least some "dependent" or "destitute" children who had two living parents. This change occurred in part because many asylum managers recognized that economic, rather than moral, problems were the most common reason poor parents needed help rearing their children. By 1900, destitution was as likely as a parental death to be the reason a child entered an asylum.

From the 1870s to the 1930s, admission standards became more bureaucratic and standardized in response to attacks from child-placing advocates and other asylum critics, who pushed asylums to investigate applicants more carefully. In some cases, this may have resulted in children being turned away who would have been accepted decades earlier. However, the expansion of public outdoor relief in the form of mothers' and widows' pensions, along with the expanding number of private charities after the turn of the century, meant that by the 1910s poor parents and their children were able to turn to a number of sources. The proliferation of public welfare departments, private charities, and juvenile courts also meant that by the early twentieth century, a growing number of children entered orphan asylums through intermediary agencies.

Orphan asylums spread in the middle and late nineteenth century as immigration rose and industrial capitalism helped create both great wealth and concentrated urban poverty. Overwhelmed by the number of applicants for admission, especially during the era's regular economic downturns, asylum managers sometimes developed connections to other agencies and institutions. Courts, for example, supplied asylums with children deemed to be deserving. In turn, asylums could refer children they themselves could not accept to asylums of different religious backgrounds, child-placing agencies, and eventually state bureaucracies that administered mothers' pensions. One thread remained constant from the 1830s to the 1930s. Since asylum managers usually held less harsh views of poor parents seeking help than did other agencies dealing with poverty, they were less likely to automatically assume parents were "unworthy" of aid. Just as importantly, because orphan asylum managers focused on *children* more than on their parents, even when they did assume parents were "unworthy" of receiving help, that was usually taken as meaning the children should be admitted into the asylum and thereby removed from their parents' "immoral" influence.

From the moment children entered an asylum, they were enveloped in an environment geared (however successfully or unsuccessfully) toward preparing them for their day of departure. Children were taught moral values, religious faith, and skills such as reading and writing to prepare them for life after the asylum. The situations into which children were discharged changed somewhat over time, though only slowly. In the antebellum period, many children were indentured, while others were placed in free homes, where their value to their new family was expected to be more emotional than fiscal. By the late nineteenth century, indenture was becoming relatively rare in many states, and asylum managers who placed children actively sought free homes, where children would be taken in for love rather than as workers. Partly because of the difficulty of finding good free homes, boarding homes that were paid to take children into their families became more widely used. In the twentieth century, this form of child care, increasingly known as foster care, became common.

From the antebellum period to the 1930s, however, most children leaving asylums were discharged to return to their own families. As the percentage of full orphans in asylum populations decreased after the Civil War, the number of asylum children with families to return to increased. By the start of the twentieth century, the vast majority of discharged children were being reunited with their families. Recognizing that parents usually wanted to reclaim their children as quickly as possible, asylum managers developed more favorable attitudes toward poor parents. By the 1920s, almost all asylums tried to encourage ties between their children and surviving relatives. The time children spent in orphan asylums often served, in the long run, to preserve poor families.

Seeking Admission

Children who had lost both parents were often brought to asylums, especially if they were from poor families; no other child was seen as more deserving than a full orphan. More often, however, children were brought to an asylum by a parent pleading for the child's admission. This was true in the early nineteenth century, and became even more common by 1900 as mortality rates dropped. Parents remained the main source of applications for admission into orphan asylums throughout the nineteenth century. Government officials, courts, other institutions and charities, and churches also brought children to orphan asylums. However, these agencies often served merely as intermediaries between parents and asylums rather than as independent actors seeking to remove children from their parents.

Destitute parents often used asylums as temporary homes for their children while they got back on their feet economically, physically, or otherwise. The death of a spouse could easily leave a widow or widower unable to both care for small children and earn a living, particularly in the case of widows. But even working-class households with both parents present were hardly guaranteed a decent, steady income sufficient to support a family. Unemployment, whether caused by illness, economic downturns, or other factors, created a terrific strain. This was particularly true for families led by a semiskilled or unskilled worker.[1] Such families had few economic options, especially if there were no children above ten or eleven able to enter the workforce and supplement the family's income. By the middle of the nineteenth century, irregular, insecure employment was a standard part of working-class life in urban America. In addition to the constant danger of unemployment, work-related accidental deaths took the lives of numerous working-class fathers in the nineteenth century.[2] As time passed, more and more asylum managers recognized and accepted this reality, and viewed helping such families as one of the chief purposes of their institutions. As the Brooklyn Home for Destitute Children's annual report for 1880 put it regarding the children that had come under its care,

> Some of these are the children of worthy and respectable people, who, through sickness or some casualty, suddenly find themselves unable to provide for their families, and need temporary relief. Others are placed here by parents who earn their living at service, or in other ways which either prevent them from having homes, or, if they have such, from being at home during the day to look after their children.[3]

While asylum managers believed that some of the parents of their children were "worthy," in the late nineteenth century many managers still saw parental immorality as a major cause of child poverty. "Character flaws" such as unemployment or a love of alcohol were often blamed for a child's presence in an asylum. The Home for Destitute Children's 1880 annual report went on to state that the "largest class" of children it cared for came from families where "the demon of strong drink has made a victim of father or mother or both." On the other hand, a few asylums refused to accept children who had such "unworthy" parents. The Chicago Nursery and Half-Orphan Asylum, an unusual asylum in a number of ways, refused to aid children unless their families were deemed "worthy" of aid.[4]

Whatever asylum managers thought, parents did not in most cases surrender their children easily. They were forced to do so by their own desperate situations and their knowledge of the options that nearby charities and institutions offered to them.[5] In some cases, these options might include outdoor relief or, later, mothers' pensions. Or they might include nothing better than a stay in an almshouse, especially in the antebellum period. Orphan asylums provided poor families and their children with another, often better, option, but it was hardly one they were happy about. As Alexander Keyssar has written about relief more generally, "for virtually all the unemployed, institutional relief was a last resort." In studying a sample of the Hebrew Orphan Asylum of New York's children in the period 1901–1922, Reena Sigman Friedman found that almost one-fourth of the children's families had managed to stay together for *at least* three years after a family crisis, before finally having to turn to the asylum for help. Another one-fourth had stayed intact for between one and three years before turning one or more children over to the asylum.[6] Placing children in an orphan asylum, where they would receive an education and be housed and fed, was better than going into an almshouse or onto the street, especially if an asylum's policy allowed children to be reclaimed by their parents. Placement in an orphan asylum was not a desirable option, but it might well be the best one available.[7]

Some poor parents probably responded to the negative assumptions many asylum managers held about them by lying about their economic status or by dishonestly claiming to have been deserted, in order to have their children admitted. Because poor people generally knew the rules involved when seeking aid from private or public auspices, applicants were often able to manipulate the system to serve their own interests more than those of the agency or institution they were dealing with.[8] From the perspective of asylum managers, parents doing so were unworthy, immoral liars. But from the perspective of poor families, it was a question of survival. Barbara M. Brenzel has found that many parents used the State Industrial School for Girls in Lancaster, Massachusetts, as a means of caring for children they could not care for themselves.[9] Similarly, many parents brought their children to orphan asylums because they had no other choice.

Lynn Lees has found that in nineteenth-century London many poor workers felt that they had some right to relief aid. This may also have been true of some parents who brought their children to orphan asylums, particularly parents who turned to an institution managed by members of their own religion. Forced to relinquish their children, even if temporarily, some desperate parents may have presented their situations in a way that they knew would be seen as "deserving." Few poor parents saw themselves as "undeserving" of aid, whatever middle-class asylum managers thought of them. Instead, parents in desperate straits saw placing a child inside an asylum for a time as a legitimate, if somewhat desperate, option to be used if other opportunities, such as sending an older child out to work, were not available.[10]

The reasons children entered orphan asylums changed somewhat over time, but in the 1920s they were still similar in important ways to what they had been fifty, or even one hundred, years before, though families now fell apart less often because of death than due to other reasons. One San Francisco orphan asylum's annual report for 1928 stated that "the usual causes of children coming under our care and protection are often broken or unfit homes" or "mental or physical disability of parents." Of the 164 children cared for by another California orphanage in 1930, sixty were there because at least one parent had died. Forty-two gained entrance because of "broken homes," and another twenty-nine were accepted after "desertion." Broken homes and desertion were constant problems for poor families, and the root cause of each was, in many cases, financial, just as it had been decades before when the reason cited for a child's admission was "destitution." But the frequency of desertion did rise around the turn of the twentieth century. As Linda Gordon writes, "the combination of urban anonymity and geographical mobility meant that men could 'disappear' in a way that was impossible in small-town and agrarian communities." Perhaps more importantly, from 1867 to 1929 the number of marriages ending in divorce rose so dramatically that by the latter year, more than one out of every six marriages was ending in divorce. Health problems, which in earlier times had often been the unmentioned cause of a parent's unemployment, continued to be an important reason for children's arrival at asylums. In particular, tuberculosis remained the nation's most dangerous disease into the 1910s and continued to be a serious health problem into the 1930s.[11]

The idea that parents who sought to have their children admitted to an orphan asylum were immoral people never completely vanished. Even in 1930, one asylum manager wrote about "unworthy parents" whose "evil intent" was being thwarted by asylum investigations, which managed to keep children of such parents from being accepted.[12] As always, such views misunderstood the central mission of most orphan asylums, which existed to care for children, either temporarily or permanently, if they did not have a home. Since poor children were, by and large, not held responsible for their parents' flaws, in one sense it should not have mattered why a parent claimed to need help. But most asylum managers saw the "fact" that certain parents were "unworthy" and full of "evil intent" as proof that their children would be better off in a good institution. Among both asylum managers and child-placing advocates, there was a continuing debate over the meaning of a parent's supposed immorality. Some thought that the children of such a parent were particularly deserving of care, while others insisted that any parent capable of caring for his or her children should be made to do so. The charitable desire to aid the needy and the judgmental desire to make "unworthy" people bear their own burdens were in direct conflict, as always in the history of welfare in America. In the case of orphan asylums, unlike many other charity and welfare institutions, the desire to aid the needy usually won.

Agencies that Institutionalized Children

The line between "private" charity groups and "public" welfare bureaucracies that placed children in orphan asylums was fluid. Government officials and asylum managers often developed relationships that were beneficial to both. City, county, and even some state governments used private agencies, including sectarian orphan asylums, to provide a public service by caring for dependent children. For example, in the 1840s roughly half the children in the privately managed Cincinnati Orphan Asylum had been committed by the Cincinnati township trustees, who paid the asylum for each dependent town child placed there. Other agencies and institutions also became involved in placing children in orphan asylums. By the late 1870s, New York City magistrates and the Society for the Prevention of Cruelty to Children (SPCC) were committing needy Catholic children to Catholic asylums. Asylums performed a public service more cheaply than government could have done, and governments often paid the asylums accordingly.[13]

By the late nineteenth century, courts and private organizations were both regularly placing children in orphan asylums. In 1893, for example, the SPCC sent over four thousand children to "Homes and Institutions" in New York City. In fact, from 1875 to 1903 the New York SPCC sent nearly 100,000 children to various institutions, in many cases orphan asylums. At the same time, New York's courts were committing children directly to asylums such as St. Agnes' Home, a Catholic coed institution where most admissions came from the legal system. The combination of court involvement and public per capita payments filled some of

New York's largest asylums, many of which were Catholic. In 1897, St. Joseph's at Peekskill contained over 1,500 children, almost all of whom had come from the court and were therefore supported by public funds. Partial public funding for asylum children was only one of the reasons so many of New York's poor children were institutionalized. The active involvement of courts in committing children to asylums was another reason. Courts could send children to asylums knowing the asylum could afford to keep them, since the state or county government would pick up much of the tab.[14]

Problems could arise when children were accepted into an orphan asylum through an intermediary such as a court, rather than by their own admissions committee or superintendent. In 1875, Kings County, New York, abolished its public nursery and had to find another home for its dependent Protestant children. The Brooklyn Home for Destitute Children offered to take them in on similar terms to the boarded children it already cared for, with the county acting as parent and making monthly per capita payments to the home. The home's next annual report stated that the home had been criticized for placing county wards out in families. The home defended itself vehemently, claiming that the children had been placed in the home by the Commissioners of Charity subject "to the already existing rules" of the institution and that therefore the children could be placed out. However, the home does not seem to have placed out other children whose board was being paid; its managers apparently felt they had more control over county wards than over other boarded children. The Commissioners of Charity disagreed and stopped placing children in the home. By 1880, the home was again caring for county wards but was presumably not placing them in boarding homes.[15]

By the early twentieth century, though many children were still being brought in by a parent, more and more were entering orphan asylums through the adult court system, juvenile courts, and private charity organizations. Despite this shift, most asylums did what they could to maintain authority over admission decisions. In 1907, the Children's Bureau of Philadelphia was created to receive and investigate children for one asylum and the Children's Aid Society, with the idea that it would decide where children should be placed. Other asylums were expected to make extensive use of the Children's Bureau, but this never happened.

Most asylum managers wanted to maintain their independence, though a number of asylums in Philadelphia did receive children via the bureau on occasion.[16]

A survey conducted by Robert Briggs of eighty Catholic orphan asylums in the mid-1910s showed that courts were the most common source of children arriving in the asylums in his sample; more than one-third of the children entering had been committed by a court. Parents and social agencies were the next most important sources, with each accounting for just over one-fifth of admissions. However, the number of commitments that began with a parent's request is understated in Briggs's study, since parents initiated many applications that then went through a court or other agency, and such cases are not listed in Briggs's survey as coming from parents. Pastors and friends of the children were also important sources of requests for admission into orphan asylums (see Table 4.1). In 1919, to give just one example of the importance of courts, the Angel Guardian Orphanage received 580 children from courts and 409 via "private arrangements."[17] Though the published results of Briggs's survey do not reveal differences between Catholic asylums in different areas, it is likely that courts and social agencies were represented particularly highly in major urban areas such as New York City and Chicago. Applications from pastors, parents, and friends may have played a more important role in smaller cities and states where government was less active.

Indeed, the 1910 census of institutions reveals a somewhat different picture than does Briggs's survey. It lists the sources bringing children who were entering orphan asylums for the first time, broken into five categories: public officials, institution officials, child-placing agencies, relatives, and "other agencies." On the average, in 1910 orphan asylums received twenty-five first entrants from relatives, fifteen from public officials, and just seven from the other three sources combined. Catholic asylums each averaged more than forty-three new children from relatives in 1910, compared to just under twenty-five per asylum from public officials. Protestant asylum entry was even more dominated by relatives, with more than seventeen children being received from relatives, compared to just seven from all four other sources. Jewish asylums were more evenly split, receiving an average of thirty-six children from relatives and thirty-one from public officials; they also were the only asylums to receive significant numbers of children from child-placing agencies, an average of eleven per asylum. Fraternal asylums received virtually all their children from relatives, while county and city asylums received the majority of their new children from public officials. State-managed asylums also received most of their new children from public officials, averaging seventy per asylum, but they also received almost thirty-five children per asylum from relatives. Despite the growing number of children entering orphan asylums in the early twentieth century from government officials, other institutions, and agencies, more than half the children entering orphan asylums across the nation in 1910 were still being brought in by their relatives (see Table A1 in the Appendix).

Rules Governing Admission

A few orphan asylums were exactly that: homes for full orphans exclusively. But this type of asylum was already in the minority by the 1850s. Orphan asylums that depended largely on court recommendations for their admissions developed in some large cities, especially after the beginning of the twentieth century as juvenile courts appeared. Some public asylums, especially in the county systems of Connecticut and Ohio, also seem to have relied on admissions from courts. For these asylums, as for those accepting only full orphans, each new application did not require careful consideration by asylum managers. From the early 1800s through the early 1900s, however, most orphan asylums had to examine each individual applicant. And since there were often more applicants than a given asylum could accept, each institution developed its own rules governing admission.

For the first orphan asylums, the question was usually whether or not to admit half-orphans. In 1800, the Boston Female Asylum's managers decided to accept half-orphans, along with full orphans, when they realized that there were more half-orphans than full orphans and that the former were often just as needy as the latter.[18] Not all early orphan asylums decided to help half-orphans, however. The New York Orphan Asylum, a Protestant institution founded in 1806, apparently sent any children within its walls found to have a living parent to the almshouse during its early years. New York's Roman Catholic Orphan Asylum, founded a few years later, also limited its admissions to full orphans. New York's Catholics eventually realized that there were many needy half-orphans, and in 1835 opened an asylum specifically for them. In

1852, the two Catholic asylums were united, and half-orphans were accepted only if their surviving parent could pay something toward the child's support.[19]

Southern asylums were more likely than their northern counterparts to limit admission to full orphans.[20] But as had happened in the North, the widespread existence of poverty eventually led most southern asylums to accept at least some half-orphans. In the 1890s, the Lutheran Children's Home of Virginia tried to accept only full orphans, though in "special cases" half-orphans might occasionally be admitted. The Colored Orphan Industrial Home of Lexington accepted only "orphan children" in the 1890s but included half-orphans in that definition. At the same time, a Baptist asylum in North Carolina accepted full orphans and half-orphans, if the mother was the living parent. (Living fathers were apparently expected to be able to support their children.) Whether or not other asylums in the South or North preferred to accept half-orphans whose fathers were deceased over those who had lost their mothers is not clear; most probably did not distinguish between the two.[21]

By the 1850s, orphan asylums that accepted only full orphans were undoubtedly in the minority in most regions of the nation. When the Orphans' Home and Asylum opened in New York City in 1852, it accepted orphans and half-orphans, as did many northern asylums by that time.[22] After the Civil War, asylums that accepted only full orphans became even less common in the North. However, many continued to refuse children with two living parents, though asylum managers acknowledged that such children could be quite destitute.[23] Of course, the fact that an asylum accepted children from several categories did not necessarily mean that children from each of those groups had an equal chance of being accepted. New York City's Roman Catholic Orphan Asylums—a group of three single-sex asylums, two for girls, one for boys—accepted both orphans and half-orphans in the 1870s but clearly favored the former as being more in need. In 1874, the asylums received thirty-five applications to accept full orphans and issued "orders of admission" for thirty-four of them, all of whom did enter one of the three institutions. In that same year, there were 153 applications in behalf of half-orphans (some of which were subsequently withdrawn); 106 "orders of admission" were issued, and ninety of the half-orphans actually entered an asylum.[24]

The Brooklyn Hebrew Orphan Asylum, officially "limited to the admission of orphans," actually accepted both full and half-orphans but turned away children with two living parents. Similarly, the 1897 annual report of the Colored Orphan Industrial Home of Lexington, Kentucky, stated that "None except orphan children shall be admitted into the Home," but the term included half-orphans, who actually made up the majority of the home's population. The use of the word "orphans" to include half-orphans was fairly common by the 1890s. As the reality of huge numbers of half-orphans and destitute children with two living parents became increasingly apparent, the term "orphan" was often used to distinguish between children who had lost at least one parent and those who had not rather than between those with no living parents and those with at least one parent still alive, as it had usually been used earlier in the century.

By the dawn of the Progressive Era, Brooklyn's Home for Destitute Children seems to have decided to accept only children with two living parents, and referred orphans and half-orphans to the Orphan Asylum Society. The presence of several orphan asylums within a city meant that each could specialize in the way that best fit its managers' attitudes toward poor children and their parents, as well as the social realities of the community. The pattern was not always one of movement toward more open admission policies; in the 1870s, the Rochester Protestant Orphan Asylum, having had problems with the parents of half-orphans in its care, decided to accept only full orphans.[25]

Some historians have argued that it was during and after the 1890s depression that the environment came to replace individual moral flaws as the most common explanation for poverty. For example, in his excellent history of social work, John Ehrenreich writes that at the end of the nineteenth century

> [T]he old Social Darwinist explanations characteristic of the late nineteenth century, which saw individual physical, mental, or moral weaknesses as the source of economic disadvantage, went into eclipse, and the dominant modes of social thought shifted to environmentalist explanations. The poor came to be seen as victims of external forces—unemployment, bad housing, disease, and accidents—which they could not be expected to control through strength of character alone.[26]

While Ehrenreich is basically right, it is important to note the word "dominant." In fact, throughout the nineteenth century most reformers held views that mixed individual and environmental explanations of poverty. Many individuals who dealt with the urban poor came to a largely environmental viewpoint long before 1900, chiefly because of their direct contact with the poor. As Ehrenreich writes of settlement house workers in the 1890s, "in getting to know people and communities it became impossible to continue to see poverty as simply the fault of the poor."[27] It was not actually impossible—some who dealt with poor people on a daily basis continued to view them harshly—but it was certainly more difficult. The two ideas, one blaming the poor themselves and one blaming their surroundings, existed side by side from the antebellum years into the twentieth century, though their relative influence shifted. Where an asylum manager stood on this issue obviously had a strong impact on which children would be admitted.

By the 1860s, some asylums such as the Protestant Orphan Asylum of St. Louis accepted poor children regardless of their parental status. The economic downturn of the 1870s "opened an era in which the involuntary idleness of wage earners began to receive serious and sustained attention in the United States," and by the 1880s many asylums had opened their doors to destitute children of all sorts. St. Benedict's Home, a Catholic asylum opened in New York City in 1886 to care for "destitute colored children," was such an institution. At least some fraternal organizations' orphan asylums also had broad admission policies. The Oxford Orphan Asylum, a North Carolina asylum managed by the Order of Free Masons, accepted children whether or not they were related to Masons from its beginning in 1873.[28]

Publicly managed asylums were especially willing to accept children from a wide variety of parental situations. The public homes for dependent children founded in Connecticut in the 1880s and 1890s accepted children if they were "of the classes hereinafter described, to wit: waifs, strays, children in charge of overseers of the poor, children of prisoners, drunkards or paupers, and others who are or may hereafter be committed to hospitals, almshouses, or workhouses, and all children within said ages, deserted, neglected, cruelly treated, or dependent."[29] Public asylums were almost always coed, accepted children with two living parents as well as orphans and half-orphans, and were far more likely to mix children of color and white children together than were most private orphan asylums. In 1900, the superintendent of the State Orphans' Home of Montana noted approvingly that the home's trustees had "made destitution and dependence the sole price of admission."[30] Some asylums held out much longer before accepting "destitute" children with two living parents. The Cleveland Jewish Orphan Asylum did not accept children with two living parents until 1924, except in cases where the parents were "mentally ill."[31]

Connecticut's private orphan asylums, like its public asylums, seem to have been fairly liberal in accepting children with living parents, so long as the children were "homeless or destitute." They did place other limitations on who could be accepted, however. The New Haven Orphan Asylum, a Protestant institution, required children to be New Haven residents. Likewise, the Hartford Orphan Asylum accepted only Hartford residents, though children from other parts of the state could be admitted if board was paid for them. Some of Connecticut's Catholic asylums had similar limitations. In 1904, St. James Asylum, also of Hartford, hoped to care only for children from its own parish. And St. Francis' Orphan Asylum of New Haven accepted only children whose parents were Catholic and state residents. These attempts to care only for one's "own," whether defined by location or religion, were emblematic of the role that orphan asylums played as community institutions.[32]

One of the most difficult questions to answer about "typical" asylum admission patterns is whether or not many orphan asylums accepted "illegitimate" children, and whether this changed over time. Most asylum reports never mention out-of-wedlock children as a category, so it is not clear whether they were banned or instead were simply accepted and categorized as "orphans," "half-orphans," or "destitute." At any rate, at least a few asylums did acknowledge accepting children born out of wedlock. For example, in 1903 St. Mary's Orphanage of Providence announced that of the last 139 children it had accepted, 26 had been "Illegitimate."[33]

In the early 1880s, the Chicago Orphan Asylum, like many late-nineteenth-century homes for children, accepted three categories of children: orphans, half-orphans, and "destitute" children. By the late 1880s, "deserted by parent" had replaced "destitute" in the asylum's annual description of nonorphans. This may have reflected an increasingly harsh attitude toward poor parents. If so, the asylum's adult clients were probably aware of the change and what it meant for their families. Children who might have been accepted as "destitute" a decade earlier might be turned down, and some mothers may have lied, perhaps claiming falsely to have been deserted by their husbands, in order to receive aid for their children. In 1895, the Chicago Orphan Asylum's admission policy became more restrictive, accepting only orphans and half-orphans. Two reasons were given in annual reports. The first was that the new policy fit the original design of the asylum's founders, even though the avowed purpose of the institution in the 1850s seemed to state that abject poverty was as good a reason as any to accept a child. The other reason given was that the change would be "an important step in the direction of grading institutions" within the city. There may have been some validity to the second reason, though the real driving force behind the change seems to have been the increasing demand on the asylum's resources that had come with the 1890s depression. Helping only children who had lost a parent made it easier to automatically rule out some applicants.[34]

In his excellent study of several Progressive Era institutions for children, LeRoy Ashby argues that around the turn of the century there was a "tendency to blur the lines between delinquency and dependency." While this was certainly true of many institutions for delinquent children, it was not the case for most orphan asylums. (The institutions Ashby examined, such as the Ford Republic and the Good Will Farm, were atypical in whom they accepted as well as in other important ways.) Though some institutions accepted children deemed "delinquent" as well as those considered "destitute," most orphan asylums avoided the former as much as possible. Many asylum managers realized that the reason children needed aid was often poverty, whether they were seen as "problem" children or not. Nonetheless, orphan asylum managers generally tried to limit their admissions to children whose main problem was poverty and who did not have serious behavioral problems. This was true throughout the nineteenth century and remained true for most asylums after the turn of the century. Ken Cmiel writes that the Chicago Nursery and Half-Orphan Asylum "rather firmly maintained the boundary" between dependent children and delinquent children. Similarly, into the 1920s and 1930s, some of Connecticut's asylums consciously avoided accepting children with severe retardation or behavioral problems.[35]

Most orphan asylums had age limits for both admission and discharge. Unless they had a baby nursery, asylums usually would not accept children under three or four years of age, or would accept small children and immediately place them out in homes. At the start of the nineteenth century, for example, the Boston Female Asylum accepted no children under the age of three.³⁶ A century later, most Jewish asylums still refused children under three; asylum managers recognized the problems entailed in caring for babies. In the 1910s, the Angel Guardian Orphanage accepted "children as young as two years of age" and kept children from two to six "in a specially equipped building, the baby-house." Adolescents might also be turned away. In the 1860s, Brooklyn's Home for Destitute Children, like the Boston Female Asylum sixty years before, would not accept children older than ten. As apprenticeships vanished and the expected extent of schooling for children increased, eleven- and twelve-year-olds became admissible in many, though not all, orphan asylums. In 1860, the Orphans' Home and Asylum refused children over nine unless it was given the right to retain them until they were fourteen (in the case of half-orphans) or to place them out in homes (if they were full orphans). At the end of the nineteenth century, the Colored Orphan Industrial Home of Lexington would not accept boys over nine or girls over ten "without consulting the Board." Similarly, the San Francisco Presbyterian Orphanage and Farm would not accept children over fourteen unless it was given the legal right to place such children in homes. By the 1920s, the average age of children in most asylums was probably around ten, whereas sixty years before it may have been as low as seven or eight. In 1926, 40 percent of the children in North and South Carolina's orphanages were between six and twelve, while more than 45 percent were over twelve years of age.³⁷

A parent's ability to pay something toward a child's board sometimes influenced whether or not that child would be admitted, particularly if the asylum was operating on limited resources. St. Mary's Home for Children in Chicago, an Episcopal asylum for girls that was better off financially than many institutions, nevertheless had to turn down some children largely because their parents could not afford to pay partial board. The home had to "receive some paying children to keep the pot boiling for the rest." More than half the children at St. Mary's Home were "free of charge" in 1907, while the rest had parents or relatives helping to support them. In 1914, well over one-third were "full pay" children, slightly more than one-third were "under pay" children whose parents contributed something, and just over one-fourth were "free" children completely supported by the home. Financial strain meant that many asylums had to reject exactly those children who were most desperately in need of aid—children whose parents could not afford to contribute anything toward their support.[38]

After the turn of the century, the increasingly complex network of charity, welfare, and social work organizations meant that when an orphan asylum had to reject a deserving applicant, it could often send the child elsewhere for aid.[39] In 1928, the San Francisco Presbyterian Orphanage and Farm found 169 applicants to be "deserving admission to the home" but could accept only 38 due to "limited facilities." Fifty years before, the rejected children, and their families, might have been left to their own devices. By 1928, however, the orphanage could often help them find other aid. "Plans for the care" of the 131 rejected but "deserving" applicants "were worked out by our Welfare Department in co-operation with other agencies."[40] By the 1920s, many children admitted to orphan asylums had already had some contact with other agencies. All but four of the forty-four children admitted to the San Francisco Protestant Orphanage in 1930 were already "known to some social agency, many to as great a number as 10 or 12."[41]

Race, Ethnicity, and Gender

As Chapters 1 and 2 describe, a great many orphan asylums were founded by and for a particular ethnic and/or religious group. Jewish asylums generally fit this description, as did virtually all Catholic asylums and many Protestant asylums. St. Vincent's of Philadelphia was founded by German Catholics, and from its beginning in the 1850s to the turn of the century it admitted children only from "German parishes" or of "German descent." Some asylums founded and run by a specific group accepted children from outside their ethnicity or religion, but did so less readily than they accepted their own children. In the 1850s, the Orphans' Home and Asylum of New York, an Episcopal institution theoretically open to all applicants, admitted that many of the children it had been forced to turn away due to overcrowding had been from "various denominations of Christians" rather than Episcopalians.[42]

By the twentieth century, at least some—and probably most—asylums had shifted toward a more open admission policy regarding ethnicity, responding to the increasingly complex ethnic structure of their communities. For example, in 1919 the Angel Guardian Orphanage, a German Catholic institution, was caring for children of "twenty nationalities" besides German. The next year, 55 percent of the orphanage's children were of German descent, while 45 percent were not. In 1930, the orphanage had 454 German children, 130 Italian children, 98 Irish children, 92 Hungarian children, and an additional 166 children from seventeen other groups, including 16 Mexican children and 1 Japanese child—but, like most orphan asylums, no black children.[43]

The vast majority of children in all kinds of asylums in 1890 were white and born in the United States (see Table 4.2). Only Jewish asylums held large numbers of foreign-born children. However, most children in asylums seem to have had at least one immigrant parent, although the high number of asylum children whose parents' birthplace was reported as unknown clouds the picture considerably. Still, some things do emerge clearly. Catholic asylums contained a strong majority of children whose parents were immigrants, but also contained a number of children whose parents had been born in the United States. Jewish asylums held almost no children whose parents were native-born, at least in 1890; this situation probably changed gradually after the turn of the century. On the other hand, Protestant asylums on the whole seem to have held a fairly even balance of white, native-born children whose parents were native-born, and white, native-born children whose parents were immigrants. Fraternal asylums held more children of native parentage than of immigrant parentage, as did county and city asylums; the huge number of parental "unknowns" reported by state-managed asylums leaves little that can be said about them. All in all, the results are hardly surprising, since from their first explosive growth in the 1830s most asylums had been important parts of ethnic and religious communities with high numbers of immigrants.

Black children were rarely admitted to asylums designed to care for white children in 1890, and while the situation changed somewhat over the next four decades, the majority of orphan asylums remained institutions for white children of various ethnic backgrounds in 1933 (see Table 4.3). Peter Holloran found that Boston's Catholic orphan asylums *did* accept black children in the late nineteenth century. But the situation in Cleveland was more representative of the nation. Marian Morton writes that "despite the growing number of Black migrants from the South," none of Cleveland's private asylums would accept their children.

Most "mixed" asylums held very few nonwhite children; the majority of children of color in orphan asylums in 1890 and 1910 were in the several dozen asylums built specifically for them. The number of asylums for children of color more than doubled between 1910 and 1923 but still remained at just ninety in 1933, compared to more than seven times that many asylums solely for white children. At least part of the reason for the increase in asylums for nonwhite children was the appearance of asylums for Japanese, Chinese, and Mexican children in California and other western states, where Japanese, Chinese, and Mexicans made up the foreign-born labor force.[44] This increase clearly does not mean that the nation as a whole was suddenly taking better care of dependent black children. In addition, asylums for nonwhite children were on average noticeably smaller than those for white children or the numerous interracial asylums dominated by white populations. In many cases, smaller asylums provided better homes for children than did large asylums; in this case, however, asylums for children of color tended to be unusually poor and thus even more restricted in what they could provide for their children than were most asylums.

Many of the "mixed" asylums that contained one or two minority children had probably accepted them due to the children's desperate situations rather than because the asylums had unusually open admission policies. Some asylums did consciously choose to be interracial, however. Nancy Hewitt found that the Orphan Asylum Association begun in Rochester in the 1830s cared for both black and white children, though Hewitt suspects that there was "substantial resistance" among some board members to accepting black children.[45] It is unfortunately not surprising that, like the rest of American society, orphan asylums tended to be highly segregated and far more available to white children than to nonwhite children. It is also unsurprising that this situation did not change all that much between the mid-nineteenth century and the 1930s.[46] In fact, it may be that the larger a city's black population became, the more likely it was that orphan asylum managers would decide to exclude blacks. Ken Cmiel found that the Chicago Nursery and Half-Orphan Asylum accepted black children in the late nineteenth century and continued to do so until at least 1914. By the mid-1920s, however, black children were no longer welcome. "In retrospect," Cmiel writes, "the integration of the nineteenth century was largely dependent on the small number of Blacks in Chicago."[47] Even where black children were few in number, however, white asylums were more likely to exclude them than to admit them.

In 1890, 44 of the 120 asylums that held "mixed" populations were run by counties or cities, while 31 were of unknown management and 23 were Catholic. Thirteen of the sixteen state-run asylums also held both white and black children. Twenty of the twenty-seven asylums for black children were of unknown management type, while six were Catholic. The number of asylums holding mixed populations had risen noticeably by 1910, while the number of Protestant asylums for black children had risen from one to eight. (In all likelihood, many of the "unknown" asylums for black children were also Protestant.) By 1933, almost half of the Catholic asylums whose policies are known accepted at least some nonwhite children, while the vast majority of Protestant asylums were still white-only. As was discussed in Chapter 1, these racially mixed asylums rarely held more than one or two black children (see Appendix, Tables A2–A5).

Many antebellum orphan asylums were single-sex institutions and more likely to care for girls than for boys. In particular, many early Catholic asylums were for girls; in many cities, Catholic asylums for girls were founded more than a decade before Catholic asylums for boys were built.[48] By the 1860s and 1870s, however, most asylums were coed, which continued to be the case thereafter. From 1890 to 1923, the percentage of asylums that were coed gradually rose. There were also a considerable number of asylums for girls only, and a smaller number of asylums that accepted only boys. As asylums continued to be founded across the nation between 1890 and 1923, the number of coed, girls-only, and boys-only asylums all rose with each new census, though the gap between girls' and boys' asylums had narrowed somewhat by 1923. Interestingly, boys-only asylums were on average consistently quite a bit larger than other asylums, and by 1910 coed asylums were larger than girls' asylums (see Table 4.4).

The management type of an asylum had a good deal to do with whether it was likely to be coed or not. In 1890, 100 of the 175 Catholic asylums were single-sex; two-thirds of these were for girls. On the other hand, 94 Protestant asylums were coed, versus 25 for girls and just 7 for boys. Jewish, fraternal, and public asylums were virtually all coed. The situation had changed little by 1910, when 201 of the 263 Protestant asylums were known to be coed, while just 110 of the 260 Catholic asylums were clearly coed. Not surprisingly, matters were much the same in 1923 (see Appendix, Tables A6–A8).

Decision-makers

Before the Civil War, decisions on whether or not to accept children were sometimes made by a single individual, usually a matron or superintendent. For example, in the 1820s the head sister of New York's Roman Catholic Orphan Asylum had final say on all admissions and removals. At some asylums, applications for admission were made to the board of trustees or an admissions committee. Even so, antebellum admissions committees did not perform detailed investigations of applicants. At the start of the nineteenth century, the Boston Female Asylum's committee simply checked an applicant's date of birth and legitimacy, and then sought legal control from a relative.[49] By the late nineteenth century, the responsibility for admission decisions was usually in the hands of a reception committee, which sometimes, though not always, performed a more thorough investigation. Community leaders sometimes carried a great deal of weight in this process. In the 1880s, children were admitted to the Roman Catholic Orphan Asylum via its Committee on Admissions and Binding only "upon the recommendation of the priests of the Archdiocese."[50]

Unlike individuals making admission decisions alone, committees usually followed a somewhat standardized admission process. A set of rules, however flexible, replaced a single person's decision. As time passed, investigations became more systematic and thorough, though the change was gradual and uneven. The rules followed by the Maria Kip Orphanage of San Francisco were fairly typical for the 1890s. No children over twelve were accepted unless the orphanage had the right to place them out in a family. No children were admitted without a doctor's examination proving them free from contagious disease. Unless immediate relief was "imperative," no child would be admitted until the committee had received the board of managers' approval.[51]

While actual investigations into children's backgrounds were rarely thorough before 1900, by the 1890s many asylum managers were coming to realize that knowledge of an applicant's family situation was important. It mattered in deciding whether to accept a child or not and, if the child was accepted, in determining how the child should be treated. This realization probably came about in response to the heavy criticism orphan asylums faced that they accepted everyone who applied (which was patently untrue) and that poor parents were using asylums as free, temporary homes for their children (which was certainly true, though many asylum managers saw this as a desirable goal). As a result, by the 1910s most orphan asylums were investigating applicants and keeping records on their children. Fifty-three of the eighty Catholic institutions surveyed by Briggs in the mid-1910s made their own independent investigations of the children to be admitted, unless they were sent by a court. Sixty-four of the eighty asylums kept records on all the children they admitted.[52] This was impressive given that Catholic asylums were notably lax at record keeping throughout the nineteenth century.

It would be a mistake to assume that asylums' investigations of their applicants were truly thorough by the 1920s. The director of St. Paul's Catholic Charities noted in 1925 that a survey conducted of "eight child caring institutions in a city of the Middle West" three years earlier had shown that none of the asylums studied their applicants very carefully. In over 80 percent of admitted cases, the asylums "lacked sufficient social history to warrant the separation of the child from his parent or parents." The arrival of thorough record keeping and admission investigations in orphan asylums was uneven, to say the least.[53]

By the 1930s, many orphan asylums had given up much of their autonomy over admission decisions. They were working closely with other child-care agencies and charities, juvenile courts, ethnic and religious organizations, and local and state government agencies in deciding whom to accept. In the nineteenth century, whatever investigations were conducted by orphan asylums had been performed at least partly to avoid admitting children whose parents were capable of supporting them. In the 1930s, however, a more humane rationale, reflecting the growing importance of social work, was being offered to justify more thorough investigations. As the San Francisco Protestant Orphanage's annual report put it in 1931, "Because the application for admission is always an indication of a serious breakdown in a family group, a thorough investigation and study of each case is made by a trained social worker. A plan for the rehabilitation of the family, if that is at all possible, is a part of the program. If taking the child into the Home is necessary in the proper treatment of the case, he is admitted."[54] Investigations conducted from the 1930s onward were, at least in theory, to determine the best possible care for the child.

Parental Rights

Some asylum managers wanted legal guardianship of all the children they accepted. They hoped this would help them to avoid interference by parents while the child was in the asylum. It would also make it easier to discharge children as apprentices or, in later years, to free or board homes. The desire to gain legal control over children was evident in some of the earliest orphan asylums. Suzanne Lebsock found that the Female Orphan Asylum of Petersburg, Virginia, sought complete legal control over children when it opened in the 1810s, but the asylum was not quite successful in doing so. It could place children as apprentices, but the local court retained the power to interfere "if the child was mistreated" while serving the apprenticeship.[55]

In the antebellum era, the Charleston Orphan House only accepted children if their parents were willing to relinquish all legal rights to the children. Beginning in the 1850s, the Chicago Orphan Asylum arranged for the city's mayor to be considered legal guardian of any child being admitted to the asylum without a parent on the scene, whether or not the child's parents were actually dead.[56] When a child entered the asylum, the child's parent or legal guardian (which could be the mayor) was required to sign an agreement of surrender, which admitted the parent's failure to care for the child and surrendered all legal parental authority to the asylum. A time limit was established for the asylum to care for a particular child. If his or her parents did not reclaim the child by the end of that time, the surrender stipulated that the Chicago Orphan Asylum became the child's legal guardian.[57]

The surrender agreement had obvious advantages for the asylum, but it also offered parents limited rights. The specified length of time before the Chicago Orphan Asylum gained permanent legal guardianship allowed parents to use the asylum as a temporary aid during difficult times. If parents were unable to reclaim their children, however, the agreement gave the asylum's managers the power to indenture the children. In fact, many of the asylum's children were boarders (usually half-orphans whose living parent paid a small monthly fee), and as such would become wards of the asylum only if their parents failed to keep up their payments. In the 1860s, Brooklyn's Home for Destitute Children also accepted children as boarders; like the Chicago Orphan Asylum, when board payments were not made the home sought legal control over its children. Each asylum had its own views on what rights it needed, and which rights parents could safely maintain. Boston's Church Home for Orphan and Destitute Children recognized parents' right to visit their children but expected a complete surrender of all other parental rights. Children still in the Church Home six months after the original time limit that had been stipulated when they entered the home were "given up to the Home" permanently. Like most Protestant asylums, many Catholic institutions held mainly children who were either boarded or legally under the asylum's guardianship, and sometimes actively sought the latter authority if no board payments were being made. St. Vincent's Orphan Asylum of Philadelphia hoped to have children whose parents were unable to make board payments "bound" to the asylum, though St. Vincent's accepted some children without either board payments or a transfer of legal authority.[58]

The question of whether or not to seek legal control over children remained pertinent for many asylum managers into the 1920s. Gaining legal guardianship over children who were not full orphans was often difficult, and some asylum managers feared that taking away a parent's legal right to his or her child might damage the emotional bonds between parent and child, thereby reducing the likelihood that children and parents would reunite. For asylum managers who wanted to help families rather than break them up, this was a critical concern. On the other hand, asylum managers often had to surrender children to parents who did not yet seem ready, in the asylum manager's eyes, to take on the burden of raising a child properly. Obtaining guardianship protected asylums from this problem. In general, after 1910 asylums were less concerned with gaining legal control over children than they had been throughout the nineteenth century. But as long as some managers viewed impoverished adults as inherently bad parents, some asylums would try to dictate who could care for the children once they were discharged.

In some cases, decisions concerning guardianship were taken out of the hands of orphan asylums, especially when children were placed in an asylum by the court. Connecticut's public orphan asylums became legal guardians of all children committed to them, though there were restrictions on the asylums' ability to place children out for adoption.

The families of children in these institutions did retain some rights. Relatives could petition the court for return of a child, and might succeed if they could show that the original reason for commitment was no longer in effect. Similarly, children committed to an asylum by the court in New York in the 1920s could be reclaimed if their parents could convince the court that they had become fit parents.[59]

Asylum managers dictated the extent of asylum children's contact with the outer world, including visits with their parents. Visiting hours for parents and relatives varied widely. In some cases, parents had legally abandoned all rights to their children and were generally not allowed to visit at all. At most asylums, however, parents still retained some legal rights to their children and were allowed to visit occasionally, typically on one or two specific days of the week. The extent of visitation rights partially depended on asylum managers' views of poor parents.

For much of the nineteenth century, some asylum managers did what they could, short of banning all visits, to strictly limit child-parent contact. The Boston Female Asylum was sympathetic to parents at its founding, but by the 1810s it had "moved inexorably toward a policy of keeping their children away from their parents" by limiting parental visits. This attitude was still prevalent in many orphan asylums a half-century later. In the 1860s, Brooklyn's Home for Destitute Children allowed parents to visit their children "on the first Wednesday of every month." This limitation apparently applied even to parents who paid board for their children and retained legal guardianship. At the same time, the Cincinnati Orphan Asylum allowed parents just a single one-hour visit on the first Wednesday of each month. Visiting policies tended to become more liberal toward the turn of the century, but this was not always the case. In 1895, the Chicago Orphan Asylum shortened "the visits of parents and guardians" to two hours on Thursday and Sunday afternoons. This was supposedly done "by the advice of physicians, for sanitary reasons," but since the general public was allowed to visit at any time, the limited parental visiting hours were apparently meant to keep asylum inmates from spending too much time with their families. Still, compared to a one-hour visit once a month, four hours a week was quite a bit of contact between children and parents.[60] That many asylum managers felt the need to impose such restrictions demonstrates that at least some parents tried to stay in regular contact with their children. This is the opposite of what many asylum critics would have expected, since they often claimed that poor parents had placed their children in asylums because they did not love their children.

Beginning in the early twentieth century, more and more orphan asylums encouraged frequent visits by parents and relatives, both for the child's sake and to maintain family ties. The Orphan Asylum Society of New York at Hastings-on-the-Hudson tried to strengthen family ties in the 1910s "by an elaborate system of visiting" during the summer and at Christmas, when children returned to their parents' homes for brief stays.[61] In the late 1920s, the San Francisco Presbyterian Orphanage and Farm's policies demonstrated how much things had changed since the Civil War era; the orphanage had visiting hours every afternoon except Saturdays.[62] By the early twentieth century, many asylum managers were doing what they could to facilitate the reestablishment of the parental home. Liberalizing visiting hours was one of the easiest ways they could work toward this goal. In general, visitation rights increased in the late nineteenth century as more asylum managers recognized, and accepted, that most children were returning to their families upon discharge. During the 1910s and 1920s, visiting policies changed dramatically. By the late 1920s, visiting hours at most orphan asylums had become extremely open, and children and parents were often encouraged to spend as much time together as parents could manage.

Length of Stay in the Asylum

Most children returned to their parents or were placed in other homes within one to four years of entering orphan asylums; in many cases, this happened within a year. However, many other children remained in asylums for five years or longer. The length of a child's stay and how the child was discharged were connected. Children who had two living parents may have been most likely—though by no means certain—to stay a short period, from a month or two to a year, or perhaps even two years. They then usually returned to their parents once the family crisis that had led to the child's institutionalization had passed. Children without any family to return to, such as many full orphans, might also leave the asylum quickly, *if* the institution was one that placed children in homes. If they were young, they might be placed out in a free home or, later, adopted. If they were twelve or thirteen years old, throughout most of the nineteenth century they were likely to be indentured after a relatively short stay in the asylum. By the turn of the century, however, older children without any family were increasingly likely to stay for several years if they entered an asylum.

Since a significant number of children either remained institutionalized for years or entered asylums at a fairly advanced age, asylum managers had to decide how old children should be before they had to leave. In the 1890s, the Maria Kip Orphanage's upper limit was fourteen years old, after which children unable to return to their own homes were indentured. Schooling often played a role in how long children were kept in asylums. At St. Vincent's of Philadelphia, children were to be kept until they finished elementary school, which usually happened when they were twelve years old. When compulsory attendance laws called for children to stay two more years in school, however, St. Vincent's began keeping their boys until they were fourteen.[63] In general, discharge age rose from ten or twelve to fourteen over the course of the nineteenth century, and to sixteen or even older by the 1920s. This is hardly surprising, given that in the early twentieth century reformers and social scientists came to the conclusion that there was a period "between childhood and adulthood," which was deemed adolescence.[64] In the mid–nineteenth century, fourteen-year-olds were not seen as belonging in an asylum; they were old enough to be out working. By the 1920s, however, it was generally agreed that children that age should still be in school and living under adult supervision—be it at home or in an asylum.

The length of a child's stay in an orphan asylum also depended on when they were in the asylum and the asylum managers' goals. In the first few decades of the nineteenth century, most of the Boston Female Asylum's children stayed an average of two to three years; they would have stayed even longer had they not often been indentured at the age of eight or nine. By the 1840s, as the asylum began keeping girls until they were twelve or thirteen before indenturing them, most children stayed in the asylum for at least six years.[65]

Prior to 1880, the three orphan asylums in New Orleans studied by Priscilla Clement kept children an average of two to four years. The Poydras Home continued to keep children for between two and three years, on average, through 1910. In the other two asylums Clement studied, the average length of stay dropped noticeably over time, in one case from 2.5 to 1.3 years and in the other from 4.1 to 2.5 years. The former change occurred at the Asylum for Destitute Boys because it had limited funds after the Civil War and responded by charging parents board to care for their children, sometimes discharging children whose families were unable to pay. In the latter case, the length of stay of children at St. Mary's dropped when a new order, which was less willing to keep children for extended periods, took over the asylum. From 1877 to 1903, the average length of stay in the Albany Orphan Asylum was 2.7 years, with 40 percent of the asylum's children staying less than one year. As in the New Orleans asylums, the average length of stay declined toward the turn of the century, dropping to an average of less than 1.5 years from 1900 to 1903. One of the reasons for the shorter stays seems to have been that more asylum children had two living parents. Children from such families had usually entered the Albany Orphan Asylum because a disaster left their parents temporarily unable to keep them. But two-parent families could get back on their feet more easily than one-parent families, thus increasing the chance of a quick family reunion. However, not all asylums saw shorter average stays as the years passed. At the St. Louis Protestant Orphan Asylum, twice as many children entering late in the nineteenth century stayed more than a year as had in the middle of the century.[66] Catherine Ross found that in New York's asylums in the late nineteenth century, the average length of stay was higher, at four years. She also found that the number of children staying institutionalized for more than five years "grew significantly with the passage of time."[67]

After the turn of the century, the average length of stay for children in most asylums continued to be in the one-to-four-year range. In the late 1920s, more than half the children cared for by the San Francisco Protestant Orphanage Society left the asylum within three years, including about 20 percent who stayed for less than one year. Marshall Jones has found in his study of fourteen asylums in Pennsylvania that the average length of stay varied between three and five years, until it shot up in the 1930s. Some asylums had much higher average lengths of stay. In the early twentieth century, the Cleveland Jewish Orphan Asylum kept its children an average of seven years.[68]

Not surprisingly, children's average length of stay in asylums rose during depressions. The chances of indenturing or placing a child decreased when the economy took a downturn, and so did the likelihood of families recovering quickly from whatever problems, especially unemployment, had led them to turn to an orphan asylum in the first place. In 1933, with the Great Depression at its worst, the average length of stay in one San Francisco orphanage, which had been decreasing across the 1920s, began to rise "because of the insecurity which most parents feel."[69]

Another way of examining how long children remained in asylums is the turnover rate of asylum populations. Roughly one-fourth to one-third of the children cared for in the Albany Orphan Asylum were discharged each year between 1875 and 1900. After 1900, the average discharge rate rose to about 40 percent per year. In New York State, between 1900 and 1929 roughly one-third of the children within asylums during any year had been discharged by the end of the year.[70] If this turnover applied equally to all children, then the asylum would have a completely new population every three years, and every child in an asylum would have stayed approximately three years.

While informative, the average length of stay of children in asylums and the turnover rate do not answer a number of important questions. An average length of stay of two years could mean that virtually all children stayed in the asylum between one and three years. However, it could also mean that the majority stayed a year or less, while a significant minority remained in the asylum for five or more years. Similarly, knowing that one-third of the children in an asylum had left by the end of the year could mean that almost all children stayed approximately three years, or it could mean that one-third to one-half of their children received short-term care while others stayed for many years.

In fact, orphan asylums served both purposes: they provided short-term care for the majority of their populations, while also providing long-term care for a significant minority. Some asylums specialized in either short-term care or long-term care, but most—perhaps nearly all—asylums provided both. Orphan asylums were not the only institutions that cared for both the long-term and short-term poor. For example, the majority of almshouse residents were institutionalized for a relatively short period, whereas a significant minority stayed for a year or more.[71] Unlike many other social welfare institutions, however, asylum policies were generally not designed to punish those requiring long-term care. Education, religious training, food, clothing, and housing were all necessary for a child's well-being, regardless of whether he or she was likely to stay three months or six years. And in most cases, children returned to their families when their families were once again able to care for them. For other nineteenth-century institutions, such as mental hospitals and juvenile reformatories, release often "depended on the inmate's ability to convince the administration that he or she was now prepared to conform to the expectations of decent folk."[72] Orphan asylum managers, however much they might worry about this issue with some of their children, rarely kept children institutionalized because they thought the children needed to be reformed or cured.

Indenture

A legacy of the colonial era, indenturing or apprenticing children was an important method of caring for dependent children, particularly full orphans, throughout much of the nineteenth century. When Ohio became a state, it based its charity legislation on the laws of older eastern states, especially Massachusetts. When other midwestern states, such as Illinois and Michigan, entered the Union, they used Ohio's laws as well as eastern precedents to write their own welfare legislation. Indenture was always a part of these laws. However, as the nature of the economy changed during the course of the nineteenth century, asylums used indenture less and less; by the end of the century, it had fallen out of use in many asylums outside of the South, though it continued to be used sporadically throughout the nation. In 1927, twelve states still allowed the children within their public institutions to be indentured, though whether this was done regularly is not clear.[73]

Indenturing children to homes where they would work in return for receiving shelter, food, and an education flourished in the antebellum years. Antebellum asylum managers used indenture to place children in homes when they left the asylum. The Charleston Orphan House bound out boys at fourteen and girls at twelve. In 1820, the New York State Legislature gave the Roman Catholic Benevolent Society, which had just opened an orphan asylum, the same power as the city almshouse to bind out children. Nashville's Orphan Society stopped indenturing girls under fourteen when it found that there were problems with girls bound out at too young an age and without proper training, as the Charleston Orphan House also discovered. Children leaving the Boston Female Asylum left as apprentices, sometimes to their own families. In the early nineteenth century, the asylum's managers often indentured girls at eight or nine years of age, but they soon decided children would benefit from longer stays in the asylum and stopped apprenticing children under ten. By the 1840s, most girls were twelve or thirteen when they left the Boston Female Asylum. Prior to the Civil War, many Protestant asylums cared for young children while indenturing children who were thirteen or fourteen.[74]

Children did not always use the skills they had been provided in the way that asylum managers intended. In the first four decades of its existence, the managers of the Boston Female Asylum intended their girls to become domestic servants to middle-class families in the asylum's immediate vicinity—in other words, to their own social class and network. This often happened in the asylum's earliest years, but by the 1820s many Boston Female Asylum graduates left their place of indenture to "take advantage of one or more of the new opportunities available to urban women." In recognition of the actual desires of their graduates and of the growing number of Irish domestic servants becoming available in Boston, after 1840 the asylum began to encourage its children to prepare for skilled jobs, especially needlework. Decades later, the Cleveland Jewish Orphan Asylum trained its boys to be skilled workers, yet only 14 percent of its graduates worked in the trades, while a much larger percentage worked in white-collar jobs, especially as clerks or salesmen.[75]

Asylum managers sometimes used indenture to provide children with more than just skills. Susan Lynne Porter has argued that the managers of the Boston Female Asylum believed that they provided their girls with "a valuable educational framework for imparting training and moral values," but that children were indentured to families where they could "learn about social relationships in a world which, unlike that of the Asylum, included men." Indenture would prepare the asylum's children for adult life, not by providing skills but by teaching them about families and relationships.[76]

Like many other asylums, the Chicago Orphan Asylum had the legal power to bind children out "to some suitable employment in the same manner as poor and indigent children may now be bound out according to the laws of this State." As was common for orphan asylums, the Albany Orphan Asylum received more requests for indenture than they could fill in the late nineteenth century. However, the asylum's managers recognized that many such families simply hoped to bring in unpaid labor, and resisted indenturing children to some homes for this reason.[77]

By the late nineteenth century, decisions about allowing children to leave asylums were often made by committees rather than by a superintendent or matron, just as had happened concerning admissions. Some asylums had already put discharges, especially as apprentices, in the hands of committees prior to the Civil War. The Cincinnati Orphan Asylum had a Binding Out Committee from its founding in the 1830s.[78] However, in the antebellum period such committees' main function was to find homes that would take children; toward the end of the nineteenth century, after considerable criticism of indiscriminate placements, these committees were expected to investigate homes thoroughly before allowing children to leave the asylum. The committees also became far more likely to stay in touch with children after they had been placed.

Most asylums developed rules to protect children being indentured, though these rules were generally ineffective. In the antebellum period, the measures taken were informal. The directors of the Poydras Home in New Orleans visited any home or business that wanted an apprentice before sending a child out. In the 1840s and 1850s, the Charleston Orphan House sent out "Lady Commissioners" to visit apprenticed children and examine their situations. In 1844, and again in 1851, at least some of these women resigned in opposition to the policy of apprenticing children under the age of fifteen.[79]

After the Civil War, methods of keeping in contact with children who had been apprenticed or placed out gradually became more careful. In the 1860s, the managers of New York's Roman Catholic Orphan Asylum created a standing committee to visit orphans who had been indentured. In the 1890s, the Maria Kip Orphanage indentured children with a six-month-long trial period, and indentured only children who were at least twelve years of age and "capable of writing a legible hand." The orphanage also limited indentures (and adoptions) to members of the Episcopal Church, a protection common among religious asylums. St. Vincent's Orphan Asylum, a Catholic institution in Philadelphia, apprenticed a number of boys to "bakers, gardeners, tailors, and barbers" among others, all of whom were "good Catholic persons." Even so, the asylum laid down rules of how and when masters were to pay their apprentices, and no child was to be apprenticed "without the permission of the pastor in whose parish he was to live." More important, every apprenticed child had a member of the asylum's board of trustees appointed as his guardian until the apprenticeship ended. Once a Catholic industrial school for boys opened in the area, however, St. Vincent's sent children to it rather than apprenticing them, and the industrial school then tried to find the children places.[80]

Though some asylums, such as the Maria Kip, were still indenturing children at the turn of the century, many had abandoned the practice earlier. New York's Roman Catholic Orphan Asylum was placing children in free homes by the 1870s, and using indentures only rarely. The Cincinnati Orphan Asylum began to encourage adoption over indenture in the late 1880s. At the St. Louis Protestant Orphan Asylum, there was a "dramatic decline" in the use of indenture after the Civil War. From 1847 to 1865, the asylum indentured 32 percent of the children who left it, but between 1871 and 1895 it indentured just 3 percent of the children discharged. Reform schools seem to have been more likely to continue apprenticing children than were orphan asylums in the last few decades of the nineteenth century.[81]

Once children without families to return to reached sixteen or seventeen years of age, they were discharged from asylums. Rather than being placed in a home where they would work, they were usually expected to find jobs and fend for themselves. The kinds of training children received while in asylums, described in Chapter 6, were given with this future in mind. By the late nineteenth century, most boys too old to remain in asylums left for factory jobs or, if they were fortunate, office jobs. Girls were still likely to wind up as domestic servants, though they too found more openings in factory work as time passed.[82] It is not clear how many asylum managers chose to not place girls out of anxiety about their safety, but it is reasonable to assume that this was one factor for some asylums that did not do any placing. It is certain that some asylum managers did what they could to protect children during their first year or two outside the asylum. In the early twentieth century, the directors of Baltimore's Hebrew Orphan Asylum discussed what they could do to find jobs, places to live, and expense money for the boys they were about to discharge. In the 1910s, one Catholic asylum in Albany established a boarding house for its discharged boys. In addition, the asylum tried to find the boys jobs as they were discharged.[83] Other asylum managers also opened boarding homes where older boys or girls lived as they began to work in full-time jobs outside the asylum. In most cases, however, the most that older children leaving an asylum could hope for was help in finding work.

Placing out and Boarding out

Between 1865 and 1900, most orphan asylums that placed children out shifted from indenturing children to placing them in free homes. This was more than a semantic change. It meant finding families willing to take in and care for children for emotional reasons, presumably treating them as family members, rather than indenturing children for the express purpose of providing them with job training. Economic relationships were to be replaced by emotional ties. However, the number of good free homes was well short of the number of children needing placement. In response to this problem, some orphan asylums and child-placing agencies began using boarding homes, where families were paid to care for children. It was this system that gradually became known as foster care in the twentieth century.

Two factors prompted orphan asylums to shift away from indenturing children to placing them out. The first was the growing recognition that childhood was a separate, and distinct, phase of life, and that children should not be overworked at an early age. In the late nineteenth century, middle-class society was increasingly coming to view children as emotionally valuable rather than as economic assets.[84] Asylum managers shared this change in viewpoint and actively sought homes where children would be treated as beloved family members rather than as workers. The second important factor was society's shift toward factory work and an industrialized workforce. If twelve- and thirteen-year-olds should not be placed on a farm or with a tradesman, it seemed even more clear that they should not be working long hours in a factory.

In the late nineteenth century, many public asylums relied heavily on finding free homes in which to place dependent children. Between 1884 and 1892, roughly half of the children discharged from Connecticut's public asylums were "placed in respectable families and removed from the pauper list."[85] The large state asylums in Michigan, Wisconsin, and several other states also sent most of their children out to private families. Some public asylums, particularly Ohio's county homes, seemed more willing to return children to their own parents.

The greatest problem in placing children in free homes was in finding enough such homes. Asylum managers regularly complained about the lack of good, Christian homes desiring to take in their children. Another problem was that asylums often lacked the legal power to place children out. Since most asylum children had at least one living parent, especially by the 1860s, gaining legal guardianship was a difficult but necessary step before an asylum could hope to place children with someone other than their own families. The surrender agreements of some asylums, such as the Chicago Orphan Asylum, required parents to give the asylum this legal right before a child could be admitted. By the early twentieth century, the Chicago Orphan Asylum was claiming that it could "always find good homes" for full orphans, particularly if they were young girls. The St. Vincent de Paul Orphan Asylum of New York had also found in the late nineteenth century that homes were much easier to find for girls than for boys.[86]

Child welfare activists in Massachusetts had responded to the difficulty "not to say impossibility, of finding homes for a limited number of children from private institutions" in the 1870s by advocating the boarding-out system, which was already in use in Great Britain. In 1880, the Massachusetts State Legislature authorized the state primary and reform schools to pay board to families willing to take dependent children into their homes. Visitors were to observe the homes, which were not allowed to care for more than two children at one time unless the children were siblings. As usual with asylum opponents, the speaker who informed the National Conference of Charities and Correction of the advantages of the boarding-out system over orphan asylums believed that "a poor home is better for the rearing of a child than an institution."[87]

By the mid-1880s, a number of asylum opponents were proposing boarding children in homes as a solution to the lack of free homes, and some cities outside of Massachusetts were responding. In Hartford, Connecticut, one reformer claimed that boarding out had led to the development of strong emotional ties between families and boarded children that usually led to adoption. The children were treated "in every way as their own" by the families boarding them, with "the children soon forgetting all other associations." Some asylums also favored boarding out as one option; Reena Sigman Friedman writes that Jewish orphan asylums "were among the first American child care institutions to establish extensive boarding-out programs in the late nineteenth century."[88]

From early placing efforts to modern foster care, people trying to place children recognized that a child's age greatly affects how successfully children and foster parents would respond to one another. Asylum managers had long known that young children adapted to new homes far more easily than children of eleven or twelve. Social workers in the 1920s used new language to describe an old fact. A report on foster care at the 1924 National Conference on Social Work stated that children placed when less than five years of age "showed a marked superiority in development" compared to children placed at an older age. In the 1910s, the Catholic Children's Bureau found that children under the age of eight placed in homes were far more likely to be adopted by their placement families than were children placed at an older age.[89]

When children were placed in homes other than their own, through whatever method, asylum managers hoped that emotional ties would develop between the placed children and their new families. Some asylum managers had considerable success in getting children adopted, chiefly with small children. Even in the 1830s, for example, the Boston Female Asylum managed to have almost one-fifth of its departing children adopted. Though it became somewhat more prevalent toward the end of the nineteenth century, before the twentieth century adoption was never nearly as common as returning children to their own homes or placing them in homes for temporary care. In 1879, the Rochester Orphan Asylum discharged eighty-two children, nineteen of whom were adopted. In 1903, eight of the fourteen children leaving St. Mary's Orphanage of Providence were being adopted. Few asylums did better; adoption was really only an option for young children who were full orphans.[90]

The 1910 institutional census gives some insight into which kinds of asylums placed children, and how often they did so. Of the 885 asylums that reported back to the census, half, 438, had placed at least a few children in homes the previous year. (The census did not distinguish between free and board homes, though in 1910 the majority were likely to have been free homes.) Just over 40 percent of the Catholic and Protestant asylums placed children in homes, but of those, Catholic asylums on average placed more than fifty children, while Protestant asylums on average placed just fourteen children. Catholics may have generally opposed placing as a *replacement* of institutional care, but when they were in charge of it themselves and could ensure that children were placed in Catholic homes and that siblings were kept together, Catholic asylum managers placed far more children than did their Protestant counterparts.

Only one-fourth of Jewish and fraternal asylums placed children, with Jewish asylums that did place averaging seventy-eight placements in 1910, while the five fraternal asylums averaged just sixteen placements. Public asylums were far more willing to place children in homes. Seventy-five of the ninety-three reporting county and city asylums placed, a much higher percentage than was found in any category of religious asylum. However, county and city asylums placing children averaged only twenty-seven placements, far fewer than Catholic or Jewish asylums. Since many state-managed asylums were de facto placing agencies as well as institutions, it is somewhat surprising that only eleven of the sixteen reporting state asylums placed children. However, as would be expected, they placed far more children than any other kind of institution, an average of over 137 (see Appendix, Table A9).

In the 1920s, social work techniques began to help shape asylums' placing-out and foster care programs. After placing children out, many orphan asylums continued to check on the homes, and in many cases they carefully inspected prospective foster homes even before providing them with children. At the end of 1930, the Chicago Orphan Asylum's Boarding-Out Department had thirty-seven children boarded out. To find these homes, the asylum had investigated 285 potential boarding homes.[91] Even many Catholic child welfare workers had come to accept that placement in homes was often superior to institutional care. A speaker at the National Conference of Catholic Charities argued in 1923 that most dependent or mildly delinquent children should be placed in "carefully selected foster, boarding or free" homes if they could not be returned to their own families.[92] Nonetheless, Catholic asylums were far more reluctant to completely abandon an institutional approach in the 1930s than were Protestant and public asylums.

Since many orphan asylums had always tried to place at least some of their children in homes, it is not surprising that a number of asylums transformed into foster care agencies or adoption agencies as institutional care for dependent children became a less desirable option. St. Mary's Home for Children retained its name in the mid-1940s, but by then it was chiefly a foster care agency. The new, relatively small building was to "be auxiliary to a boarding home program." Similarly, by 1944 the Chicago Orphan Asylum had become a foster care agency and adoption service, and the only institutional setting it provided was temporary care for babies. Small religious asylums in smaller towns also changed. The Mennonite Children's Home of Millersville, Pennsylvania, had placed children in private foster homes right from its opening in 1911. By the early 1950s, the majority of children under its supervision were living in foster homes.[93]

Returning to Family

Most children in orphan asylums had relatives who hoped to reunite with them. Almost all orphan asylum managers came to recognize this fact; some did so happily while others hoped to prevent children from returning to their parents. At the start of the nineteenth century, the Boston Female Asylum preferred to indenture its girls to middle-class families that wanted a domestic servant rather than return the girls to their own families. Starting in the 1820s, however, the asylum's policy changed because its managers decided that family ties, whenever they existed, might well be more important to a child's happiness and future success than training in a middle-class home. Between 1838 and 1855, nearly one-third of the children leaving the asylum returned to relatives.[94]

Though all orphan asylums tried to make some sort of provision for departing children who lacked families to return to, the most common departure entailed a child returning to its family. In the decades after the Civil War, the Orphans' Home and Asylum placed a number of children in free homes, but in most years they returned far more children to their relatives than they placed in other ways. In 1866, for example, twenty-four children were "returned to their friends" (including family), while only six were placed. In 1880, "situations" were found for two children, but the other forty-one who left the asylum were again "returned to their friends." In 1887, thirty-one of the thirty-seven children who left the asylum "returned to their friends or to parents who have made a second marriage." Other asylums also eventually sent most of their children back to their families in the late nineteenth century. "The vast majority of discharges" from New York's Roman Catholic Orphan Asylum were to "parents or other relatives." In 1891, twelve children left the Maria Kip Orphanage, all of whom were "removed by parents or guardians." As the Maria Kip grew, it began to place more children in homes, but the vast majority of children leaving were still returning to their families. In 1898, fifty-one of the sixty-one children who left the orphanage "were reclaimed by relatives or friends." Similarly, 108 of the 145 children leaving the Chicago Orphan Asylum in 1896 were "taken by parents or friends." Not all asylums in this period sent a clear majority of their children back home. In the late nineteenth century, 43 percent of the children discharged from the Albany Orphan Asylum returned to their own homes; more than 50 percent of children less than five years old returned to their own families. On the other hand, by the 1910s, virtually every one of the several hundred children leaving the Angel Guardian Orphanage each year were returning to their families.[95]

Many children returned to their families once they were old enough to work and help support the family. Asylums were widely criticized for letting children go back to families that then sent them out to work, on the basis that this showed parents did not really care for their children. In many ways, it was more an indictment of working-class life than of orphan asylums. After all, working-class families regularly sent older children out to work to help the family; in this regard, asylum children who returned to their families at fourteen or fifteen years of age and took a job while living at home were no different than their peers in the neighborhood. In many instances, asylum critics disliked working-class culture and failed to recognize the economic realities within which the working class lived.[96]

As the idea of keeping families together became more widely accepted in the early twentieth century, the percentage of children who returned to their own families upon leaving orphan asylums rose. The majority of children leaving most asylums returned to their parents, though this was not the case in every asylum. Overall, however, it is clear that a central purpose asylums served for the children they cared for was to return them eventually to their kin; this became even more true in the twentieth century than it had been in the nineteenth century. For example, more than three-fourths of the children leaving California's orphan asylums in the year ending June 30, 1916, returned to "parents or guardians."[97]

Conclusion

Parents who tried to place their children in orphan asylums were often viewed as bad parents; they were immoral, unloving, and lazy, according to child-placing agencies, public welfare officials, and other critics of orphan asylums. Parents' willingness to abandon their children to an institution seemed to many middle-class observers further proof that they were not worthy of aid, though their children might be innocent and deserving. Yet deciding to part with one's child is never easy, whether one is middle class or working class, native-born or foreign-born, female or male, black or white. From the perspective of an orphan asylum manager, an application for a child's admission was the first step. From a parent's perspective, however, it was often the final, desperate step in a series of attempts to deal with poverty brought on by some sort of family calamity. Parents who tried to place their children within orphan asylums were far more likely to have been driven to make such a move by the death or illness of a mate, or the lack of a steady income, than by lack of love for their children. In many cases, parents and asylum managers agreed that the institution would serve as a temporary home for a child until the parent could again care for a family. But other asylum managers saw a need to tear poor children away from their parents and provide them with a fresh start. These different attitudes toward the poor were clearly reflected in the admission policies orphan asylums adopted.

By the 1920s, the idea that poor parents were often good, or at least not bad, parents who were financially (rather than morally) unable to care for their children was becoming widespread among asylum managers and other people working with poor children, if not in society as a whole. The San Francisco Protestant Orphanage annual report for 1931 stated that

> [I]n our large family there are few full-orphans; about six per cent are in this class. The remainder are half-orphans or have both parents living. It must be kept in mind that while the great majority of our children are the victims of misfortune, poverty and neglect, we have many who have parents, who, under normal circumstances, are quite

responsible, and, are in fact, anxious to meet their duties in the fullest measure.[98]

What is most notable about this positive view of the poor, however, is that growing numbers of orphan asylum managers had held it long before the Progressive Era. The widespread belief that children and parents should be kept together if possible, and that poor parents might also be "worthy" parents, was not simply a product of the early twentieth century. Instead, it was the gradual triumph of one long-standing strand of thought over another. Over time, virtually all orphan asylum managers abandoned the harsh view that destitute families seeking public or private aid to survive were unworthy of aid. Some orphan asylum managers had abandoned this belief before the Civil War, while others developed a benevolent view toward the working poor only in the twentieth century. By the 1910s, almost all asylums were doing what many had already been doing for decades: caring for children until they could be reunited with their families.

The ways in which children left asylums depended on a number of factors. The most important, of course, was whether or not they had living relatives, particularly parents, who could reclaim them. The attitudes that asylum managers held toward poor relatives of their children had a great deal to do with how children were discharged: asylum managers who viewed poor adults as unworthy of aid were less willing to return children to their parents than were managers who saw poor parents as struggling under difficult circumstances. And the national economy and nature of the workforce also mattered. Full orphans were more easily indentured than other children in the first half of the nineteenth century, and far more easily placed in free homes or adopted from the Civil War era to the 1930s. Children with two living parents, on the other hand, were always likely to return to their parents after a year or two in an asylum. Half-orphans were dealt with in a variety of ways, but by the late nineteenth century they too were generally returned to a parent when they left the asylum.

Throughout the nineteenth century, orphan asylum managers were generally far more willing to return poor children to their families than were child-placing advocates, who frequently hoped to separate "innocent" children from "unworthy" parents. By the beginning of the twentieth century, a relatively friendly attitude toward poor families was becoming more and more widespread among asylum managers. By the 1920s, children leaving orphan asylums were almost always being returned to their families, usually in accord with the expressed wishes of asylum managers.

Table 4.1. Sources of admission to eighty Catholic orphan asylums, mid-1910s.

Source of request for admission	Number of children admitted	Percent of total number of children admitted*
Committed by courts	7,174	36.7%
Parents' application	4,288	21.9
From social agencies	4,127	21.1
Pastors' recommendation	2,484	12.7
Friends' application	1,472	7.5
All admissions	19,545	100.0

Source: 4th *NC Catholic* (1916), p. 173.
*Column does not add up to 100% due to rounding.

Table 4.2. Mean number of children in orphan asylums by parentage, and by management type, in 1890.

	White native-born				
Management	With native-born parents	With one or two foreign-born parents	Parents' birthplace unknown	White, foreign-born	Other/Unknown
Catholic	17.7	53.5	36.6	9.8	8.9
Protestant	20.4	17.9	14.3	4.4	4.5
Jewish	0.9	60.3	49.8	48.1	0.1
Fraternal	30.8	16.3	11.8	1.8	3.8
County/City	18.3	1.6	20.9	0.4	5.5
State	29.6	13.3	149.3	3.1	24.5
Unknown	18.9	13.0	12.2	2.3	9.5
All asylums	18.9	26.1	25.9	5.6	7.9

Source: *Eleventh Census: 1890.*

Table 4.3. Total number of orphan asylums by race accepted, 1890–1933.

Year	White only	Nonwhite only	Mixed or all races	Unknown
1890	490	27	120	7
1910	585	36	349	2
1923	939	85	296	7
1933	663	90	239	329

Source: *Eleventh Census: 1890; Benevolent Institutions, 1910; Children Under Institutional Care, 1923; Children Under Institutional Care, 1933.*

Table 4.4. Total number of orphan asylums by gender accepted, 1890–1923.

Year	Coed	Girls only	Boys only	Unknown
1890	393	105	53	12
1910	667	130	88	87
1923	975	204	147	1

Source: *Eleventh Census: 1890; Benevolent Institutions, 1910; Children Under Institutional Care, 1923.*

5

Routine, Discipline, and Improvements in Asylum Life

Life in an institution was rarely full of pleasant surprises and meaningful choices for inmates. Orphan asylums were no exception, especially in the nineteenth century. The larger the asylum, the more likely it was that children followed a familiar routine from one day to the next, from one week to the next, and for month after month. They usually ate a meager diet, and in larger asylums wore uniforms that decreased their sense of individuality and marked them as "asylum children" to outsiders. Discipline remained an important part of most asylum managers' thinking well into the twentieth century and was at times harsh and brutal.

By the 1890s, asylums were being criticized regularly for raising "institutional" children unprepared to face independent life as adults. These critics, many of whom were child-placing advocates, also attacked asylums for accepting children too readily, thus allowing presumably undeserving parents to escape their responsibilities, and for then keeping children too long. Finally, the regimentation and often harsh discipline within asylums were criticized as being far from the "homelike" ideal asylum managers had long claimed.

Asylum managers responded to these criticisms by opening up their institutions and sending their children out into the broader world more often, as is described in the next two chapters. They had always tried to improve their institutions, both out of a desire to better care for their children and out of pride in what they provided to their communities, but these constant attacks led some asylum managers to reshape the very nature of their institutions by adopting the cottage system. Under the cottage system, children would be kept in groups of between fifteen and thirty in what amounted to semi-independent, small asylums, each run by its own matron who would be a surrogate mother to her children. By 1910, only a small proportion of asylums had managed to make the switch to a true cottage system, but asylums across the nation were slowly moving away from rigid regimentation toward a more humane approach focusing on children as individuals who needed attention as much as they needed structure.

Daily Routine in the Asylum

The daily schedule of asylums before the Civil War was almost certainly monotonous. At the Boston Female Asylum in the 1800s, from April to October the girls woke at 6:00 A.M., said their prayers, washed with cold water, and cleaned their rooms before having breakfast at 8:00 A.M. After eating, the children played until 9:00, when they were read a Bible chapter and again said prayers before attending school until noon. Dinner was at 1:00 P.M., followed by a little more playtime, and then by school from 2:00 to 5:00. Another hour of play was presumably followed by supper; after praying again, the girls were in bed at 8:00 P.M. During the long Boston winter, the schedule was similar but shortened, with children going to bed at 6:00 P.M. and staying there until 7:00 A.M.[1]

Late nineteenth-century asylums had similar schedules. At the Cleveland Jewish Orphan Asylum in the 1870s, boys and girls awoke at 6:00 A.M. in the winter and at 5:45 A.M. in the summer, and were given forty minutes to wash, dress, and be inspected for cleanliness. After fifteen minutes of prayer, they marched to the dining hall, where they ate in silence. They finished eating at 7:30; younger children then had seventy-five minutes to play, while children eight and older performed household chores. From 8:45 to 11:45, they all attended school, with one twenty-minute recess. From 11:45 A.M. to 1:45 P.M., they ate their main meal and then returned to their play areas, where they might play or be put through military drills and parades. School resumed and ran from 1:45 to 4:45, with one thirty-minute break during which they were given a snack. From 4:45 to 6:00, the younger children played while the older ones again performed chores. Supper, a light meal, was served at 6:00, after which children returned to classrooms to prepare their lessons for the next day. From 7:30 to 9:00, children were sent to bed in shifts, the youngest first, after saying their evening prayers. This schedule was adhered to from Monday to Friday throughout the year, aside from a few holidays and a six-week summer vacation. Weekends were spent in religious services and instruction, lessons in Jewish history, and needlework for girls.[2]

St. Vincent's Orphan Asylum in Philadelphia, a Catholic institution, had a similar schedule in the 1880s, though it was more heavily weighted toward prayer and religious ceremony than most other asylum schedules. At St. Vincent's, the children woke early, with the older children expected to dress quickly and then help the younger children with their clothes. At 6:30 A.M., all the children went to chapel for morning prayers and stayed through mass, which apparently did not even begin until 7:30. The institution was German Catholic, and so all prayers were said in German. Then the morning session of school ran until 11:30; presumably the children were allowed to eat breakfast at some point, though it is not certain that they ate before the noontime meal. There was "spiritual reading" throughout both the noon and evening meals. There was apparently an afternoon session of school as well, then prayers before and after supper.[3]

The daily schedule of children in Virginia's Lutheran Children's Home in the 1910s will sound familiar. Children rose and cleaned their rooms and the halls from 6:00 to 7:00 A.M., then ate breakfast and prayed until 7:40. They cleaned the tables, washed the dishes, and cleaned other parts of the home until 9:00 A.M., then attended school until just after noon. From 12:10 to 2:00 P.M., the children ate dinner, cleaned dishes again, set the table for supper, and then played. From 2:00 to 5:00, children either attended school or work; at 5:00, some ate supper while others played. At 6:00, those who had not yet eaten did so; then there was a worship service, after which the younger children went to bed. From 7:00 to 8:30, the older children studied; 9:30 was their lights-out.[4]

These may seem like harsh routines, but compared to the daily routine of reform schools in the same era, orphan asylums had much more time devoted to education, a reasonable amount of time allotted to recreation, and notably less time spent working on chores. At the Massachusetts State Reform School for Boys in the 1850s, for example, the boys awoke at 5:00 or 5:30 A.M., dressed, washed, prayed, ate breakfast, and then worked from 7:00 to 10:00. School ran from 10:00 to noon, followed by a meal and a brief recreation period; then they went back to work from 1:00 to 4:00 P.M. After another hour split between eating and recreation, the boys had evening lessons from 5:00 to 7:00, followed by prayer and moral lessons, and then went to bed.[5] Orphan asylums in the nineteenth century rarely allowed children to do whatever they chose, but they presented their children with schooling and recreation as well as regimentation and punishment. This was true in most families as well, but in asylums there was one major difference: it was not the children's real parents who were rearing them.

Mealtime reveals a great deal about what life in an asylum was like. The kind of rowdy, playful scene that often occurs in late-twentieth-century school cafeterias probably never happened in nineteenth-century asylum dining halls. But the extent to which children were allowed to interact while eating varied quite a bit. In some asylums, such as the Cleveland Jewish Orphan Asylum and the Chicago Nursery and Half-Orphan Asylum in the late nineteenth century, children were not allowed to speak to one another at all while eating.[6] In smaller asylums, children were probably allowed somewhat more freedom while eating. For that matter, smaller asylums may have had a generally more relaxed atmosphere than could institutions holding one hundred or more children.

Children were always fed in asylums, but that does not necessarily mean they received either the quality or quantity of food they might have liked. The diet of children at the Boston Female Asylum at the dawn of the nineteenth century was probably representative of most asylums' meals for decades. Except for Sundays, breakfast and supper consisted of "hasty-puddings, boiled rice with molasses, or milk, or milk-porridge, as the season will admit." The day's main meal, dinner, varied somewhat: on Monday and Wednesday, soup; for Tuesday, boiled meat, and sometimes vegetables; Thursday, beans or peas, with pork; on Friday, mutton broth or lamb broth; and fish on Saturday. Sunday was not much better; roast meat and pudding for dinner, and slightly better morning and evening meals including bread. The Cincinnati Orphan Asylum's historian believes that in the 1830s the children there ate mostly bread and molasses, and drank water or "weak coffee." In 1875, the Chicago Orphan Asylum tried to improve the quality of its meals by "procuring a liberal supply of vegetables, fresh from the farmer producing them." The asylum's physician claimed that "the effect speaks for itself." In 1881, the Michigan State Public School also added vegetables to what was already a somewhat less monotonous diet: milk or coffee, bread, and either rice, oatmeal, or hominy for breakfast; a noontime dinner of bread, potatoes, pork and beans or fish or soup, and fruit; and a light supper of bread, milk, and sometimes biscuits or mush. In 1900, Minnesota's State Public School took the unusual step of furnishing both its children and its officers food of identical quality; though small children could not be fed exactly the same meals as adults, the food was "prepared from material taken from the same packages."[7]

By the middle of the nineteenth century, virtually all orphan asylums had access to some kind of medical care for their children. (Whether the care actually did much good in the earlier years is of course another question.) Lists of asylum officers at the start of annual reports almost always showed at least one physician (who usually donated his time and was often the husband of an asylum trustee); as time passed, larger asylums might list several specialists and dentists as well. In 1860, Boston's Church Home for Orphan and Destitute Children, just three years old, listed two physicians at the bottom of a long list of officers, just above the home's matron! St. Mary's Home for Children, a moderately sized asylum in Chicago, listed one "Physician" and two "Consulting Physicians" in 1906. The home's managers expressed their gratitude to the doctors, including a fourth who was not mentioned on the list but who had "been very kind in caring for our children's eyes during the last year."[8]

Access to medical care was crucial for orphan asylums, which had always suffered high death rates. Throughout the nineteenth century, asylums struggled to keep their children alive. Of the eighteen children who "departed" the Colored Orphan Asylum of New York in 1842, nine had died, most apparently from scarlet fever or the measles. Five years later, after the asylum had tripled in size and held 144 children, 24 children died. In 1849, another twenty died, nine from cholera.[9] Mortality rates may have improved somewhat by the last decades of the nineteenth century, but in many asylums they were still high. The Chicago Nursery and Half-Orphan Asylum was more dangerous than most asylums in the 1880s, because it focused more on caring for small children than did most asylums. Twelve children died in 1886, eleven in 1888, fourteen in 1890, and nineteen in 1892. The victims were chiefly in the asylum's nursery and "were under six years of age."[10]

Availability of medical care was crucial to asylums, since if one child caught a serious contagious disease, it might well sweep through the entire asylum population. For example, a scarlet fever epidemic hit

Chicago and swept through St. Mary's Home in 1907. Fifteen of the twenty-nine children infected were cared for in the home, while the other fourteen were sent to the county hospital; apparently, all survived, though one of St. Mary's children did die that year "due to capillary bronchitis following measles."[11]

Asylums that accepted babies had much higher mortality rates than other asylums, but all asylums seemed to expect some deaths and congratulated themselves if "only" one or two died a year. In 1882, the superintendent of Michigan's State Public School wrote that "only" six deaths over the previous five years was "the highest endorsement of our dietary, and the sanitary arrangements of this institution." In 1896, five children died in the Chicago Orphan Asylum's care, all "under two years of age"; the asylum's annual report referred to this as "only five deaths." The asylum enjoyed the voluntary services of a number of specialists, including a surgeon, an oculist, and a dentist. Two years later, three children died in the asylum's care, the oldest five years old. Even so, the asylum's managers were "thankful" because no epidemic had struck that year, though there had been cases of whooping cough, diphtheria, and chicken pox. A full-time trained nurse had been hired to help carry out the orders of the various doctors, especially regarding the care and nursing of infants.[12]

The disease that rampaged through the institution in 1899 showed why the asylum had been "thankful" the previous year. At one point, there were "thirty-six cases of measles, two of scarlet fever, one of diphtheria; and one with pneumonia, all needing the best of care." The asylum stopped accepting new children for several weeks while dealing with the ill children and felt "proud" that only two died. The asylum's managers even tried to dodge responsibility for those deaths, by saying that the deceased "had been hospital patients from the time they were received into the Home."[13] Many asylums were less lucky when disease struck. In 1884, just two years after the Michigan State Public School congratulated itself for averaging only about one death a year, a diphtheria outbreak struck, killing seven children.[14]

As time passed, asylums began taking precautions regarding the health of new children. Some asylums had given children medical examinations upon admission in the 1860s and 1870s; after 1900, this became common. In the 1910s, children entering the Angel Guardian Orphanage were examined on admission and then were given "periodical examinations" by doctors and dentists. By 1930, the Chicago Orphan Asylum gave each child a complete physical examination, "including vaginal smears, Wassermans [sic], and toxin and anti-toxin followed by the Schick test in six months." Children then had annual physicals near their birthdays.[15]

Large asylums in the nineteenth century did a number of things that depersonalized children. Upon entering the Cleveland Jewish Orphan Asylum, children had medical exams, had their hair cut short, were "put into drab gray, coarse second-hand uniforms, and assigned identifying numbers."[16] In most congregate asylums, children slept on rows of small, uncomfortable beds; there might be as many as one hundred children in the same large, overcrowded room. Adults or older children often served as monitors to make sure that children remained quiet until they fell asleep. Children might bathe once a week in groups, sharing bathwater and towels as well. In the early 1900s, "bath night" at the Fred Finch Children's Home saw seven or more children sharing a tub.[17]

In many asylums, children wore uniforms that gave them little sense of themselves as individuals and clearly distinguished them to community members. Smaller asylums were probably much more likely to let children dress individually, at least to some extent. For example, the Chicago Home for Jewish Orphans, which held thirty-six children in 1899, sent their children to public school "clothed in different styles, and not in uniforms" to keep its wards from being "singled out from their more fortunate comrades." But the larger Cleveland Jewish Orphan Asylum's children did not exchange uniforms for individual outfits until 1919–1920, when the asylum's school was largely shut down and the children were sent out to public schools from the third grade onward.[18]

In coed asylums, children were often segregated by sex for most or all of the day, especially prior to the Progressive Era. Under its first superintendent after its founding in 1868, the Cleveland Jewish Orphan Asylum separated boys from girls during meals, in chapel, in school, and at playtime as well as in their dormitories. Some asylums allowed boys and girls to play together until they were five or six years old and began school, at which point segregation was common.[19] Catherine Ross found that in the late nineteenth century, the sexes were separated in almost all of New York's orphan asylums. Of course, it was not just orphan asylums that separated the sexes; for example, mental hospitals did the same, probably much more thoroughly than most asylums for children.

In addition, asylum children sometimes chose to keep separate from the opposite sex. At the Cleveland Jewish Orphan Asylum, older boys did what they could to keep younger boys from interacting with girls, and of course refrained from doing so themselves as well.[20]

Discipline

Asylum children, like most children, often acted in ways that their parental figures did not approve. These actions ranged from the mild, such as not having one's clothes as clean as a staff member wished or whispering to another child when one was supposed to be eating in silence, all the way to blatant lack of respect for an asylum manager or running away from the asylum. Managers reacted in a variety of ways, but in general, discipline in nineteenth-century asylums, as in many families at the same time, could be quite harsh.

Running away seems to have been a particularly important problem, for an obvious reason. By leaving on his or her own, a child was disproving asylum managers' claims that they were creating a loving home where children were happy. Managers sometimes treated runaway children very harshly, even though that in turn may well have led to more children running away. Asylums where discipline was particularly strict, such as the Cleveland Jewish Orphan Asylum in the late nineteenth and early twentieth century, were never able to completely prevent children from "running out" through their strictness. Some asylums tried other tactics. In 1904, New York's Hebrew Orphan Asylum tried to discourage parental approval of running away—the asylum found most runaways with their families—by announcing it would not readmit runaways no matter how desperate their family's problems might become in the future.[21]

Most, perhaps nearly all, nineteenth-century asylums' managers felt they had no choice but to be strict with some children. This may have been especially true in asylums where older children were retained. In the 1850s, the Charleston Orphan House was already sending some children to high school and thus occasionally had to deal with rebellious adolescents. In 1857, one boy treated the asylum's matron so disrespectfully that he was placed in solitary confinement (in a cellar "prison") and given just bread and water, until he apologized a few days later.[22]

Corporal punishment was undoubtedly the most common method of dealing with disobedient children. In the 1870s, boys at the Cleveland Jewish Orphan Asylum were whipped when they misbehaved; perhaps girls faced somewhat less harsh punishment when they disobeyed. By 1900, at any rate, girls there did not face corporal punishment, although unacceptable behavior was punished through an extensive system of demerits. Paddling was still very much a part of a boy's life if he disobeyed. New leadership at the asylum in the 1910s finally ended the use of corporal punishment.[23]

In the late nineteenth century, most asylum managers moved gradually toward rewards and reason to shape their children's behavior but did not hesitate to use physical punishment whenever they believed it necessary. In 1880, the Brooklyn Home for Destitute Children's annual report stated that "the matron appeals to their sense of right before she resorts to corporal punishment. It is pleasant to find that there are as many boys and girls among this class who respond quickly to such an appeal, as there are those who have only a craven fear of punishment."[24] The home's managers held a harsher view of the poor than many asylum managers by the 1880s, but the assumption that some children would only improve their behavior because of a "craven fear of punishment" was still widely held by asylum superintendents and matrons prior to 1900. The superintendent of Michigan's State Public School expressed similar views in 1882. "The majority" of the school's children obeyed its rules, but some children were "very disobedient and vicious, destructive of property, overbearing and oppressive towards their fellows, untruthful and dishonest" and needed to be dealt with accordingly. The superintendent proceeded to doubt that any asylum in the country actually forbade the use of corporal punishment, whatever some managers might claim.[25]

In 1896, the New York State Board of Charities banned the use of corporal punishment in the state's orphan asylums. Some asylum superintendents felt this undermined their ability to discipline their children effectively; most apparently responded by relying more heavily on other methods of punishment such as extra chores, less food, or solitary confinement. Catherine Ross found that the Colored Orphan Asylum responded more humanely to this law than the other asylums she studied, often relying on rewarding good behavior rather than simply punishing disobedient children.[26] Even when staff members did not resort to beating, they often relied on humiliating a child as a way to improve his or her behavior. Gary Polster argues that in the 1890s at the Cleveland Jewish Orphan Asylum, "the goal was to make the orphan ashamed about their behavior" so that they would seek to reform and view the asylum as their friend. In the same era, the Fred Finch Children's Home responded to children who swore by having a "mouth wash day."[27]

Children whose behavior became too disruptive to an asylum's routine or who were seen as bad influences on other children were often sent away. Four of the twenty-nine children who were dismissed from the Orphans' Home and Asylum in 1858 were "dismissed for bad conduct," though the annual report does not describe what they had done.[28] This is hardly surprising in light of the fact that asylum managers tried not to admit children who were seen as "delinquent" rather than dependent. Similarly, Barbara Bellows argues that the commissioners who managed the Charleston Orphan House dealt with unacceptable behavior on the part of children by expulsion.[29]

Over time, most asylums developed systems of rewards and punishments. By the late 1850s, the Charleston Orphan House's commissioners were already using a demerit system; children who misbehaved were apparently allowed to acquire one hundred demerits before they "faced immediate indenture and the end of childhood." In many cases, these systems coexisted with corporal punishment, at least for boys. In the first years of the twentieth century, the Cleveland Jewish Orphan Asylum gave demerits to children of both sexes who misbehaved (while still beating boys who tried to run away). Too many demerits would mean that a child would either be expelled from the asylum or be allowed to stay but lose the right to enjoy various privileges, such as the outings described in Chapter 7.[30]

Asylum children did not only have to worry about being hurt by asylum staff; in many instances, they had even more to fear from older children. Violence was often a part of a boy's normal life in poor neighborhoods,[31] and asylum life was no different. At the Cleveland Jewish Orphan Asylum, children sometimes "protected" younger children from other bullies, in exchange for favors such as shoe shines or food. In addition, the asylum had a formal monitoring system; boys and girls who did well in school and showed good conduct became monitors and helped the asylum staff keep order. In New York's Hebrew Orphan Asylum, older children regularly threatened or attacked younger children, especially new arrivals, and even stole their property.[32]

One of the reasons sometimes given for the kind of regimented daily schedule outlined at the beginning of the chapter was that busy children had little time or energy to get in trouble. (Assigning children extensive chores, as is described in the next chapter, was very much a result of this thinking.) After the superintendent of Montana's State Orphans' Home described work performed by older boys and girls, he wrote that "this also goes far toward settling the question of discipline. Keep the boys and girls busy and you largely solve that problem. The busy man has no time to quarrel with his neighbor. Keep children employed, either at work or play, and they have little opportunity, or desire for wrong doing."[33] This did not mean that the home's managers never used corporal punishment on children, simply that it was "the dernier resort." "Kindness, reason, and persuasion" were used to elicit "order, promptness, regularity, and obedience" from the children; punishment occurred only if these superior methods failed.[34]

From a late-twentieth-century perspective, the kinds of discipline used in many orphan asylums in the nineteenth century seem quite harsh. It is clear that at times the treatment of asylum children was indeed severe. Many Progressive Era asylum managers agreed, and lessened or abandoned the use of corporal punishment. But looking at what nineteenth-century reform schools sometimes did to discipline their children may provide a useful balancing perspective. An investigation into a Massachusetts reform school in the 1870s found a very severe environment. Flogging with a heavy leather strap was a common form of corporal punishment, and not the worst. Children were also placed in straightjackets and gagged or, for the worst offenses, placed for hours in the "sweatbox," which was twenty-one inches by sixteen and a half inches. Yet the report praised the overall condition of the reform school; investigations into orphan asylum conditions over the next few decades expressed dismay with more humane methods. Of course, reformatories dealt with older children, many (but not all) of whom were considered disciplinary problems, while the vast majority of orphan asylum wards in the nineteenth century were twelve or younger. Still, strict discipline in most orphan asylums was not all that unusual for the era, in many cases was probably similar to that experienced by many working-class children in their own homes, and was far from what children in reform schools underwent.[35]

Attacks on the Asylum

Charles Loring Brace, the nineteenth century's most important advocate of placing children in homes, was also the most outspoken critic of orphan asylums. The combination was hardly a coincidence; the two methods of caring for dependent children were in competition for decades. Brace and the Children's Aid Society originally focused on street children, who were presumably not being cared for by their families; he left asylums to their own devices. By the 1870s, however, Brace was attacking New York's asylums as impersonal institutions that harmed children and failed to prepare them for independent adulthood. He also claimed that they encouraged dependency at the public's expense by allowing parents to temporarily escape their natural duties to their own children and then regain their children when they wished. Brace, who was vehemently anti-Catholic, was especially unhappy that Catholics were allowed to put their children in New York's Catholic asylums for years if they wished, while the public footed a large part of the bill. Placing out, according to Brace, was better for children, since it separated them permanently from their parents. Just as importantly in Brace's mind, placing children in homes would be much less costly to the public purse. At the same time Brace was mounting his attack on orphan asylums, his Children's Aid Society was also facing a "rising tide of criticism." (By the late 1890s, however, as asylums were becoming much less popular at national gatherings of charity workers, the Children's Aid Society was receiving much stronger support.)[36]

By the 1890s, orphan asylums were regularly being condemned at national and state charity conferences, usually by placing-out advocates. One of the most common condemnations of orphan asylums was that they created an "institutional" type of child who lacked individuality. Even those who supported orphanages tended to agree with this charge. One speaker at the 1890 National Conference of Charities and Correction praised orphan asylums and their generally "wise and competent matrons and superintendents" for their "good work in the care bestowed upon the little ones." But she also believed that "the training of the institutional child does not tend to individual development, under the forced and requisite obedience to the systematic rules and regulations which must prevail" when dozens, or hundreds, of children were being raised together. Other critics, especially advocates of placing out, were less kind, seeing orphan asylums as overly expensive and artificial environments.[37]

Two other frequent criticisms of orphan asylums in the last decades of the nineteenth century were interconnected: that they accepted children too easily and that they held children too long. William Letchworth was repeating an often-stated belief when he announced at the 1886 National Conference of Charities and Correction that "among the temptations to over-retention is a pride in numbers."[38] Many asylums also came under fire for their sometimes harsh methods of disciplining children and for their strict segregation by sex, which was seen as an unnatural way for children to grow up. These criticisms of institutional life were also aimed at other institutions, especially those for the mentally ill, during the last few decades of the century.[39]

Public funding of private institutions was also heavily criticized in the states where it was provided. In New York, government funding of private orphan asylums (and some other institutions) was attacked in the 1880s and 1890s on two fronts. Some reformers, who accepted the idea of public responsibility for dependent children, felt that asylums should be more closely regulated by the state, since they were fulfilling a public duty with public money. Other reformers argued against public funding of institutions that were, in most cases, clearly sectarian in nature.[40] Much of this criticism stemmed not from the fact that asylums were religious in nature, but instead from the fact that many were Catholic; Brace was hardly the only child-placing advocate who was also anti-Catholic.

New Jersey's Commission on Defective, Delinquent, and Dependent Children in 1897 was a typical government response to institutional care for poor children as the nineteenth century came to a close. Its report praised the Children's Aid Society and the Charity Organization Society, but also commended the state's private orphan asylums while criticizing almshouses that still held children. However, despite its praise of New Jersey's private asylums, the report strongly criticized neighboring New York's method of supporting private asylums with public funding. It went on to favor placing children in homes over institutional care; free homes were best, but paying boarding homes to care for children would also be preferable to asylum care.[41]

There was considerable truth to some of these charges. Even many asylum managers agreed that large institutions sometimes failed to develop children as individuals. The managers of the Brooklyn Industrial School Association's Home maintained "that years of institution life unfit the child for the place it should occupy in the family."[42] Asylums' constant attempts to become more "homelike" were, in large part, an attempt to meet this criticism. There is no question that the monotony and discipline of life in asylums were often their greatest flaws, particularly in large institutions. By the 1890s, many asylum managers were responding to these attacks by softening their disciplinary methods and allowing boys and girls to interact with one another, and with the outside world, more often.[43]

It was also true that many orphan asylums were overcrowded, and they often did keep children longer than asylum critics would have liked. However, the reason was rarely pride in numbers, or the belief that asylums were the best possible place for children. Most orphan asylums were regularly turning down "worthy" candidates because they had no extra room. They were often overcrowded because of frequent economic downturns and the extent of urban poverty, not because their managers wanted to brag about how many children they had helped. In the 1880s, the Bishop Armitage Orphanage of California accepted both boys and girls. In 1889, it was decided, because of overcrowding, that the Maria Kip would be founded to care for the Bishop Armitage's girls. This was expected to leave ample space for boys in the Bishop Armitage and create more space for girls in the new building. But the number of needy children quickly outstripped the Maria Kip's means. Thirteen children entered in 1889 from their previous quarters, but a year and a half later the Maria Kip, which had been "compelled to convert every available space into dormitories," held forty-one girls. A year after that, it held sixty-two girls, had converted its "large airy attic" into an additional dormitory, and was actively seeking to increase its building fund so that it could purchase land and erect a larger building.[44] Asylum populations grew quickly in California and New York because, in those states, asylum managers had relatively little trouble finding enough money to care for all the needy children they were faced with, not because public funding somehow encouraged large numbers of children to seek institutional aid.

When orphan asylums kept children for long periods of time, it was usually due either to the difficulty in finding good homes for children or to the fact that most children in asylums had at least one living parent. When a half-orphan's parent was unable or unwilling to care for the child, most private orphan asylums lacked the legal right, and often the desire, to place the child elsewhere. Most half-orphans—the majority of children in most asylums for decades—remained there until their parent could afford to reclaim them or until they came of age. In some instances, however, asylum managers believed that the only way to have a strong, positive influence on children was to keep them in the asylum for a number of years. In 1859, the president of the Orphans' Home and Asylum of New York wrote proudly that the asylum was keeping more of its children for lengthy stays than it had in the past; as a result, the asylum was helping "an increasing number of those destitute ones whom it can hope to benefit only in proportion to the length of the period during which it can control them."[45] Some asylum managers undoubtedly still felt this way in the early twentieth century. Nevertheless, the majority of children who stayed in asylums for more than a year did so because of the basic, overarching reality that there was nowhere else for them to go.

Another important attack on asylums focused on the parents of asylum children. Critics charged that parents used asylums to care for their children until the children were old enough to work and help support the family; only then did parents reclaim their children. This had some truth to it, but that this was somehow evil on the part of parents is not as self-evident as critics believed. Lack of money often forced families to make the difficult and emotionally charged decision to place a child in an asylum. Once the child was old enough to contribute to his or her own support, both the child and the parents might be better off financially and emotionally if they were reunited. The idea that these parents were reclaiming their children only to put them to work, and not for any emotional reasons, was rooted in a harsh view that presumed that parents had abandoned their children due to their own moral flaws. As we have seen, this was a view that many asylum managers, who actually worked with dependent children and met their parents, had abandoned after the Civil War.

Improving the Asylum

Asylum managers had no trouble finding uses for any money left over after children were fed, clothed, and educated. Throughout the nineteenth century, children in many asylums faced primitive conditions. Prior to the mid-1850s, children at the Charleston Orphan House apparently slept on "vermin-infested wooden cots." A few years before the Civil War began, these cots were finally replaced by "iron beds" as part of the city council's attempts to improve the Orphan House.[46]

Like private homes, orphan asylums gradually incorporated the advances of the day. St. Vincent's Orphan Asylum of Philadelphia received its first bathtub in 1869, added "modern" plumbing and a drainage system in 1884, and brought electricity to the boys' building in 1920. Five years later "shower baths" were added to the girls' building, and in 1929 the boys also received them, allowing for "quicker and more frequent bathing for the children than formerly when bath tubs were used." In 1888, the Chicago Orphan Asylum proudly announced its newly installed "unique and complete wash-rooms, where each child has its individual wash-bowl and toilet articles, and should sound its voice in the chorus: 'Cleanliness is next to Godliness.'" In 1892, it added a fire escape. Many asylums improved more slowly. In 1889, Chicago's Angel Guardian Orphanage was connected to the city water system, and the next year a hot water system was installed. In 1902, the Fred Finch Children's Home in California improved the asylum's sanitary conditions by building new outhouses; indoor lavatories apparently arrived in 1913. In the 1910s, the Cleveland Jewish Orphan Asylum installed showers and changed from huge dining tables to smaller ones seating fourteen children each. In the same decade, Baltimore's Hebrew Orphan Asylum installed fire escapes and new shower baths in the process of renovating its building.[47]

Asylums were continually raising money for new, and not coincidentally larger, buildings, or for additional buildings to supplement their existing physical plant. The Chicago Home for Jewish Orphans opened in the mid-1890s and held just three dozen children in mid-1899; by 1926, it had grown dramatically, holding 208 children at year's end. In the late 1890s, St. Vincent's of Philadelphia's greatest problem was overcrowding; in 1901, a new, large building was finally completed to ease the congestion. In 1927, a two-story annex was added to the boys' building so that older and younger boys could be separated "in order to give them more specific attention" and, in all likelihood, to protect the younger boys from bullying by the older wards. In the 1910s, the Lutheran Children's Home began seeking funds for new buildings. It did so in part because overcrowding had forced it to turn down many deserving applicants and in part because the current building was "inadequate" and "a more modern plant was needed." Fund raising went slowly, but the cornerstone of the new building was finally laid in late 1925. Even though—and perhaps because—social workers and state charity boards had been opposed to institutional care of children for decades, asylums across the country were busily trying to improve themselves. In 1923, the San Francisco Protestant Orphanage Society proudly announced that work on its new location had begun. The next year's annual report boasted that the seventy-four-year-old society was "now represented by an Orphanage which is the last word in institutional construction."[48]

This kind of growth happened again and again as asylums became overcrowded (even though they turned away many children who needed help for lack of space), raised funds for new buildings, and then quickly filled the buildings with needy children. Critics of asylum growth in New York and California, who claimed it occurred because of the availability of public per capita payments to orphan asylums, apparently did not notice that large asylums sprang up even in states that gave little or no money to private asylums.

Some orphan asylums were continually tempted by the idea of extending their services to babies. After years of wanting to add a baby nursery to its institution, the Chicago Orphan Asylum finally did so in 1886. Part of the managers' reasoning was that the asylum received many applications from families with several children, often including a baby. A baby nursery would allow the asylum to keep all the children of a family together. The managers feared that the high mortality rates common in baby nurseries would damage their reputation, but after another year they announced that the four deaths that had occurred (out of ten children taken in) was a "success" compared with other institutions.[49]

Virtually all orphan asylums hoped to build an infirmary or hospital room to isolate their children during epidemics and, later, to isolate newcomers from the rest of the asylum population until it was determined they were healthy. After an 1874 outbreak of scarlet fever that left five children dead, the Brooklyn Industrial School Association's Home reiterated its long-standing desire to add a "hospital-room." Many asylums did manage this addition in the nineteenth century, while others had to wait; St. Vincent's Orphan Asylum finally built an infirmary in 1930, though its managers had apparently wanted one for decades.[50]

Orphan asylums became more tightly connected to other agencies and institutions in the 1870s and 1880s. New York's Society for the Prevention of Cruelty to Children (SPCC), founded in 1875, favored institutional care and often placed children in asylums. In fact, the SPCC disagreed with reformers who attacked asylums because of children's lengthy stays. The SPCC, which received children from the court, argued that a lengthy stay was needed to make sure that the child came out changed. If children were removed from asylums too soon, the SPCC argued, they stood at risk of reverting to their previous bad habits; an important job such as child saving should not be left half finished.[51] This argument showed the SPCC's relatively harsh view of the poor, but it also worked in favor of New York's asylums.

Asylums could coexist by focusing on different populations. The Brooklyn Industrial School Association's Home viewed itself as filling a niche that the newer, larger Orphan Asylum Society did not. The latter accepted orphans and half-orphans, while the former accepted children with parents "who for various reasons can either partially provide for them, or who need such temporary assistance as will bridge over for them a hard winter, a time of sickness, or inability from any cause to obtain work." A child with two living parents would have been turned down by the Orphan Asylum Society in the 1870s, but not at the Brooklyn Industrial School Association's Home.[52] By the 1870s, New York's asylums were becoming increasingly specialized, filling what they perceived as special needs. In other cities, which usually supported far fewer charity institutions than New York, most asylums continued to accept children from a variety of family situations. Of course, most continued to serve a specific religious and ethnic group, as they had always done, though as urban populations became increasingly diverse, so did many asylum's populations.

One of the most important changes many asylums made in the 1910s and 1920s was to improve the quality and quantity of food they offered their children. The Cleveland Jewish Orphan Asylum is an excellent example. A 1920 Ohio Bureau of Health survey of the asylum showed that more than half its children were undernourished. The asylum's new superintendent, who had moved quickly to improve the asylum in a number of ways, hired a professional dietician. Milk, eggs, and other items were served for the first time or in much greater amounts, with noticeable results. Fifteen months after the survey, only one-sixth of the asylum's children were still considered undernourished.[53]

In 1924, the Cleveland Jewish Orphan Asylum made another important change, one that was particularly significant for the direction many asylums would take over the next three decades. It brought in a psychiatrist to help children suffering from personality or behavioral problems. As Gary Polster writes, "the orphanage slowly began to shift its focus from a home for biological orphans to one for psychological orphans." The same year, the asylum's admission policy was broadened to include children with special needs or behavioral problems. As Chapter 1 discussed, these types of changes signaled the beginning of some asylums' evolution from institutions for poor, dependent children to other functions.[54]

The Cottage System

The most widely talked-about advance in asylum life in the Progressive Era was the shift away from large congregate institutions, holding an asylum's entire population in one or two buildings, toward cottage-based institutions, where children lived in small groups of between fifteen and thirty. Each cottage had its own matron and, often, its own eating and recreation facilities. The cottage system was the chief answer of institution supporters to the criticisms aimed at large congregate orphanages in the late nineteenth century. Some of the asylums for delinquent children built in the postbellum era had been based on the cottage system; prior to the Civil War, the State Industrial School for Girls in Lancaster, Massachusetts, had opened as a cottage-based institution in 1856, with each cottage's matron referred to as the "mother." Other kinds of institutions had also occasionally been cottage-based. For example, the Willard Asylum for the Chronic Insane developed an extensive cottage system long before it became common among orphan asylums. Orphan asylum managers hoped to bring the system's presumed advantages to dependent children. According to its supporters, the cottage system would make a truly homelike atmosphere possible, though as critics were quick to point out, few families had anything like twenty-five or thirty children.⁵⁵

Shifting to the cottage system was no easy task, since it involved raising funds for an entirely new set of buildings that would cost even more than erecting a new congregate institution. When the Albany Orphan Asylum changed to the cottage system, it had to dismiss almost two hundred children because building enough cottages to handle all its children was not financially feasible. The Lutheran Children's Home of Virginia spent more than a decade raising money and planning for the cottage system, which it finally adopted in 1926. The Angel Guardian Orphanage, a large Catholic congregate asylum in Chicago, made halting moves toward adopting the cottage system starting in the 1910s. In 1914, two cottages were built "more or less as an experiment." In 1929, more cottages were built: five new buildings to hold ten groups of schoolboys, plus additional dining rooms, based on "the experience of the intervening fifteen years." However, the depression put a stop to Angel Guardian's spending on large-scale improvements such as new cottages. In 1930, the Chicago Orphan Asylum had built three new cottages: they were located in a suburb west of the city, "about six blocks apart" from one another, with two adults caring for twelve children in each cottage. The rest of the asylum's children remained in its older congregate setting or were placed out in homes.⁵⁶

Some asylums did manage to change to the cottage system relatively quickly and easily. When the San Francisco Protestant Orphanage Society, which ran the city's oldest orphan asylum, prepared in 1923 to erect a new home, its plans (and the aspirations behind them) were fairly representative of asylums able to make the change to a cottage system. "There will be an Administrative Building containing offices, class rooms, gymnasiums, infirmary and Superintendent's quarters, six cottages, and a laundry and heating plant, as a nucleus for what we trust will be one of the noblest and most useful centers of our community life."⁵⁷

The switch to cottages did unquestionably improve life within an orphan asylum. When the San Francisco Protestant Orphanage Society's new buildings were finished, each cottage was occupied by ten boys and ten girls, who were to be raised by a cottage mother responsible for their "care, discipline and training" and an assistant who would handle cooking duties and otherwise help the cottage mother. Siblings were kept together, and each cottage held children of varying ages. In many ways, cottage life probably was like living in a small asylum of a few dozen at most. At the same time, the children continued to enjoy the advantages of larger asylums, such as extensive playgrounds.[58]

Most asylums that shifted to a cottage or "group" system still segregated children by age, by sex, or by both. The San Francisco Presbyterian Orphanage and Farm had a nursery for its twenty children under six years of age as well as four separate departments for boys under eleven, girls under twelve, and older boys and older girls. Montana's State Orphans' Home mixed boys and girls under five years of age in the same cottage but had separate cottages for older girls and boys.[59]

The 1910 census of benevolent institutions recorded whether or not each orphan asylum operated in the cottage system, and if so how many cottages it held. Despite the assumption of some historians and many observers at the time that the cottage system was being widely adopted, in actuality only 125 (13 percent) of the 972 orphan asylums listed were cottage institutions as of 1910 (see Table 5.1). Roughly one-quarter of Protestant, fraternal, and public orphan asylums employed the cottage system, but only a handful of Catholic institutions had shifted to the newer, more respected system. As with the Angel Guardian Orphanage, Catholic asylums interested in adopting the new system were often large institutions with severely limited funds, unable to quickly replace their current buildings with numerous new cottages. Most asylums that managed to adopt the cottage system did so later, in the 1910s and 1920s.

Being unable to fully develop a cottage asylum did not stop some Catholic asylums from seeking a more homelike atmosphere based on smaller living units. In 1915, at the beginning of its long, halting shift toward the cottage system, the Angel Guardian's managers introduced "the home or group system, a modified cottage system." The children in its congregate institution were divided into "families," each of which shared a "living room, sleeping room, dining room, and wash room." Each "family" had a nun acting as its mother. In 1920, the orphanage's superintendent felt that this group system—by then misleadingly called simply "the cottage system" in annual reports—was a success. He wrote that "the 'cottage Sister' can give the children more individual attention; there is a marked improvement in their conduct; they are more contented and they make better progress in school and there is much less sickness." While this new system probably did provide children with more individual attention, the size of the "families" left much to be desired. The 1922 annual report stated that groups consisted of "thirty or forty" children, while the 1924 report seems to imply that over the ten years of its existence, the group system had divided children into groups of between forty and forty-eight. The same report described the success of the group system glowingly. "The institutional character has almost entirely disappeared in the living quarters of the children and a home atmosphere has been created. Pot plants are hanging from the ceilings or are lined up on the window sills, knick-knacks fill the corners of the room, there are shelves lined with toys, there is the family bookcase, the graphaphone and the radio."[60] While it is unlikely that a "home" of forty children was what the cottage system's supporters usually had in mind, the group system probably did provide children with more individual attention than they would have received in earlier years.

In the 1920s, a group of Catholic child-care advocates developed what they called the small-group system in an attempt to gain most of the benefits of the cottage system within large buildings. It mixed old asylum precepts with the newer, more scientific social work view of proper care, along similar lines to what the Angel Guardian Orphanage had begun implementing in the mid-1910s. Under the small-group system, asylum managers supposedly had to have a deep affection for their children and provide a thorough religious and moral training. They needed to develop an intimate knowledge of each child and provide individualized treatment based on that knowledge. All these goals would be met by group mothers, each of whom would care for at most thirty children. Every group would have its own living and dining rooms, bathrooms, and bedrooms, thereby subdividing the asylum into separate units. This separation into groups of roughly thirty would presumably replicate the cottage system effectively, though few cottage advocates thought groups of more than twenty or at most twenty-five to be desirable. But just as many asylums were unable to switch to the cottage system, the lack of a sufficient number of nuns could sometimes prevent a Catholic asylum from adopting the small-group system.[61]

The switch to cottage asylums for Jewish institutions was already being suggested in 1902 at the National Conference of Jewish Charities. The committee for dependent children gave a classic statement of why cottages were preferable to large institutions, but then explained that since Jewish asylums were "homes" they did not need to switch to the cottage system.

> It is axiomatic to state that where the institution is required, the best possible results will be obtained from the cottage plan, through a system of small detached houses, rather than one large building, under which all the children are housed. Such a plan is the closest approach to the home that can be attempted. It is a satisfaction to know that while none of the Jewish asylums have attempted such a plan the reason therefor is obvious. Jewish institutions have never been institutions, but homes, and most worthily have Jewish family ideals been fostered and perpetuated by them.[62]

In fact, many Jewish asylums were among the largest and least "homelike" of all orphan asylums at the turn of the century. Although their educational facilities and the medical care provided their children were among the best in any asylums, other asylums often had a greater claim to being "homes" than did Jewish asylums.

The introduction of the cottage system sometimes went hand in hand with other improvements. A new building that placed two to four children in a bedroom might also contain luxuries such as a closet for each of the children.[63] However, not all "improvements" led to greater interaction between asylum children and the outside world, or with each other. When St. Vincent's Orphan Asylum of Philadelphia moved into its new building in 1902, one of its "advantages" was "the complete separation of boys and girls into two different buildings."[64] In general, however, new purchases or additions to asylums after the turn of the century improved the lives of the children within, just as they had done in the nineteenth century. Unlike other Progressive Era reforms that "did not significantly improve inherited practices," the ways in which orphan asylums changed after the turn of the century made them better institutions, largely because they became less and less institutional as they became more integrative.[65]

Conclusion

Life in orphan asylums was certainly harsh by late-twentieth-century, middle-class child-rearing standards; this was especially true prior to

1910. But how asylums cared for their children also needs to be viewed relative to the times in which they lived. By the standards of the growing urban middle class, asylum children received little individual attention, poor food, and overly harsh discipline, all of which were serious flaws in institutional care. But these were all issues that varied from one asylum to another, just as they varied from one immigrant group to another, and indeed from one household to another. And compared to life in most working-class communities of the nineteenth century, the food, clothing, and housing asylum children received were generally quite good, as asylum managers were quick to point out. It was the lack of individual attention and the weakening or severing of family ties that made asylum life "institutional" for children, not the material surroundings of the asylum itself.

Asylum managers did what they could to improve the lives of the children under their care. Alongside the monotonous routines and often harsh discipline, opportunities to interact with the broader society multiplied in the late nineteenth century and blossomed in the Progressive Era. As time passed, more and more asylum children went to public schools, attended church in the community, and even took summer vacations. These changes are described in the next two chapters.

Table 5.1. Total number and mean population of asylums, cottage and congregate, in 1910.

	Cottage asylums		Congregate asylums	
Management	Number of asylums	Mean population	Number of asylums	Mean population
Catholic	7	311.1	253	156.2
Protestant	47	109.9	216	85.3
Jewish	—	—	21	213.7
Fraternal	4	181.5	14	89.1
County/City	13	58.1	84	42.3
State	11	286.0	6	215.0
Unknown	35	95.4	261	51.1
All asylums	117	130.8	855	95.7

Source: *Benevolent Institutions, 1910.*

6

Education and Building Character

Molding their children's characters was a central concern for all orphan asylum managers. From the early nineteenth century through the 1930s, asylum superintendents and matrons tried to shape children into disciplined, religious, respectable, hard-working citizens. They did this in a variety of ways. Building character was seen as the chief function of education, as well as being an important part of religious training. Even children's chores, which saved asylums money and supposedly prepared children for later jobs, were seen as a way of encouraging the proper development of moral, industrious citizens.

Providing dependent children with an education was one of the two central goals of most orphan asylums, along with creating a home where children would be fed, clothed, and housed. To asylum managers, educating children meant providing moral values and a religious faith as much as it meant teaching reading, writing, and arithmetic. Giving children a moral education continued to be an important goal for most asylum managers into the 1930s, even though by 1900 many asylum children were being sent out to public schools rather than attending asylum schools, as they had done for most of the nineteenth century.

Religious training also remained at the core of most asylum managers' thinking for over a century. Unlike schooling, which gradually shifted from the asylum itself to other institutions, religious training was provided to children in a variety of ways. Some asylums already sent their children out to church long before the Civil War, while others still held religious services and religious training classes inside the asylum in the 1930s.

Having daily chores to perform was one of the most common aspects of orphan asylum life across time, region, and type of orphan asylum. Asylum children, like children in the kinds of working-class families from which virtually all asylum children came, scrubbed floors, dusted, did laundry, sewed and mended clothes, helped cook food, and performed other tasks to keep their large households functioning. This was almost as widespread in the 1920s as it had been in the antebellum period. Children in Catholic, Protestant, Jewish, nonsectarian, and public asylums in the North, South, and West performed chores to learn good work habits, to stay out of trouble, and to earn their keep. These chores were usually segregated by gender, with boys and girls each doing the type of work asylum managers, and society, saw as appropriate for them.

In important ways, asylum schools reflected changing educational practices and ideas in the broader society. When manual training appeared in the late nineteenth century, some asylum schools developed manual training programs. Other asylums began justifying children's chores as a form of manual training, particularly in the case of girls' domestic chores. As high schools became more widespread around the turn of the century, many asylums began sending a few of their children to public high schools, even if younger children were still being educated in an asylum school. Different religious groups responded to public schooling in very different ways, however. Catholic asylums were far more reluctant to enroll their children in public schools than were Protestant asylums, which usually made use of public schools whenever they were available. Jewish asylums often embraced public schooling, but they also continued to conduct evening classes in Bible study and Hebrew within the asylum to make sure that their children were receiving a proper religious education.

Education and Religious Training in Antebellum Orphan Asylums

Education in antebellum orphan asylums meant far more than learning the basic skills of reading, writing, and arithmetic. Religion was central to most asylum managers' conceptions of education. Children were expected to develop a strong work ethic, respect for the value of property, and appropriate gender roles. These values tended to be fairly similar across religious groups, however different the specific religious doctrines being taught were. Michael Katz writes that in the middle of the nineteenth century, "Public school systems existed to shape behavior and attitudes, alleviate social and family problems, and reinforce a social structure under stress. The character of pupils was a much greater concern than their minds."[1] The same could be said of asylum schools throughout the century, except that in asylums the religious aspect of character training was usually even stronger than in public schools. Because education was such an essential part of asylum managers' attempts to form children's characters, almost all asylums provided their children with at least a few years of schooling.[2]

Most antebellum asylums tried to provide a secular education, religious training, and a specific, internalized sense of values by separating children from the outer world. In some cases, this might mean blocking them off from the families and neighborhoods from which they had come. The Cincinnati Orphan Asylum wanted to isolate children "from their former associates and protect them from the 'evil influence' of the city" as well as remove parental authority over children's lives. The asylum required a written pledge from parents and guardians that they would not interfere in its rearing of their children.[3] This was a tactic that many isolating asylums used in the nineteenth century, though it became somewhat less common by the end of the century as the shift toward integrative asylums began. Protective asylums, especially Catholic ones, also kept their children in asylum schools. Public schools were usually seen by Catholic asylum managers as Protestant, and therefore unfriendly, institutions. As David Nasaw writes, "the Irish believed that the common school had been invented for the express purpose of turning their children against them."[4]

Antebellum asylums usually had to provide schooling if their children were to receive any formal education. The Boston Female Asylum, which opened in 1800, had little chance to send its children to Boston's public schools since they had space for only a fraction of the city's children. In a city where most poor girls received little or no education, and in an era when most children spent a few weeks or a few months in school each year at best, the asylum's managers held school six hours a day, six days a week, and taught arithmetic along with reading, writing, sewing, and various domestic skills. They sought to provide a moral education so that their children would be virtuous, hard-working, and skilled. Character was to be built through an ordered, disciplined environment and constant work—methods public schools would employ toward similar goals throughout the century. Children also attended worship services on Sundays, though the specific church varied from week to week. The Boston Female Asylum was unusual for its day; by the late nineteenth century, many asylums would adopt the same style of nondenominational Protestantism.[5] But the asylum was typical in its desire to provide an education that was both moral and practical. In many asylums, such as the Colored Orphan Asylum in New York City in the 1840s, the "moral and religious culture" of children was even more important than developing literacy and specific job skills, although these were also seen as important. This belief in the central importance of moral education was also held in antebellum common schools, where, as Carl Kaestle writes, "morality was the most important goal of common education."[6]

In the Orphans' Home and Asylum, an Episcopal institution founded in New York City in 1851, education and religious training played a central role in asylum managers' thinking. The first thing done by the home's managers, after securing a building, was to establish the "schoolroom" in which "the regular daily instruction of the children" would occur. The home had been created because of the "unquestionable need" of the church's flock, who had "only the Church to look to" in times of trouble. Children whose parents were members of the Episcopal Church would have first right to aid in the asylum, though others would also be admitted.[7] The Orphans' Home and Asylum was typical; many asylum schools, like the asylums themselves, existed chiefly to protect specific religious (and often ethnic) heritages. Even though they might disagree on what exactly should be taught, the Catholic Church, various Protestant groups, and most orphan asylum founders and managers were in agreement: sectarian religious training was crucial to society's stability and morality.[8]

The education provided in the Orphans' Home and Asylum in the 1850s and 1860s is fairly representative of asylums in the middle of the century. Children were taught "reading, writing, spelling, geography, arithmetic, and Church Catechism; and [were] learning various necessary household duties." The asylum's goal was "to send them forth from this Institution having all the characteristics of the useful member of society—healthy in body, healthy in mind, and, above all, healthy in soul." Though unlikely to achieve middle-class status, the asylum's children were expected to become self-supporting and to remain faithful members of the church.[9] Few goals were more widely shared among various orphan asylums than this one, and few endured longer. Even in the 1920s, most orphan asylums were religious institutions that still hoped to raise hard-working, respectable church members.

Religious Training After the Civil War

Few aspects of asylum life changed less between the middle of the nineteenth century and the 1920s than the emphasis placed on religious training for children. Throughout this period, children in Protestant and Catholic asylums were reared within specific traditions, attended religious services every week (in some cases every day), and went to Sunday schools. Children in Jewish asylums received equally heavy doses of religious training, supplemented by related courses in Hebrew. Children in nonsectarian asylums were also taught a specific, though perhaps less narrowly defined, set of religious beliefs that was vaguely Protestant, as were children in most publicly managed asylums.

Children in asylums run by a particular religious group were usually encouraged to join that denomination, and in some cases had no choice. In the 1890s, every child who entered the Maria Kip Orphanage, San Francisco's Episcopal asylum for girls, was required to be christened. Unconsecrated children were admitted if they were needy, but were also immediately "admitted into the fold of Christ's flock." Though the religious beliefs of the child's family were ignored if other than Episcopal, once the Maria Kip had made its children into Episcopalians it jealously protected that faith. Children could not be adopted by or indentured to anyone who was not a member of the Episcopal Church. St. Mary's Home for Children, an Episcopal asylum for girls in Chicago, took similar efforts and even had its own chaplain in the 1910s.[10]

Many orphan asylums held religious services within the asylum at least once a day, a practice that continued in the twentieth century. In the 1920s, St. Mary's Home still held religious services for its children twice a day, provided classes in religion weekly, and sought to have all its children baptized. Protestant, Catholic, and Jewish asylums all took active measures to provide their children with very specific religious training. And most "nonsectarian" asylums also taught moral and religious lessons that were distinctly Protestant.[11]

For most asylum managers, having children pass through rites of confirmation such as baptism was a crucial step in their development. Annual reports regularly boasted about the number of children recently confirmed. Furthermore, an asylum's other children were likely to be at confirmation ceremonies, which would enhance their own faith and give them a memorable goal to seek for themselves. St. Vincent's Orphan Asylum of Philadelphia, a Catholic institution, started its day with morning prayers in the chapel, with children "remaining until after mass which began an hour later." All the asylum's services were still being performed in German at the start of the twentieth century, though the increasing number of Italian Catholic immigrants in the neighborhood would eventually end that policy. Religion was at the center of its reason for existence; St. Vincent's would not discharge children until after their first Holy Communion at the age of twelve. Asylums connected to one particular Protestant church or run by a Catholic order of nuns had people at hand to provide religious training. Other asylums brought in a variety of clergymen to provide their children with a religious education. Local clergy gladly donated time for this purpose. In 1862, the Orphans' Home and Asylum thanked "several of the clergy, who have, in rotation, given a portion of their time to catechizing and conversing with the children."[12]

Many orphan asylums, like St. Vincent's, conducted their own religious services. Some did so without adequate chapel facilities, but most either had or hoped to build space specifically for religious purposes. Soon after its founding in the late 1850s, the Church Home in Boston had its own chapel. Only a few years after its founding in 1890, the Maria Kip Orphanage's children had formed a society to raise funds for a chapel. Within five years they had succeeded, presumably with considerable help from adults.[13]

Some asylum managers preferred to take their children out to church on Sundays. In the early 1860s, the children of the Orphans' Home and Asylum attended church outside the asylum. The home's managers "greatly prefer that, when practicable, they should go out to church on the Lord's Day, as in this way can best be preserved in their minds the distinction between the public worship of a congregation and the family worship in which they are accustomed to unite every morning and evening." However, the afternoon closing of churches in the mid-1860s hindered this practice, and the Orphans' Home's managers arranged for services in the asylum until the children could again attend outside church services every Sunday.¹⁴

Many asylums ran their own Sunday schools. In the 1880s, the Orphans' Home and Asylum held one every Sunday afternoon. Half a century later, the San Francisco Presbyterian Orphanage and Farm's pastor conducted a weekly Sunday school. In many cases, asylums that did not run their own Sunday school sent their children out to one run by a nearby church. The Lutheran Children's Home of Salem, Virginia, sent its children to church services and Sunday school at nearby College Church in the early twentieth century. The Chicago Orphan Asylum sent most of its children to the Christ Church Sunday school in the 1890s; when twenty-two children graduated to "a higher class," each child was given a new Bible as a reward.¹⁵ Connecticut's county asylums also sent their children out to church. In 1904, the Middlesex County Home sent its children to church in Middlesex every Sunday, where the children also attended Sunday school. In the same year, the Hartford County Home sent its children to churches in "the village, Protestant and Roman Catholics going to their respective churches."¹⁶

Religious training remained central to the mission of many orphan asylums well into the twentieth century. In 1920, the California State Board of Charities and Corrections required asylums to provide their children "moral and religious instruction," so long as children did not have a religion other than that of their parents thrust upon them.¹⁷ Catholic and Protestant asylums tended to avoid this problem by accepting only children of their own faith. Some nonsectarian orphan asylums went out of their way to give children options regarding religious services. This became more common after the turn of the century, but some nineteenth-century asylums were sensitive to their children's backgrounds. The Poydras Home of New Orleans, a Protestant asylum, allowed children to attend the church of their choice on Sundays. But many nonsectarian asylums were less flexible. For example, the Rock Nook Home of Norwich, Connecticut, sent all its children to Sunday services and Sunday school at a Congregational Church in the early twentieth century.¹⁸

Marian Morton argues that in Cleveland's orphan asylums, the "primary official goal was religious instruction and conversion." While this was true of some asylums, in most cases religious instruction was one of several central goals so tightly intertwined with one another that to elevate one goal over others misunderstands how asylum managers viewed their children, especially in the nineteenth century. Learning to read and write, learning right from wrong, and learning the word of God were all part of the preparation that asylum children needed to be honest, hard-working, God-fearing, self-supporting adults after they were discharged.[19] And it is important to remember that, for the vast majority of asylum managers, the issue was one of *protecting* children's religious heritages, *not* of converting children away from their parents' beliefs.

Chores

Asylums created before the Civil War depended heavily on their children to perform the institution's upkeep. Asylum managers rarely had enough extra money to hire many servants. It was up to children to sweep, dust, make their beds, do laundry, and perform other chores that working-class children often did in their own homes. The Cincinnati Orphan Asylum, founded in 1833, was typical. Its girls were taught to sew as soon as they were old enough to learn, and the children all helped out around the asylum as soon as they were of "sufficient age" to do so.[20]

Throughout the nineteenth century, children did many of the basic cleaning chores in most asylums.[21] These chores were usually gender specific. In 1860, the Orphans' Home and Asylum used its boys and girls to do "the daily work of the house," including making beds, sweeping, and washing and mending clothes. At the Chicago Orphan Asylum in the early 1880s, boys and girls did all the sweeping and dusting together; older girls also helped in the kitchen, and older boys did much of the asylum's "outside work." At a rural California Methodist asylum in the 1890s, boys helped with farm duties, including milking cows, caring for poultry, and working in the garden. Girls worked within the house, sewing, mending, knitting, and helping in the dining room. Forty years later at another California Protestant asylum, girls' chores were much the same. They were "busy in their own sphere, being trained in home making, learning to care for little children," as well as keeping up on schoolwork. Southern asylums also relied on children's labor. As in most asylums of the time, the Lutheran Children's Home of Salem, Virginia, divided boys' and girls' labor at the turn of the century. Arthur E. Fink has found that in several North Carolina orphan asylums chores were "an essential part of the program of each institution from its inception."

Few experiences were more universal for children in asylums than performing chores.[22]

Catholic orphan asylums were even less likely to hire help than other types of asylums, so for them children's labor was particularly important. In the 1880s and 1890s at St. James' Home, a Catholic asylum for girls in New York State, the children did all the housework under the supervision of the Sisters of Charity. At St. Vincent's in Philadelphia, boys and girls joined to clean the asylum and make their beds. Boys also worked on the farm and painted the asylum, while girls washed dishes and made clothing. This partial division of labor existed from St. Vincent's founding through the 1930s.[23]

Even the richest of orphan asylums, including many Jewish asylums, made sure their children did housework. Chores were considered important training for the future as well as character-building exercises. In 1897, the president of the Ladies' Auxiliary for the Brooklyn Hebrew Orphan Asylum argued that since homemaking had become a science, the older girls should be taught housekeeping and cooking in preparation for becoming "useful helpmates in respectable families." What exact difference the increasingly "scientific" bent of homemaking made was not clear; the housekeeping chores the children performed had not changed, even if managers' ideas about those chores had. A California Jewish asylum's superintendent wrote in 1908 that his institution's children "have been taught, as in years past, everything that pertains to house-keeping." Children in the Baltimore Hebrew Orphan Asylum had chores both before and after school in the early twentieth century.[24]

By the 1920s, older children often worked part-time outside the asylum in addition to the chores they performed within the asylum. The Chicago Orphan Asylum's boys sometimes ran errands, delivered goods, or cleaned stores to earn extra cash. Older girls sometimes helped local housewives with their housework or in caring for their children. Doing chores prepared children to enter the work world during their teenage years.[25] Chores were also justified on several other grounds, which varied somewhat over time and from one institution to another.

The Rationale for Chores

Asylum managers assigned children chores for several reasons. Most fundamentally, they believed that working helped build character and instill a work ethic in asylum children. Children's work also saved money, allowing the asylum to spend its limited resources on necessities such as food and shelter. Children who cleaned house, cooked meals, and did laundry were contributing to their own upkeep and, in some cases, helping to make the very existence of the asylum possible; many asylum managers openly recognized this. Developing a work ethic in children and saving money for the asylum remained important justifications for children's labor within asylums well into the twentieth century. But other explanations appeared as well, and the ways in which chores were expected to build character evolved as society's ideas about child development changed.[26]

Asylum managers believed that chores would teach children to "acquire habits of industry and usefulness." In 1866, one asylum's annual report lamented that its children were not getting enough practice "in household duties that they need to have to fit them for usefulness in after life." It was hoped that a reorganization of the asylum would fix this problem and put children to work more effectively in "this very important element of youthful education," meaning, apparently, sweeping, dusting, washing clothes, cleaning dishes, and so on. Another New York asylum's 1863 annual report claimed, probably unrealistically, that its children performed chores "not as drudges, but cheerfully, being encouraged by the idea that they are learning to be useful and rendering some return of the kindness bestowed upon them."[27]

Another important reason for assigning children regular work chores was to instill obedience to authority. Without obedience from their children, asylums could not function. And without a sense of respect for authority, children could not become good citizens or good workers. As Daniel Rodgers writes, "Work and obedience, service and mastership, remained intricately tangled together in early nineteenth-century America, and the socialization of children followed suit in its preoccupation not with system but with submission and authority."[28] In the 1830s, the conception of children's work shifted to the use of systematic work to instill good work habits and develop self-control in children. By the Civil War, asylum managers regularly gave this reason when discussing chores.[29]

One Massachusetts opponent of institutions argued at the National Conference of Charities and Correction in 1886 that if children had to be kept within an asylum, they should be worked constantly for their own good. "Work, engrossing and continued, with the recesses necessary for rest and recreation, is the one important desideratum of institution life; occupation, from the rising in the morning till the going to bed at night."³⁰ She defined work broadly, including school study and even play if it was properly directed. This constant occupation was to keep children from dwelling on their past lives and to encourage them to think positively about the future. Exactly how constant work would cause a child's thoughts to move in this direction was not clear, but many asylums did strive to keep their children occupied. In the late nineteenth century at the Lutheran Children's Home in Virginia, "strenuous effort was made to keep the children constantly employed" through schoolwork, chores, and playtime. The State Orphans' Home of Montana also kept its children busy at the turn of the century on the theory that "the busy man has no time to quarrel with his neighbors." Children who were constantly playing or working would "have little opportunity, or desire for wrong doing." It was probably this desire to keep children out of trouble, rather than expectations of turning children's thoughts toward the future, that mattered most. After the turn of the century, this rationale appeared much less frequently.³¹

There was a distinct division of labor between boys and girls in orphan asylums. It is quite clear that most orphan asylum girls were trained to be obedient, competent servants at the worst, or obedient, competent housewives at the best. For example, in 1904 Brooklyn's Home for Destitute Children taught its girls "to wash dishes, act as waitresses, to think and plan, to be careful, prudent, deft and tidy and in every way to act as little housekeepers." Twenty years later its girls were still receiving a similar training, though the home's annual report tried to claim that it was to imbue the girls "with aspirations for better things." Despite the rhetoric, it was clear that the girls were not being prepared for careers outside the home.³² They were to be domestic servants, wives, or perhaps one and then the other. Boys, on the other hand, were generally trained to become either artisans or farmers, particularly in the nineteenth century. As time passed, boys' training gradually shifted toward preparation for more urban, but usually still fairly menial, forms of labor. The work children did as chores often reaffirmed these directions. The everyday household work children did within asylums shows that many asylum managers perceived part of their mission to be preparing children to be servants or semiskilled workers.

Chores were also justified as partial repayment from the children to their benefactors. Even more than that, a child's willingness to do the chores that were often performed by paid servants in middle-class homes showed that child to be deserving of aid. Whatever the future might hold, no child should be allowed to think that "the world owes them a living" or grow to accept "daily supplies as though they have a right to them without any obligations on their part." The San Francisco Presbyterian Orphanage and Farm's annual report for 1900 could have been that of almost any orphanage, from any year, when it argued that every child should be "taught that he has no right to accept food or clothing unless he or she is willing to work." Asylum managers saw chores as a crucial way to teach this lesson to children. It was also a part of making the asylum homelike, a preoccupation in almost all orphan asylums from before the Civil War through the 1930s. Children did chores "just as do boys and girls in their own homes."[33]

After the turn of the century, some asylums transformed the idea of children earning their board through chores into merit systems that specifically repaid work performed within the asylum. One Presbyterian asylum in California assigned each child a daily household duty "which he understands is his contribution toward the support of the Home." The duties changed each week to relieve monotony. Children were allowed to take on extra duties to earn cash, and their regular duties could also yield benefits if done especially well. Not surprisingly, failure to perform chores could cause embarrassment. A close tab was kept on each child's performance and made public, so that children were in effect competing with each other to see who would be the best worker, and to win rewards. "A daily report of each individual child's work, based on cheerfulness, courtesy, and thoroughness, is posted on the large Merit Chart on the bulletin board. On these grounds, week-end privileges, also educational excursions and camping trips, are then awarded, according to the degree of co-operation thus shown."[34] This system was designed to lead children to develop a powerful internalized work ethic. Asylum managers also regularly expressed a desire for children to learn how to handle money, and especially to save money.[35] This was a skill children would need after they left the asylum, since the jobs they were expected to take would not pay enough to allow them to squander any of their limited earnings.

Manual Training

Training children for some occupation was a constant concern of orphan asylum managers. In the early nineteenth century, this may have simply meant teaching children to read and write, to respect authority, and to work hard. When they were indentured, they would presumably learn more specific job skills. As indenture became a less viable option, children tended to receive more and more training within asylums. By the 1880s and 1890s, as manual training courses began to appear in many public schools, some orphan asylums developed similar courses to prepare their children to enter the workforce. In many cases, unfortunately, the kinds of chores described above were increasingly viewed as "training" for future jobs, rather than just as character training.[36]

Girls in the Albany Orphan Asylum helped clean the asylum, with some doing additional work in the kitchen or taking sewing classes after school. Boys also helped around the building, kept up the yard, and sometimes worked in the laundry, but girls probably bore the brunt of housework and were especially likely to be "trained" in housekeeping skills while in fact keeping an asylum functioning cheaply. In the late 1880s, Boston's Church Home expanded its effort to give girls "an elementary knowledge of cooking, in addition to the sewing and easier domestic work which they have always learned." St. Vincent's Orphan Asylum of Philadelphia discharged boys at fourteen in the late nineteenth century, but girls stayed until they were eighteen "because of their usefulness about the house."[37]

A number of asylums combined manual training with what amounted to a small business staffed by older children, usually boys. By the late 1870s, Cleveland's Jewish Orphan Asylum had an active shoe shop manned by its boys; girls also saved the asylum money while being trained in needlework. The Lutheran Children's Home of the South purchased a printing press in 1889, which gave the boys "the opportunity to make some income for the Home, as well as giving them a valuable experience."[38]

Girls received a more uniform, if not more interesting, training than boys. They were trained to be domestic servants; not coincidentally, the same skills that would make them good servants would also make them good wives. Hasia Diner argues that Irish nuns were not especially concerned with preparing immigrant women and their daughters to be good wives but were instead trying to make them self-sufficient for religious reasons.[39] Orphan asylum managers in general, however, clearly hoped that training would prepare their female wards for work as well as for marriage. Teaching a girl to be a domestic servant was a highly practical education in the mid–nineteenth century, since half of the nation's female labor force worked as domestics. It remained one of the few jobs open to women throughout the nineteenth century. Asylum managers felt confident that they were providing their girls with useful skills, and managers of other types of institutions agreed. Reform schools also trained girls to be domestics, as did women's prisons. Teaching girls to sew was another important form of job training in orphan asylums. In some of New York City's Irish neighborhoods in the 1850s, almost half of all Irish women aged fifteen to nineteen sewed for pay, as did nearly one-third of those aged twenty to twenty-nine.[40]

Not all asylums tried to combine job training with schooling. In the early twentieth century, girls at St. Mary's Home in Chicago remained in the home for two years after finishing school to be trained as domestic workers. The home's managers felt that while children were in school full time there was "little or no time for special training in any direction." In 1913, the home announced that its "crying need" was a domestic science teacher who could take girls who had finished school "and give them a thorough training in domestic work, fitting them to be wage earners, and, later on, competent wives and mothers." The following year St. Mary's received a gift of $10,000 to provide a building for training girls from sixteen to eighteen years of age in domestic science. The home's motivation was to prevent its girls from "falling into the great class of unskilled laborers" who received "barely a living wage" by providing them with "training in dressmaking, millinery, laundry work, bookbinding, home nursing and domestic arts." The Chicago Orphan Asylum began providing its girls with similar training in 1915, in schoolrooms that had been vacated when the asylum decided to send its children to public schools.[41]

Children were sometimes trained at other institutions while still living in the asylum. In 1887, fifteen boys from the Orphans' Home and Asylum were "taught carpentry at the Industrial Education Association," and fifteen girls "received lessons in plain cooking at the Cooking School." Other asylum managers wanted to give their children serious manual training but lacked the funds to do so. For example, the law that established Montana's State Orphans' Home declared that it would have training shops on asylum grounds, but a decade later no money had been provided for such workshops.[42]

As in many other areas, limited funding meant that asylums for black children offered their wards fewer opportunities for manual training than their white counterparts generally received. The Colored Orphanage at Oxford, North Carolina, still lacked any formal training programs for its children in 1933. Boys helped around the asylum with odd jobs, which supposedly made them at least somewhat skilled with tools.[43] This sort of informal training through the performance of chores had been on the decline in most asylums for white children for decades.

Manual training for both girls and boys remained an important part of many asylums' methods in the 1920s and 1930s, but by then it was widely recognized that it was only useful for some asylum children. As one annual report noted in 1930, "Although very skillful cabinet work cannot be expected from young boys, it does develop a taste for working with tools or it proves that there is neither ambition nor ability in that direction." Girls in the same asylum were "trained in home making" and in caring for little children; asylums continued to think of the girls they cared for as future mothers, and treated them as such, as they had done for more than a century.[44]

Manual training fit perfectly into the goals of most asylum managers. Though they wanted to instill their children with a distinctly middle-class set of values, they did not actually expect most of their children to wind up in middle-class jobs. Instead, children were expected to grow up to become what many of their parents had presumably failed to be: self-supporting, respectable members of the working class. The rare child capable of more than that would receive extra training. As the 1884 annual report of the Orphans' Home and Asylum stated,

> Our aim, in the secular education of these children, is to fit them for the life that lies before them, and not for that upon which they may never enter; to help them to become good and useful workingmen and women, rather than disappointed aspirants to a position which nature never designed them to occupy. Genius and great talent will always assert themselves and these would be given a fair scope.[45]

Asylum Schools from the Civil War to the Progressive Era

In the decades after the Civil War, children in asylum schools were taught the same subjects that had been provided in the better asylum schools in the late antebellum period. The curriculum gradually expanded as older children were kept in the asylum rather than indentured, but the expansion was slow. In 1878, the Orphans' Home and Asylum still focused on "spelling, reading, writing, arithmetic, geography, and history" along with sewing, which all girls and some boys were taught. In the late 1890s, the children of the Chicago Orphan Asylum were being taught "history, arithmetic, geography, grammar, physiology, reading, and writing."[46]

In the late nineteenth century, many asylum schools consciously tried to emulate public schools. The same subjects were taught, the same methods were used, and in many cases the same textbooks were employed. In 1893, the Chicago Orphan Asylum's teacher "visited other schools and compared her methods" to theirs because the asylum wanted to "follow closely the prescribed work of the school system of Chicago."[47] Asylums, like public schools, were more concerned with turning out good citizens than good scholars. This was a goal of most asylum managers long before the Civil War and would remain one until orphan asylums began to close or serve a different clientele from the 1920s onward.

Asylum schoolrooms were often crowded, with far too many students for one teacher to instruct properly. In the Chicago Orphan Asylum's school, the third and fourth grades were taught together in a class of fifty children in 1897. Overcrowding had been a problem in asylum schools for decades, just as it was in many public schools. In fact, the lack of space in public schools often kept asylum schools functioning because asylum managers knew there was nowhere else to send their charges.[48] For this and other reasons, some public orphan asylums also ran their own schools instead of sending their children out to nearby public schools. For example, in 1904 the Middlesex County Home of Connecticut had its own schoolrooms, as did the Hartford County Home. At the same time, some of the state's religious asylums, such as the Protestant Hartford Orphan Asylum managed to send all their children to public schools.[49]

Superintendents, matrons, and members of their families often served as teachers, especially in schools in small asylums. In the 1850s, for example, the Orphans' Home and Asylum's teacher was the daughter of the matron. As asylum populations rose, it usually became necessary to hire more teachers. As part of their effort to survive and provide for children on limited funds, almost all orphan asylums hired female teachers, who were paid far less than their male counterparts. (Public schools were also shifting to female teachers, for similar reasons.) These teachers were sometimes even less well trained for their profession than most public school teachers, though asylums often tried to hire teachers with experience, including ones who had taught in public schools. In 1863, the Orphans' Home, which by then held more than one hundred children, employed three female teachers along with the matron and eight other employees. Student-teacher ratios do not seem to have improved very much over the course of the nineteenth century. In 1899, the Chicago Orphan Asylum's school had just three teachers for 158 schoolchildren.[50]

Probably the greatest problem most asylum schools faced was the rapid turnover of their children. In asylums where half the children stayed less than two years, the amount of education that could be provided was minimal, and asylum managers knew it. They hoped that any education they could give children would prove worthwhile. The Chicago Orphan Asylum's 1875 annual report stated that its school was harmed by "the shortness of time that some of the children remain" in the asylum, but the managers hoped that "in years to come intellectual fruits shall grow from the beginning."[51]

The short duration of many children's stays also affected the prospects of achieving other asylum goals. Many asylum managers believed that the Americanization of their children was crucial to the asylum's mission, but children who only stayed a short while were unlikely to be strongly shaped by asylum life. Protestant asylums were especially likely to try to Americanize non-Protestant children as part of making them Protestants, but they had little success with children who only stayed a few months. Other asylum managers, especially German Jews running Jewish institutions, often tried to Americanize children of different ethnicities. This was another example of orphan asylums serving a mission similar to that of public schools. Assimilation was a central goal of public schools, and one of the major tools asylum managers used in their effort to Americanize their children was the asylum school.[52]

By the start of the twentieth century, public schools were beginning to pay more attention to children as individuals.[53] Orphan asylums also began to focus more on individual training, and probably did so more widely and rapidly than did schools. Orphan asylum schools reflected this change as they became less rigid and somewhat more attuned to children as individuals. Whether keeping children in asylum schools or sending them out to public schools, asylums in the early twentieth century paid far more attention to the needs of individual children than they had a few decades before.

The Shift Toward Public Schooling

By 1860, most states outside of the South had created public school systems that made elementary schooling widely (though not universally) available. Private schools still flourished in some areas, particularly the New England states.[54] Many orphan asylum managers moved in the late nineteenth century to take advantage of the increasing opportunities for their children to be educated outside of asylum schools, though the overcrowding of most public schools sometimes made this impossible.

There were many advantages to sending children out to public schools. One was financial, since asylums would no longer need to hire their own teachers. In addition, the problem of finding qualified teachers, always difficult with limited asylum funds, could be shifted to public schools. The use of public schools would also free up what would otherwise have to be used as classroom space in the asylum for other purposes, an important factor given the overcrowding many asylums faced in the late nineteenth century. In the 1890s, the Maria Kip sent its children to a public school for girls in San Francisco, which was nearby and "admirably suited to our needs" because it could classify children by age and knowledge far more easily than an asylum school could.[55]

The decision to enroll asylum children in a public school had a profound effect on their lives. While the curriculum and quality of teaching might be very similar to what was found in an asylum school, they now mixed with children from the neighborhood for a significant portion of the day. The Chicago Orphan Asylum, which began sending its older children to public schools in the 1890s, considered the change "an improvement and an increased advantage to the children." The managers of the Lutheran Children's Home began sending children who had graduated from the sixth grade to public schools in 1926, and found their new method so successful that in 1935 they began sending all their children to public schools. It saved the home money, and "it was also helpful to the development of the children by giving them contacts outside of the Home." This was a lesson many other asylum managers had learned over the previous five decades.[56]

Before public schools opened in New Orleans in 1841, the city's several orphan asylums schooled their own children. The asylums continued to do so until near the turn of the century because there was no room in the city's public schools. As New Orleans's school system expanded in the 1890s, some asylums saved money by shutting down their schools and sending their children out to the increasingly available public schools. Where public schools existed and had space in the middle of the century, however, some asylum managers were already making use of them. In 1863, the Church Home for Orphan and Destitute Children of Boston was sending its children to local public schools. On the other hand, and for a variety of reasons, some asylums still educated their own children more than half a century later. In 1922, seven of Connecticut's eight county asylums continued to operate their own schools, even though most of the state's private asylums had been sending their children to public schools for decades.[57]

Asylum schools in cities or states with short public school years might actually offer considerably more schooling than nearby public schools. This was particularly true in the South, where public schooling remained limited in many areas. Arthur Fink has found that in North Carolina at the turn of the century, "when the General Assembly of North Carolina was being urged to provide four months of public schooling throughout the state," many asylums had school terms that ran most of the year. Earlier, in the antebellum period, at least some asylums had also provided much lengthier school years than their public counterparts. Just as importantly, all orphan asylums could boast that their children had excellent attendance records, even when they sent their children out to public schools.[58]

The shift toward sending asylum children to public schools, while widespread, was not universal. An asylum's changing circumstances could lead it in the other direction. In 1900, the managers of the San Francisco Presbyterian Orphanage and Farm noted that their new home was almost three miles from San Rafael, where their children were still attending public school. They feared that there was "nothing to do but to build our own school-house," because the trip was too long for the children to make on a daily basis.[59]

Because Catholic asylums had schools in which nuns taught without pay, and because they were particularly concerned with controlling their children's secular and religious education in the midst of a Protestant society, Catholic asylum managers were less likely to send their children to public schools in the early twentieth century than most other asylum managers. Schools in Catholic asylums sometimes also served neighborhood children, whose parents often chose to send their children to private Catholic schools rather than enrolling them in public schools. When the neighborhood's demands on the school of St. Vincent's Orphan Asylum in Philadelphia overburdened its facilities in the early 1890s, the solution was to build a new, larger building that could teach significant numbers of the German Catholic children of the area, not to make greater use of public schools. In her study of several New Orleans asylums, Priscilla Clement found that "the managers of Protestant orphanages were much more willing than their Catholic counterparts to close asylum classrooms and integrate orphans into city schools." An extensive survey of Catholic asylums in the mid-1910s showed that only a handful sent their children to local parochial schools. The vast majority were still educating their children in asylum schools. In California in 1920, forty orphan asylums sent all their children to public schools, while just thirteen conducted grammar schools within their own walls. At least ten of those thirteen were Catholic asylums.[60]

High School and College

As high schools became more common and as asylum children became more likely to attend public schools, it was only natural that a growing number of asylum children attended at least some high school. In 1870, only 2 percent of American seventeen-year-olds were high school graduates; by 1900, it was 6 percent. Erie County was representative of this rising high school attendance: between 1850 and 1915 the percentage of children in Erie County aged fifteen to nineteen who were attending school tripled. It should be no surprise that many asylum managers made little or no use of high schools in the Civil War era, since they remained quite rare. But by the early twentieth century, many asylums sent their brightest students on to the local public high school. By 1925, the managers of one San Francisco asylum noted that they made "full use of our Public School System," including "junior and senior high schools." Most orphan asylum managers could have made the same statement by the 1920s.[61]

There were two fundamental requirements for an asylum child to attend high school. The first was that the child had to be a good student; only children who had been at or near the top of their class in earlier grades would be sent to high school. Baltimore's Hebrew Orphan Asylum sent all its children to a public elementary school; only the best students were sent on to preparatory school and high school. In the early 1900s, the State Orphans' Home of Montana tried to "give every child a common school education and an opportunity for a high school training," but in fact children had to do quite well to continue on to high school.[62]

It was also necessary that the child be a long-term resident of the asylum. For example, if a thirteen-year-old arrived suddenly at an asylum, asylums managers would probably not send the child to high school the next year, unless he or she was a full orphan who was both academically superior and likely to be in the asylum for years. Similarly, any child who arrived at an earlier age and only stayed in an asylum for a year or two would obviously not attend high school through the asylum. Asylum managers do not seem to have favored either boys or girls when it came to higher education.

Not all asylum managers agreed that public schools were better for their children, especially little children. Many asylums continued to educate at least some of their younger children within the asylum. When the San Francisco Presbyterian Orphanage and Farm constructed its new buildings in the late 1920s, there were "a number of rooms for the high school girls" who attended public schools, but they also contained a schoolhouse for the younger children. This arrangement, with children in the first six or eight grades attending school on asylum grounds, and older children going out to public schools, seems to have been fairly common by the early twentieth century. The Colored Orphanage at Oxford, North Carolina, was also sending children who had "shown ability" in the asylum's grammar school to the public high school by the early 1930s. Most, though not all, of North Carolina's asylums sent their children to public schools by the late 1940s. The opening wedge for this practice was usually sending a few older children to public high schools, since managing an asylum high school for a handful of children would have been prohibitively expensive.[63]

Catholic asylums also began sending increasing numbers of their older children to high school in the 1910s and 1920s. In some cases that meant public high schools, but whenever Catholic high schools were available they were probably used. Some children were sent to business schools instead, often on scholarships donated to the asylum. In the 1920s, St. Vincent's Orphan Asylum of Philadelphia was sending some "talented children" to Strayer's College, to the business schools of three local Catholic schools, and to "the Northeast Catholic High School for boys and the Hallahan High School for girls."[64]

Conclusion

Providing their children with an education may have been one of the goals of parents who brought their children to orphan asylums. Judith Dulberger is right that "poor families used nineteenth-century institutions to their own advantage," particularly as a school where their children would be educated.[65] The point should not be overstated, however. The fact that their children would receive an education in an asylum may have served to console parents who were forced by poverty, illness, unemployment, or the death of a spouse to separate from their children. But usually it was one of the latter causes that led to the decision to give a child up to an orphan asylum, not a calculated desire to provide that child with an education. Poor parents used institutions to overcome rough times when their first choice, to keep their families together, was no longer possible. Furthermore, since the majority of children in most asylums stayed there for less than three years, they received relatively little schooling while institutionalized.

While asylum managers tried to maintain control over their children's schooling, as public schooling became more widely available asylum managers often made use of it; the limited funding of most asylums made this an obvious decision. Catholic asylum managers were the least inclined to turn their children over to public, but basically Protestant, schools; while Protestant asylums shared many assumptions with public schools, Catholics often distrusted the intentions of public schools regarding their children.

The continuing existence of chores in the asylum closely resembled the experience of working-class children whose families remained intact. Prior to 1900, asylum managers rarely had an overarching philosophy regarding their children that went beyond a desire to make the asylum a home and to give them appropriate religious beliefs and educational opportunities. After 1900, as ideas about child rearing became more focused, asylum managers, especially in the North and West, were clearly affected. But ideas about developing children's characters through teamwork or housework did not function in a vacuum. There was usually a conflict between asylum managers' middle-class backgrounds, children's working-class backgrounds, middle-class reform theories about how children of all kinds should be raised, and the desire to send asylum children out into the world as solid, but in all likelihood working-class, children.

The nature of chores remained the same; few things were more constant in asylum life over time. And some of the justifications asylum managers gave for working their children also survived over time, especially its character-building quality and the fact that the children were helping the asylum survive by freeing up money for other needs. But as theories about childhood and character formation evolved during the nineteenth century, so too did the explanation of how chores were expected to build character.

7

Play, Holidays, and Vacations

In the decades immediately before and after 1900, orphan asylums became increasingly able and willing to have their children leave the asylum for hours, days, and even weeks at a time. The shift to enrolling asylum children in public schools, discussed in Chapter 6, is probably the most important example, but there were also other ways asylums sought to integrate their children into their neighborhoods and the broader society.

Children's opportunities to play increased greatly between the Civil War and 1900, and even more dramatically after 1900. Previously confined in their asylums by both asylum managers' wishes and limited asylum funds, by the early twentieth century many asylum children were having much more frequent contact with the outside world. They were encouraged to meet socially with other children and celebrated numerous holidays. Occasionally, they even enjoyed some of the advantages of a middle-class child's life, such as lengthy summer vacations; for weeks or even months they played sports, swam, and enjoyed other forms of recreation. In the 1910s and 1920s, asylum children were increasingly allowed, and even actively encouraged, to join sports teams, learn dancing, and enter formal youth organizations where they mixed with, and competed against, a wide variety of children.

By the early twentieth century, most orphan asylums were providing their children with daily lives that mixed aspects of middle-class and working-class life. The harsh picture of an institutionalized, regimented life so regularly described in attacks on asylums in the late nineteenth century was becoming less and less accurate for many asylums. As various forms of leisure became increasingly commercialized and more widely available, opportunities for asylum managers to send children out into society became far greater than they had been fifty years earlier. And ironically, ideas that playground reformers had developed about the necessity of play opportunities for working-class children were far easier for some asylum managers to implement than for reformers to impose on working-class families.

Playing Inside the Asylum

Even the earliest orphan asylums allowed children some opportunity to play, but playtime was not seen as a high priority or as something that would help build their characters. By the 1850s, however, asylum managers were beginning to view children's play as an important aspect of growing up. Limited asylum resources were sometimes used specifically to allow children time and space for playing. The Orphans' Home and Asylum constructed a new building in 1860 that had two "play-rooms" as large as its two schoolrooms. The grounds also had "large playgrounds" on two sides of the house. These were segregated by gender, as many asylum playgrounds would be for the rest of the century, and they saw considerable use. In 1875, the boys' playground was blocked off so that it could again be made "fit for use," and the next summer the same was done for the girls' playground.[1]

The Orphans' Home and Asylum was unusual in the 1860s; few asylums could provide their children with two playgrounds as well as two large rooms for playing inside. In the 1870s and 1880s, however, increasing numbers of asylum managers recognized that playtime was important for children, and accordingly they tried to make recreation accessible. Even so, what most asylums could provide their children was fairly limited: one playground for children of each sex, perhaps a playroom inside the asylum for use in winter or inclement weather, and a few toys and games. But even though facilities remained simple, the belief that children should be given regular opportunities to play spread. By 1896, an orphan asylum superintendent argued for the importance of children's play at the National Conference of Charities and Correction to what was undoubtedly a highly receptive audience.

> Children must have a great deal of play. Their amusements need not be expensive. They manage to extract a large amount of fun out of

simple things. A pile of sand; a few square feet of garden that they can dig, plant, water, and hoe; a few nails, pine sticks, and old lumber, out of which they can construct kites, stilts, and playhouses, not only give them great pleasure, but "keep them out of other mischief" (as an old lady once said to me when she consented to let her children attend my Sabbath-school), and will do more toward maintaining good discipline than punishments.[2]

This manager's rhetoric regarding the importance of play was something that most orphan asylum managers had accepted by the 1890s. The simple means he advised for presenting children with the opportunity to play, such as sand and lumber, were hardly state of the art or central to most asylum playgrounds by this time, though some poorer asylums probably had little more to offer children. But those that could provided much more. Despite his simple claims for what children needed to "extract a large amount of fun," this superintendent stated that toys, games, books, playgrounds, and if possible even a gymnasium should be provided for children.[3]

Giving children an opportunity to play was justified on a number of grounds by the turn of the century. Play helped children emotionally, kept them happy, made them healthier, and kept them out of trouble. Their nature demanded the chance to play, and play had important lessons to teach children about patience and achieving success. It was "as natural, necessary and beautiful for children to play as for lambs to skip or kittens to frolic." By 1900, play was coming to be seen as being almost as important to a child's healthy development as education. This aspect of asylum managers' thinking was reflective of middle-class child-rearing literature in the late nineteenth century, which advocated raising children with love and ample opportunity to express themselves, particularly through play. By the early twentieth century, the belief that physical strength "helps to make strength of mind," as one Jewish asylum superintendent put it while discussing his asylum's gymnasium in 1909, was also widespread.[4] The next year, the same superintendent summed up his reasons for encouraging children to play in a statement that most asylum managers would have endorsed in 1910: "We consider this matter of vital importance—for play is not merely pastime for the child; it is the chief method of developing health, independence, comradeship, the joy of childhood and performs an important part in character building."[5]

Though asylum resources often remained limited at the turn of the century, play was clearly important in practice as well as rhetoric in all orphan asylums. The Roman Catholic Orphan Asylum of New York gave its children four hours per day for recreation throughout the late nineteenth century. The superintendent of one Catholic asylum stated in 1912 that all orphan asylums should have large playgrounds because physical education was a crucial part of a child's education. By the 1910s, many orphan asylums were providing their children with more than the simple playgrounds that had been prevalent thirty years before. Briggs's 1916 survey of eighty Catholic asylums showed that almost all had playgrounds with facilities for baseball, basketball, and tennis. Many of them also employed playground teachers to care for children under ten while they played. Active, athletic children became a source of pride for asylum managers. The Chicago Home for Jewish Orphans, which had handball and volleyball courts, boasted that its sports teams were "formidable rivals to any challenging neighborhood or playground group."[6]

The amount of play space available for children seems to have increased during the gradual shift to cottage systems described in Chapter 5. A study in 1910 by Hastings Hart, which included seventeen congregate asylums and ten cottage system asylums, found the average indoor play space in the former to be fourteen square feet per child, whereas in the latter it was nearly twice as great at twenty-six square feet per child. Whether this was because the cottage system could more easily provide play space is not clear. It may well be that the difference came about because cottage-based asylum buildings were generally much newer than congregate buildings and were therefore more likely to have been built after asylums had come to recognize the importance of play (and when asylum resources in general were greater). Differences in available play space among asylums by type of management and by region seem to have been minimal; the financial resources a particular asylum enjoyed and the age of its buildings were what mattered.[7]

In the 1910s, orphan asylums that did not yet have gymnasiums and playing fields with swings, baseball diamonds, and other equipment often sought them as a high priority. In 1919, for example, St. Vincent's of Philadelphia finally managed to replace a "shed" in which boys and girls had used separate play areas with a modern pavilion for the asylum's girls.[8] In California in the 1910s, orphan asylums seeking state licensing, and state funds, were required to have facilities for play: "Playgrounds and playrooms, properly equipped with apparatus, games and toys shall be provided, and it shall be the duty of some one officer of the institution to supervise and encourage play activities."[9]

While some California asylums could (and did) claim much more thorough supervision of play than they really provided, they could hardly claim to have playgrounds that did not exist. Possibly in response to this new state demand, the Pacific Hebrew Orphan Asylum successfully sought funds for "playground equipment for both the boys' and the girls' side of the yard" in 1910. Not all asylums could respond so quickly. Some were unable to provide worthwhile playgrounds until years after it became a state requirement. One was finally left a $10,000 legacy in 1923 for a playground "with the thought that thereby, the children's best development, both mental and physical, will be accomplished."[10]

The shift from simple playgrounds, where children might run and play, to playgrounds with swings, slides, sandboxes, and facilities for team sports such as baseball and basketball did not occur in a vacuum. From the 1880s onward, some urban reformers urged the creation of systems of playgrounds for poor children. After the depression of the 1890s, this idea gained increased importance. Assumptions about what playgrounds could achieve were astronomical. As Paul Boyer describes it, playground leaders sought to "shape a cohesive urban moral order" through implementation of their plans.[11] While asylum managers do not show evidence of such grand goals, they certainly did see playgrounds as a way to build character in children.

Recreation within the asylum was by no means limited to physically strenuous activities. Music was an important part of both education and recreation in some asylums, particularly Jewish institutions. The Brooklyn Hebrew Orphan Asylum was able to establish a brass band in the 1890s, which the asylum's board of education felt would allow the children to "cultivate a taste for music." Within a few years of its formation, the band performed in a Memorial Day parade. Many asylums encouraged their children to form literary societies, which, like musical training, were seen as a combination of education and recreation. The Chicago Home for Jewish Orphans had three literary societies by the 1920s, with a total membership of 130 children. Asylums began to provide other activities as well. One Catholic asylum for boys gave its children dancing lessons in the 1910s in the attempt to "neglect nothing that can help to make the boys reasonably happy." The asylum held weekly dances, and the boys were encouraged to invite girls from various city parishes. In 1916, the Angel Guardian Orphanage had a film projector installed in its assembly hall, and movies "of an educational as well as an entertaining character" were shown.[12]

The children's group activities sometimes found generous sponsors. In 1897, the Brooklyn Hebrew Orphan Asylum's brass band was aided by a donor who purchased nineteen instruments for the children at a cost of $1,300. The same year, the asylum's baseball team received twenty-four baseball outfits from another patron. As with so much else that asylums tried to do for their children, facilities and equipment for play and recreation depended heavily on donations from supporters. Fortunately, gifts of this nature had a particular appeal to some donors because the results would be highly visible and personal. Listening to an asylum band play with instruments they had purchased, or watching a baseball team play in uniforms they had supplied, was not just a sign to donors that the orphan asylum was providing its children with a good life; it also assured donors that they were playing an important role in the asylum's achievements.[13]

Day Trips Outside the Asylum

In the self-contained world of antebellum orphan asylums, children rarely ventured out into the world for recreation or entertainment. The first outside trip made by the Cincinnati Orphan Asylum's children apparently did not occur until two decades after it was founded. In the summer of 1853, a railroad company gave the asylum's children a free trip to the countryside, and the next year the children had a picnic in a donor's garden. In 1856, they shared a Fourth of July picnic with children from another asylum, after which one outing each summer became the norm. The children of the Church Home in Boston in 1860 had it slightly better, since "several opportunities for recreation were provided for the children during the summer, by excursions into the country, &c."[14]

Some asylum managers were convinced by the 1860s that trips outside the institution's walls were crucial to their children's emotional wellbeing. As one put it, "we diversify the lives of our little ones from what would otherwise be a somewhat monotonous and prison-like way of life as much as is in our power. In the summer months they frequently spend the afternoon in the woods, no doubt drinking in unconsciously the sweet influences of nature."[15] Day trips outside the asylum fulfilled two crucial functions. They helped to reduce the monotony of asylum life, thereby answering, at least somewhat, one of the most common accusations leveled toward orphan asylums during the second half of the century. Outings for an "afternoon in the woods" also gave children time in rural or natural settings. Since many asylum managers, like other reformers of the era, considered anything urban to be dangerous and anything rural to be good, a trip that took children into the countryside could only be a positive experience for them. No matter how important outside ventures were deemed, however, most asylums struggled to find enough money to give their children summer holidays. In the 1870s, trips outside the asylum to anywhere but school or church were still a rarity for most asylum children.

While the contributions of donors were important to children's play opportunities within the asylum, they were absolutely essential to children's trips outside the asylum. Railroads often provided free passage to asylum children for their trips to a city park or to the countryside. Individual donors who provided a day's entertainment for children were equally important, and some fortunate asylums had several such friends. Instances of such generosity are strewn throughout asylums' annual reports. For example, through the "kindness of a friend," the Orphans' Home and Asylum was able to take 145 children on a trip to the beach in 1884.[16]

Most day trips for asylum children in the Northeast happened in the summer, since children were out of school and the weather was at its most reliable. A Vanderbilt joined with several other asylum patrons in taking all the children from Brooklyn's Home for Destitute Children to Coney Island in 1866. The children of Brooklyn's Hebrew Orphan Asylum were taken on a picnic by two charitable organizations of Jewish women in the summer of 1894, when many of them also saw a Buffalo Bill Wild West performance courtesy of two of the asylum's trustees.[17]

The ability of most urban asylums' managers to send their children to entertainments outside the asylum increased significantly over the last three decades of the nineteenth century. During this period, the number of public, commercial forms of recreation available to Americans expanded rapidly, and asylum children often benefited. The children of Boston's Church Home had one daylong trip to a country mansion in 1876; it was their only excursion that summer. Similarly, in the 1870s the Chicago Orphan Asylum could only manage to send its children out for one annual picnic each year. By 1892, however, one-third of a page in the asylum's annual report was devoted to "Entertainments Furnished the Children," each of which had been provided by an individual donor. Dozens of children went to a minstrel show, to a concert, on a lake excursion, to a casino(!), or on a car ride. The next year's annual report contained a list that was twice as long, including numerous trips to the 1893 World's Fair. By 1896, the asylum's children were receiving a wide variety of invitations to "circuses, picnics, and other entertainments," which were "quickly accepted" and "occasions of happiness" for the children.[18] As was noted in Chapter 5, some asylum managers punished children who had misbehaved by denying them outings.[19]

From the 1870s onward, children in Protestant, Catholic, and Jewish asylums all had more and more opportunities to make trips outside the asylum. Catholic St. Vincent's of Philadelphia saw an increase in "the number of friends who provided happy holidays for the children." Brooklyn's Hebrew Orphan Asylum Society thanked a donor in 1897 for the summer day trips she had provided, which had "become a fixture," while other donors gave tickets for one hundred children to attend the opera. And when the asylum's children made their annual outing to Coney Island in 1899, they "received so many invitations from the different pleasure resorts on the Island" that they could not accept them all.[20] Even so, a perennial lack of money left some asylum managers unable to provide many outings for their children. St. Mary's Orphanage of Providence sent its children to annual picnics held by two local Sunday schools in 1897, but other outings were few and far between because donors had given "very little money" for excursions.[21]

Advances in technology broadened the range of possible outings. Just as railroads had made trips to the countryside feasible, the rapid spread of automobiles in the early twentieth century allowed asylum children to take "numerous automobile rides" as a form of diversion. Again, individual donors made a great difference. A Jewish asylum in California thanked one friend in 1910 "for his extreme consideration for those of our children who have no near relatives. Throughout the summer vacation he took out little groups in his automobile and entertained them in the most generous manner."[22] In the 1920s, the San Francisco Protestant Orphanage Society owned an automobile, which was regularly used to give children rides for entertainment.[23]

In the early twentieth century, opportunities for asylums to send their children out to entertainments proliferated even more rapidly. Orphan asylum managers across the country were actively seeking to integrate children into their communities. In some cases they succeeded to such an extent that children's outings and their everyday lives were no longer clearly separable. For example, by 1930 the children of the Chicago Orphan Asylum went "occasionally to the neighborhood movies and often to the Field Museum and the parks" on their own. A virtual catalog of events inside and outside the asylum listed in the San Francisco Protestant Orphanage Society's annual report for 1923 was typical by this era. "Activities in the home aside from the routine duties of the day during the year have been many and varied. The most important were: Mr. Geary's Boys' Reading Club, Singing Class, Boys organized in the Pioneers connected indirectly with the Y.M.C.A., Moving Pictures, Dancing lessons, Manual Arts, social evenings in the Matron's room, athletic meetings of the boys at Presidio Play Grounds, many trips to the Park, museum, aquarium, Academy of Science, beach and Presidio. Our special parties on holidays and children's birthdays have been a source of much happiness."[24]

Many of these examples demonstrate asylums' continued dependence on individual donors for children's holidays. As with providing musical instruments or sporting equipment, this form of giving probably held particular pleasures for those with the financial wherewithal to manage it. Donating money that would be used to purchase food or linen for children was charitable, but actually taking a dozen (or a hundred) children to a play or picnic was far more personal. From the child's perspective, it also allowed them to spend time with adults other than the ones they saw every day. This type of highly personal giving flourished well into the twentieth century. In the winter of 1915, for example, the Chicago Orphan Asylum's children saw moving pictures thanks to one donor, took a sleigh ride with another, and were given ice cream once a month by a third.[25] The schoolboys of the Angel Guardian Orphanage saw a Chicago Cubs baseball game in 1926 courtesy of a local Kiwanis club, and the next year all the Angel Guardian's schoolchildren were taken to a circus by another Kiwanis club.[26]

In the early twentieth century, nothing demonstrated the changing nature of asylum life better than children's access to outside entertainments. In the antebellum era, few children left the asylum more than once or twice a year. After the turn of the century, most orphan asylum children had the chance to see plays, hear concerts, play in parks, go to the beach—all opportunities to mix with working- and middle-class children and adults in ways that would have been highly unlikely half a century earlier. While asylum children's lives were inherently different from those of children living with their own families, as time passed those differences gradually became less obvious.

Clubs and Sports

By the early twentieth century, many asylum managers were encouraging their children to join clubs based outside the asylum. In such groups, asylum children mingled with children from a variety of backgrounds. Numerous clubs also formed within asylums. Asylum clubs, like outside clubs that asylum children joined, were often age-graded as well as gender-specific. The variety of clubs available both in and out of the asylum increased rapidly after the turn of the century. By the 1930s, one asylum had four different clubs for its boys, depending on their ages, and girls had similar opportunities.[27] Sports teams, on the other hand, were generally for boys. Boys played baseball and basketball, and regularly engaged in both informal and league contests against other children. Girls, who were usually confined to gymnastic tumbling and other "suitable" sports, only competed against outside children at school or in musical contests, both of which were also arenas for male activity. Furthermore, while five-year-olds and fifteen-year-olds generally shared time on playgrounds, most clubs and sporting events were for adolescents, not for small children.

Paul Boyer has described "environmental moralists" who, in the 1890s, urged the formation of clubs for boys and girls in urban slums. Membership in such clubs would supposedly "help impressionable city children avoid vice" and improve their characters. After the turn of the century, asylum children increasingly joined such clubs. Club membership was seen as important for asylum children in a number of ways. Some Jewish asylum managers believed clubs would serve as Americanizing forces on their children. One Jewish asylum superintendent in New York was proud that over 90 percent of the asylum's children had joined at least one asylum club. The director of a girls' club thought it developed "leadership and interest in worthwhile things," and that these traits carried over into other aspects of girls' lives such as schoolwork and school activities. Club leaders were allowed to take their fellow members on outings "to the theater, to the museum, to various places of historic interest, to parks and playgrounds," and so on. Some clubs mixed boys and girls together, thereby helping to "establish very much more natural relations between the boys and girls."[28]

Between 1906 and 1912, the Boys Club of America, the Boy Scouts of America, and the Girl Scouts of America were all founded, and some asylum managers enrolled their children when given the chance. In the 1920s, the San Francisco Presbyterian Orphanage and Farm's older children were members of the local Camp Fire Girls and Boy Scout troops. Membership was not merely for the children's pleasure; it was also supposed to help train them for "the constructive use" of their leisure time. For the same reason, the Orphanage and Farm's children would derive benefit from lessons in gymnastic tumbling, musical instruction, and other activities such as folk dancing, swimming, and handcrafts. They could play sports on the orphanage's new ball field or use new playground equipment; a gymnasium was listed as one of the orphanage's most pressing needs.[29]

Organized sports became an increasingly important outlet for boys after the turn of the century, for asylum children as well as for the rest of society. By the 1890s, baseball was becoming a popular working-class sport, both for playing and watching. Basketball, though a newer sport and less popular as a spectator sport, was also becoming better known. By 1923, the San Francisco Protestant Orphanage Society's boys had two basketball teams playing in a Protestant Church Athletic League. The older team had practiced for two months against high school teams, usually at the local YMCA. In 1924, the same asylum was completing construction of a playground that included a baseball field, a tennis court, four handball courts, and an outside basketball court, as well as swings, slides, and other equipment for smaller children. The asylum already had an indoor gymnasium, which like the playground was paid for by a legacy left specifically to give the children better recreational facilities. Several years later, its annual report proudly announced the asylum children's victories in two track meets and in a YMCA baseball league. Even more important than that championship, however, was when the asylum's baseball team beat a team from the nearby Hebrew Orphan Asylum to win a trophy from the Masons. Another asylum encouraged its boys' interest in baseball by taking them to see professional baseball games.[30]

The increased involvement of asylum children with other children through clubs and sporting events paralleled what was happening to adolescents within families in the 1910s and 1920s. During this period, older children began to spend much more of their time outside the home, with their peers.[31] However, whereas children in families exchanged time spent with parents for time spent with peers, asylum children replaced time spent within the institution with time spent outside it. By the 1920s, the lives of children within many orphan asylums bore little resemblance to the monotonous, prisonlike existence that late nineteenth-century critics had condemned so vehemently.

Holidays

From the early nineteenth century onward, asylum managers did what they could to help their children have the same sort of holiday celebrations that they would have presumably enjoyed if they had lived in stable families. Asylums did all they could to honor certain holidays, most notably Christmas, Thanksgiving, and the Fourth of July. But the limited resources of orphan asylums in the middle of the nineteenth century guaranteed that these holiday celebrations would be rather simple. In 1860, for example, Boston's Church Home was happy that its children had "received several baskets of books and toys" for Christmas.[32]

By the 1890s, as with many other aspects of asylum life, Christmas celebrations had become much grander. The presence of donors who were determined that asylum children should have relatively normal lives often made this possible. At the Maria Kip, a California asylum for girls, there were two Christmas trees in 1897, one for the "larger" girls and one for the asylum's twenty small children. Each was decorated by ornaments and surrounded by gifts. There were also visitors to brighten the children's day, some of whom "planned and carried out many forms of entertainment" to make the day more memorable. Even an epidemic of whooping cough that forced the Chicago Orphan Asylum to quarantine itself against visitors could not stop its Christmas celebrations. Though the asylum was "obliged to forgo the usual Christmas festivities" in 1903, "the children found their stockings well filled with gifts on Christmas morning, and later a turkey dinner was served." At the Angel Guardian Orphanage in the late 1910s, each boy received a gift from the local Knights of Columbus, and each girl received a gift from the Ladies of Isabella. After 1900, many orphan asylums' Christmas celebrations had become a lengthy series of events that began four or five days early and only ended after New Year's Day. The variety of events children enjoyed was considerable. One asylum had a sixty-foot Christmas tree in 1925, and its children gave a Christmas play to visitors that was broadcast on local radio.[33]

Since most children in orphan asylums had at least one living parent, some asylums encouraged such children to spend the Christmas holiday with relatives. In the 1910s, one New York asylum used both Christmas and summer vacations to strengthen ties between parents and institutionalized children through "an elaborate system of visiting." More generally, long before most asylum children were attending public schools or making regular trips outside for entertainments, holidays served as an important connection to the world beyond the asylum's walls. Donors often came into the asylum for Christmas and Thanksgiving to watch the children enjoy their largesse. On other occasions, such as the Fourth of July, children attended celebrations along with families from the neighboring community.[34]

Thanksgiving, made a national holiday in 1863, was almost as important a holiday as Christmas in many asylums by the late nineteenth century. The central feature was Thanksgiving dinner, and every child "of suitable age" was likely to be at the table. As with Christmas, "kind and liberal friends of the cause" often contributed money for food, and sometimes provided entertainment for the children as well. In 1904, the Chicago Orphan Asylum's children had turkey dinner and "good things galore" as well as the chance to listen to a street band's music throughout their feast.[35]

Asylum children also celebrated a number of other holidays. Outings of the entire asylum to public celebrations of the Fourth of July were a regular occurrence. Washington's birthday was observed in some asylums, though in at least one, the Chicago Orphan Asylum, it was celebrated in a rather strange way: in the 1890s the children learned and sang Civil War songs as part of the festivities.[36] The number of holidays celebrated by American society rose over time, and asylums took part in this trend. By the 1920s, Halloween had become a particularly important event for children in some asylums. As one asylum manager put it, "Perhaps at no time in the year is there quite such fun and frolic in our Assembly Hall as on Hallow-een night, when the little folks in masks and costumes, surrounded by mysteries and special decorations, have an unforgettable party."[37] Another asylum's children attended a Masons' Halloween party in 1925, which "pleased the children very much."[38]

Some asylums had annual holidays connected to an event in the asylum's past or based on a day that was important to a particular donor. The Chicago Orphan Asylum began celebrating November 3 in the 1890s because one donor had left money in his will to give "the children pleasure" on what had been his own birthday. For years, one little boy (aided by his mother) gave the Brooklyn Home for Destitute Children cake for all on his birthday, "bought with money which he had saved during the year." The birthdays of asylum children were also being celebrated regularly in at least some asylums by the late nineteenth century. Children's birthdays had only become an occasion for celebration in the United States after 1800, and, as with other holidays, orphan asylums eventually followed suit.[39]

Summer Vacations

In the decades before and after 1900, summer vacations "became a mass urban custom" for middle-class families.[40] From the 1870s onward, the combination of improving modes of transportation, increasing leisure time, and growing disposable income made possible a kind of vacation still unattainable for working-class families, who were limited to one-day excursions.[41] During the decades around the turn of the century, the increased availability of long summer vacations for asylum children was less widespread, yet perhaps even more dramatic, than the growing ability of asylums to give children holidays and day trips. One of the many differences between antebellum asylums and those in the Progressive Era was that twentieth-century orphan asylums were sometimes able to give their children summer vacations away from the city. One asylum manager declared in the 1920s that "probably the greatest event in the life of the Orphanage is the annual going to our camp." From the children's perspective, this statement may well have been true.

In 1890, the Orphans' Home and Asylum of New York rented a house on Long Island to serve as a summer home. The asylum's younger children were moved there in June and stayed the entire summer. Due to space limitations, older children were brought down in groups that stayed for two or three weeks before returning to the asylum. It was seen as a successful experiment, "as shown by the children's delight when in the country, and by their improved looks" the following winter. As with so much else asylums did, the summer home had been made possible by "special gifts" from donors.[42] By the 1890s, some asylums were encouraging donors to contribute to funds earmarked for building summer homes.

From 1890 on, the children of the Orphans' Home and Asylum had a summer vacation every year. In the 1890s, the asylum purchased a house on Long Island, possibly the one it had rented in 1890. By 1900, the summer home had been sold, apparently due to financial constraints, but the asylum's managers had not given up. That same year they rented a house in Germantown on the Hudson, and the entire asylum population spent its summer within sight of the Catskills. Owning a summer home gave the Orphans' Home and Asylum flexibility. When financial necessity and an aging building led the asylum to sell its forty-year-old home in New York City, the asylum population lived on the Hudson for two years before a new home in the city was purchased.[43]

Southern orphan asylums seem to have been less likely to send their children on summer vacations. One reason is that, in general, they tended to have less money than their northern and western counterparts. As with so much else, an asylum's ability and desire to send its children on summer vacation varied from one institution to the next, and asylums with particularly generous and wealthy donors had the most options. Arthur Fink has found that for several North Carolina orphanages in the late nineteenth century, summer vacations were at best a month long, partly due to the lengthy school year of these asylums. And during their month's vacation, the children did not go away together to a camp or summer home. Instead, they usually went to visit their families for a few weeks, which served to solidify family ties as well as save the asylums some money.[44]

Asylums that could not afford summer homes on their own still did what they could for their children. By the 1920s, many asylums could manage some sort of summer vacation. For example, in the early 1920s the Brooklyn Home for Children sent its boys, though not its girls, to a summer camp. Through the aid of the Brooklyn Rotary Club and the Edwin Gould Foundation, the Brooklyn Home gained a permanent summer house on Long Island in 1925. In 1928, the Chicago Orphan Asylum's children each had at least one week away from the asylum, a few staying with a parent but most vacationing at Lake Geneva through the generosity of the Salvation Army and two members of the asylum's board of managers.[45]

Being on summer vacation did not completely change children's lives. They were able to spend more time playing and less time studying, but they were usually still expected to work. In 1925, the San Francisco Protestant Orphanage Society's children went on an eight-week-long summer vacation. The girls spent "much time in play and recreation" but also made dresses, nightgowns, and numerous other articles of clothing. All the reasons that were used to justify children's chores during the school year were also used to explain this vacation work: "This not only furnished them domestic training but gave vent to much pent up energy and also fully occupied their time." Boys were also expected to work, and in a masculine way; a few years later their main summer task was to construct a play pavilion for the asylum's younger girls.[46]

Conclusion

The changing nature and increased availability of play, holidays, and vacations that orphan asylum children experienced in the years between the Civil War and the Great Depression echoed the experience of middle-class children and, in some ways, paralleled what middle-class reformers sought for working-class children. Asylum managers wanted their children to become hard-working, God-fearing, and self-supporting. By the end of the nineteenth century, giving children plenty of opportunity to play had become part of most asylum managers' plans for developing children's characters, alongside older methods such as having children perform chores, go to school, and attend church. In the twentieth century, play became even more important as it not only helped form children's characters but also provided asylum managers with a way of treating children as individuals.

The nature of play changed along with the justification for providing it to children. Day trips, holiday celebrations, and summer vacations all became increasingly available for asylum children, just as they were becoming more common in society. More importantly, the greater access to events outside the asylum meant that asylum children were mixing into American society far more often than they had in the antebellum era. The increasing variety of ways children ventured outside the asylum from the 1870s onward reflected a society that saw leisure time both expanding and more frequently located outside the home and the workplace. Children's leisure time and recreational options also grew because asylum managers, aware that their institutions were not perfect, did what they could to improve the lives their children led. They took the opportunities offered to them. Finally, children were mixing more with the outer world partly because American society, which had always had a powerful impact on how asylums were run internally, increasingly welcomed asylum children.

Conclusion

On June 16, 1902, Lillian Scott was born in Montana, where her parents had recently moved from California. Tragically, Lillian's mother died in childbirth. Her father, an attorney and journalist, was not able to raise her himself, but it is unlikely that placing her in an orphan asylum was ever considered, even for a moment. Lillian's father was solidly middle class, and like most members of the middle class, he had both financial resources and other people he could turn to for help. In short order, Lillian was moved to California, where she was raised by an aunt and uncle who received monthly payments from her father. By the age of twenty, having graduated from Pomona College, Lillian was back in Montana, teaching English at the University of Montana.

It was not just those with money who were able to keep their children out of institutions when disaster struck. Most children who lost a parent remained with family, whether their surviving parent, a grandparent, an older sibling, an aunt (as in Lillian's case), or even a friend of the family. This was true for working-class ethnic groups, and for various racial groups, though with less certainty than for the middle class. It remains true today: most children whose parents become unable to care for them are cared for by their extended family, sometimes very broadly conceived. Orphan asylums were for those children who lacked any family or friend able and willing to take them in. Asylums were, quite literally, a last resort for almost all who turned to them.

Orphan asylums were by no means perfect places to raise children. Large asylums in particular were often highly regimented institutions where children had relatively little positive interaction with adults and limited opportunity to develop emotionally or psychologically. Discipline was often harsh, especially prior to 1900. Most importantly, there was little or no chance for children in large asylums to develop strong relationships with parental figures. For children who spent the bulk of their childhoods in asylums, these problems were severe. For many children, however, a year or two in an asylum while their families struggled to overcome some sort of disaster may have been a better fate than being with their families during that time if things were especially bad, or than living on the street.

Some asylums focused on short-term care, while others, most notably Jewish asylums, kept most of their children for at least three or four years, and sometimes much longer. Most orphan asylums served both purposes by caring for some children for short periods, often less than a year, while providing other children with long-term care that might stretch from early childhood to the teenage years. It is important to distinguish between these two aspects of orphanage care, and to recognize what each one offered to poor children and their families.

Children cared for on a short-term basis before returning to their own families were best served by the asylum. When disaster struck their families, such children were provided with food, clothing, shelter, companionship, and at least some education. If their parents (or surviving parent) were able to reclaim them and the family was reunited, the orphan asylum had played an important role in the long-term survival of the family. Scholars have noted a number of working-class strategies for dealing with insecure unemployment, illness, and other problems. For example, families often sent their children to work at an early age rather than to school, took in boarders, and relied on kin networks to see them through difficulties.[1] But they also utilized whatever nearby charity was available, and none was more useful to a family in dire straits than the orphan asylum, which could care for their children for months or years while providing them with an education.[2]

Children who spent most of their youths in orphan asylums were served somewhat differently. Compared to poor children able to stay with their own families, such children probably lacked emotional warmth from a parental figure and the opportunity to learn to act independently in society. But for orphans with no relatives able to take them in, asylums provided a reasonably stable, if not necessarily loving, environment. Children who stayed in an asylum for year after year were given an education and a sense of their place in the universe through religious training, though only small asylums could hope to replace the family in a more personal sense.[3] This was just what some children needed; for others, it was not nearly enough.

The fact that asylums could serve both short-term and long-term clients with some measure of success may have been their greatest triumph. The poor in the United States have always been divided between the short-term needy and the long-term poor, but methods of dealing with the poor, from the poorhouse to today's homeless shelters, have often treated both in the same way—by providing little for either. Institutions and policies geared to keep all but the truly desperate from applying for aid not only fail to provide adequately for the long-term poor; they also punish those who only need a temporary helping hand. As Michael Katz points out, the dominant view of the poor in American culture sees poverty as a moral condition and usually makes little distinction between different types of dependence.[4] But most orphan asylums avoided this flaw because their focus on children as innocents needing help effectively separated children from whatever shortcomings their parents might possess. When asylum managers did hold harsh views of poor parents, it led them to pursue full legal control of children far more often than it led them to reject children. Despite their strengths, however, orphan asylums shared a crucial weakness with virtually all other forms of charity and public welfare in the United States. Despite the realization of many orphan asylum managers that poverty was usually the result of unemployment or illness, rather than moral flaws, asylum managers did not attempt to deal with the underlying structural causes of poverty; they simply tried to care for those who were poor.[5]

The late nineteenth century saw a struggle between asylum proponents and advocates of placing children in homes other than their own, now known as foster care. Interestingly, when state governments became increasingly involved in trying to resolve this issue from the 1910s onward, they chose a third option, mothers' pensions, which harkened back to outdoor relief more than to either institutionalization or placing out. When substitute care was needed, foster care eventually became favored over institutional care. Asylums were local and far-flung; foster care, like mothers' pensions, was much more easily centralized and bureaucratized. Under this system, people making policy decisions were not likely to actually know their clientele; orphan asylum managers had interacted with poor parents every day.

Most social welfare institutions began as private corporations serving public interests and later became, or were replaced by, public institutions.[6] With orphan asylums, this process took nearly a century, and it only happened when asylums started offering care to a somewhat different clientele. The passage of mothers' pension laws by virtually every state government during the 1910s created a new, important, public method of caring for dependent children. Though foster care is now widespread and far more central to child welfare than orphan asylums, most of the children who would have been in asylums in the nineteenth century have been kept in their own homes in the late twentieth century through the successor to mothers' pensions, AFDC, which was ended in 1996. Between the late 1920s and the early 1960s, virtually all orphan asylums either stopped functioning as institutions or began serving a different clientele. Some became foster care or adoption agencies, and continued to deal with dependent children. Others began to specialize in specific types of children that spread (at least somewhat) across classes, such as children with severe emotional problems.[7]

Though both the elderly and children are groups that are largely defined by their ages, they have undergone very different experiences in connection with charity and welfare in America. In the late nineteenth century, the elderly were increasingly being separated from society and placed in institutions.[8] At the same time, children in orphan asylums were being given much greater contact with the world outside asylum walls than ever before. This trend accelerated in the early twentieth century, both through the integrative nature of asylums and through the creation of mothers' pensions. By the middle of the twentieth century, however, state provision for the elderly had become fairly extensive, serving, as John Myles writes, as "an adjunct of the market."[9] Because the elderly had once worked, it was seen as society's obligation to keep them out of poverty. But no matter how often advocates of mothers' pensions or AFDC claimed that rearing children was an important duty to society, the hold that poor mothers have had on the public purse has always been weak. Theda Skocpol traces the underfunding of mothers' pensions to "the gap between the political requisites of the original nationwide movement for mothers' pensions laws" and the local political conditions involved in attempts to provide adequate funding.[10] In fact, Skocpol's focus on "the polity," though broader than most other views of the developing welfare state, is too narrow. It leaves out a more fundamental reason why mothers' pensions, like outdoor relief in the nineteenth century and AFDC from the 1970s to the 1990s, have always been terribly underfunded: Americans neither like nor trust the poor, even when we deem them "worthy," even when they are children.

Not only did asylums have the difficult task of rearing children effectively in an institutional setting, they also had to care for poor children in a society that looks down on the poor. In theory, children are innocents devoid of blame for their parents' flaws (namely, poverty and the moral failings assumed to have created that poverty, such as alcoholism or laziness), but in practice virtually every method American society has ever employed to care for such children has punished them for the sins of their parents. Indenture in early America was far more concerned with preserving order in society and providing a stable workforce than with the well-being of children. Poorhouses lumped children with their parents, and treated both as deserving of nothing more than bare subsistence. Outdoor relief was seen as encouraging laziness and as too expensive, its availability was often limited, and the amount of aid given to any single family was quite small.

The first few decades after the turn of the twentieth century saw an increasing bureaucratization of America. Various institutions, such as old-age homes, reflected this change. By the 1890s, some child-placing agencies, such as Boston's Children's Aid Society, "had moved a long way toward a modern, bureaucratic approach to child welfare." But though they sometimes tried to adopt social work techniques, orphan asylums did not offer a fertile field for the growth of social work as a profession. While asylums might hire a social worker or two, they were local, charitable institutions that were likely to remain under local control. Nor was the patchwork of Catholic, Jewish, Presbyterian, Methodist, Episcopalian, Masonic, and other kinds of asylums easy to bring under centralized, bureaucratic control. On the other hand, foster care, which social workers preferred over both mothers' pensions and institutions in the 1910s, was easy to centralize and bureaucratize. It was also far easier to treat children on a case-by-case basis in foster care than in an orphan asylum.[11]

Twentieth-century methods of caring for the poor grew out of the nineteenth century, and though far more government aid is now available to the poor, welfare is still provided in degrading ways and in limited amounts. Unlike provisions for the elderly, which have been indexed for inflation since the early 1970s, AFDC payments continued to lose real purchasing power because of inflation, and the federal guarantee backing them was ended in 1996. Whereas the elderly have become an extremely effective political force, children lack the vote, and their surrogate political advocates have enjoyed relatively little success. Since the 1950s, income transfers have greatly diminished poverty among the elderly, but they have done little to move children out of poverty. In 1985, 22 percent of American children lived in poverty, and the percentage has certainly risen since then;[12] it will almost certainly rise even more in the late 1990s. AFDC, a program to aid *dependent children,* has been viewed in terms of its effects (supposedly destructive of character and initiative) on poor *parents.* It is only by viewing it this way, of course, that its critics can argue that it should be abolished and succeed. The discussion is about "lazy" parents instead of about "worthy" children.

Scholars trying to explain the welfare state who focus on politics rarely pay adequate attention to the historical roots of welfare in the United States. Weir, Orloff, and Skocpol have argued that to understand current debates on welfare policy, it is necessary to go all the way back to the 1930s.[13] But the ideas embodied in the Social Security Act of 1935 themselves had a long history in America. This was particularly true of Aid to Dependent Children, which became AFDC. All methods used to care for dependent children over the past two centuries have viewed children as innocents but have nonetheless operated in ways that reflected doubts about the worthiness of parents; modern attacks on AFDC are also part of a lengthy historical story. Methods of helping poor children have been hampered by society's unwillingness to spend what is required to provide children with a decent upbringing: a good education, nourishing meals, opportunities to develop as unique individuals, and, most of all, extensive time and concern from adults. Exactly what constitutes each of these things is debated, and in the absence of widely accepted solutions, each requires money that few are willing to spend.

In the mid-1990s, eighty-five years after the first White House Conference on Dependent Children recommended aiding mothers in their homes and pronounced foster care superior to institutional care, orphanages are back in the news. Just as in 1909, institutional care and aid to poor mothers in their own homes are seen as alternative means of caring for poor children; what has changed is which alternative is seen as superior. Calls by conservative academics and politicians for a "return to orphanages" filled the airwaves and print media at the end of 1994, as they tacitly admitted that the welfare reforms they proposed would create a need for a way to deal with children no longer receiving aid in their own homes. This fed into a less heralded discussion of a return to orphanages that had been echoing in child welfare circles for years, as the foster care population in many states exploded during the 1980s and early 1990s.

In a very real sense, orphanages never completely went away. Many institutions that function as homes for troubled children began as orphan asylums. And orphanages have never left the public's consciousness, though they are remembered in two very different ways. Some see them as Dickensian warehouses where children are virtually starved and dressed in rags, while others remember them as idealized "Boys Towns" where children are raised by a wise, loving father figure. As this work has tried to show, the truth was almost always somewhere in between. The quality of life for children in asylums improved dramatically between the 1830s and the 1930s, as did the quality of life for most children living in their own families. It is no coincidence that Dickens's vision of an asylum is from the middle of the nineteenth century, while the film of a Spencer Tracy–managed, highly successful Boys Town is from the 1930s. Now orphanages are being discussed as a partial solution to our society's current ills. But that assumption may rest on a misreading of what our current ills are; it is certainly based on a complete misunderstanding of the strengths and weaknesses of institutional care for children.

In late 1994, Congressman Newt Gingrich made the debate front-page news by suggesting that watching the movie *Boys Town* would somehow clarify for his political opponents how our nation should take care of dependent children. Like Charles Murray and others, Gingrich believes that institutions would provide stability in children's lives, and there is some truth to this. But then, the central problem of most people on AFDC has been a lack of money, not drugs or abusive behavior. Providing more money to poor families, along with serious job training and day care, would create a far better environment for children than group homes, and at far less cost. But that would involve helping poor parents, which is exactly what current "welfare reform" is trying to avoid. (And this is hardly new; orphan asylums often helped poor families in the long run by allowing them to reunite, but their method of helping in the short run was to take in needy children and leave parents to fend for themselves, not to directly help entire families.) William Bennett, former secretary of education and a long-time advocate of removing children from impoverished parents and placing them for adoption and in orphanages, stated the new conservative view of AFDC in 1994.

> Most proposals miss the essential point of welfare reform. It is not to ensure tougher work provisions and job training but to end a system that fosters illegitimacy and its attendant social pathologies. The worst problem with welfare today is not that too many unmarried women are not working; the worst problem is that too many unmarried women are having babies.[14]

Bennett's arguments harken back to the ideas of Charles Loring Brace: poor parents are to blame for everything and should under no circumstances be helped to care for their children. The assumption is that helping poor parents, or for that matter poor people in general, is the worst possible thing to do, for it just encourages them. Instead, parents needing help should have their children taken away and given to someone else. In an era long before AFDC existed, Brace sent children out of the city to be placed in homes, and fervently opposed orphanages; in the 1990s, Bennett and Murray oppose directly aiding poor mothers so they can retain their children, seeking instead to take children out of their homes and place them in institutions.

Virtually all the evidence about why people are poor, how AFDC affects their lives, and what is good for children points in one direction: maintaining families when possible. Managers of orphan asylums often started out thinking poor parents were uncaring, drunken, and totally unfit. But they also usually came to the conclusion that unemployment and illness were far more likely to be at the root of the troubles faced by poor families than were "moral flaws," and that most poor parents loved their children and wanted to reunite with them as soon as possible. Similarly, the evidence today points toward poverty as the central cause of what, over time, has indeed become a tangled web of problems faced by the urban underclass, and more broadly by impoverished parents throughout the nation. With huge, isolated, impoverished communities in virtually every urban center, it seems clear that poverty is nothing less than central. We have come full circle, once again blaming the poor for their poverty and their inability to support their children properly. The lessons learned by orphan asylum managers–that poor people loved their children and were far more likely to be poor due to circumstances largely or completely out of their control than because of moral flaws— have been rejected, even as institutional care itself is being reconsidered.

The actual strength of orphan asylums lay in two factors: their nature as community institutions, and the fact that most of the children they cared for were in asylums for a year or two or three at most, and then returned to their families once the family had overcome whatever disaster had led it to seek institutional care in the first place. A return to widespread institutional care today, by building numerous new group homes, would lack both of these strengths. It goes without saying that today's asylum advocates are at least as determined to remove children from their neighborhoods as from their parents. And once a child entered such an institution, he or she would be unlikely to leave any time soon.

This does not mean that a movement back toward institutional care would lack all ties to the past. Even before the federal commitment to AFDC ended, its funding had failed to keep pace with inflation, and this stinginess would undoubtedly be true of funding for new asylums as well. As in the past, a lack of funds would severely limit the quality of care institutions could actually provide. Hiring good staff would be almost impossible. Today, group homes for children are often impressive, "homelike" settings that would have warmed the hearts of the best asylum managers of the Progressive Era. But they are not without problems, and they are most definitely not for everyone, as their managers openly admit. The growth in the nation's foster care population is driven by infants, but institutions serve troubled teenagers far better than they serve young children and babies. And the institutions that currently exist are already drawing heavily on charitable resources in their states (as well as government funding through foster care); if they had to double or triple current capacity at the same quality of care, they could not do it. Even tripling the availability of care would not make space for one-tenth of the children that will need homes if states slash their welfare programs and family breakup is instituted as national policy. Institutions play an important role in foster care systems, mostly by caring for emotionally troubled teenagers. Building more to serve the same function is perfectly reasonable as a small part of improving the nation's foster care system. Yet to most observers, even if the money were somehow found, building institutions to replace AFDC would be a step backward.

How a nation cares for its poor, and particularly its poor children, is an important marker of just how civilized and humane that nation is. The United States had a mixed record on this score in the nineteenth century, by that era's standards. Since the New Deal, the record has been better, but hardly admirable; now it has taken another turn for the worse. Building more modern versions of the orphan asylum might help us take better care of some children who are already "in the system," but it also could easily lead to a system of warehouses for children whose real need is for a home.

American society is far more ready to respond to disasters than to prevent them. Like every other method that has been employed to care for dependent children, orphan asylums were to be employed after some tragedy had already struck a poor family. Their greatest strength was that, often against the initial assumptions of their founders, asylums served to help families temporarily until they were back on their feet. But like other methods that have flourished more recently, asylums never addressed the causes of poverty. Until we are ready to do so, any method of child care we develop—whether it provides funding to poor parents, places children in foster homes, or returns to institutional care—will ultimately fail. The least we can do, as a society, for dependent children is to remember that the central question in debates about both welfare reform and foster care must not be, *How do we reform parents?*, but instead must be, *How can we best help children?*

Appendix
Notes
Bibliography
Index

Appendix: Supplementary Tables

Table A1. Mean number of children entering asylums for the first time in 1910, by source of entry and management style of asylum.

Management	From public officials	Via institution officials	From child-placing agencies	From relatives	From other agencies
Catholic	24.4	4.6	1.9	43.4	6.6
Protestant	2.9	2.3	0.4	17.6	1.5
Jewish	30.6	1.1	10.9	36.1	0.2
Fraternal	0.8	0.0	0.0	22.1	1.3
County/City	20.9	2.5	0.2	5.5	2.0
State	70.2	3.5	0.1	34.5	0.0
Unknown	10.0	1.9	1.1	21.4	1.9
All asylums	14.5	2.8	1.2	25.3	2.9

Source: *Benevolent Institutions*, 1910.

Table A2. Number of asylums accepting children of specific racial groups, by management style, in 1890.

Management	White only	Black only	Mixed	Unknown
Catholic	142	6	23	4
Protestant	121	1	8	0
Jewish	9	0	0	0
Fraternal	2	0	1	1
County/City	27	0	44	0
State	3	0	13	0
Unknown	105	20	31	2
All asylums	409	27	120	7

Source: *Eleventh Census: 1890.*

Table A3. Number of asylums accepting children of specific racial groups, by management style, in 1910.

Management	White only	Black only	Mixed	Unknown
Catholic	158	8	93	1
Protestant	217	8	37	1
Jewish	21	0	0	0
Fraternal	16	0	2	0
County/City	26	1	70	0
State	1	0	16	0
Unknown	146	19	131	0
All asylums	585	36	349	2

Source: *Benevolent Institutions, 1910.*

Table A4. Number of asylums accepting children of specific racial groups, by management style, in 1923.

Management	White only	Nonwhite only	Mixed/All	Unknown
Catholic	248	27	69	1
Protestant	298	20	45	2
Jewish	40	0	0	0
Fraternal	79	3	6	2
County/City	29	1	71	0
State	7	2	16	0
Unknown	274	43	91	2
All asylums	975	96	298	7

Source: *Children Under Institutional Care, 1923.*

Table A5. Number of asylums accepting children by specific racial groups, by management style, in 1933.

Management	White only	Nonwhite only	Mixed/All	Unknown
Catholic	104	17	79	62
Protestant	205	8	47	40
Jewish	38	0	0	0
Fraternal	67	3	9	11
County/City	16	4	4	96
State	7	4	8	7
Unknown	226	54	92	113
All asylums	663	90	239	329

Source: *Children Under Institutional Care, 1933.*

Table A6. Number of asylums accepting children by gender, by management style, in 1890.

Management	Coed	Girls only	Boys only	Unknown
Catholic	72	65	35	3
Protestant	94	25	7	4
Jewish	9	0	0	0
Fraternal	3	0	0	1
County/City	68	0	2	1
State	16	0	0	0
Unknown	131	15	9	3
All asylums	393	105	53	12

Source: *Eleventh Census: 1890.*

Table A7. Number of asylums accepting children by gender, by management style, in 1910.

Management	Coed	Girls only	Boys only	Unknown
Catholic	110	77	54	19
Protestant	201	33	11	18
Jewish	19	1	0	1
Fraternal	18	0	0	0
County/City	92	0	1	4
State	16	0	0	1
Unknown	211	19	22	44
All asylums	667	130	88	87

Source: *Benevolent Institutions, 1910.*

Table A8. Number of asylums accepting children by gender, by management style, in 1923.

Management	Coed	Girls only	Boys only	Unknown
Catholic	146	107	85	7
Protestant	286	54	15	10
Jewish	39	0	1	0
Fraternal	77	1	2	10
County/City	97	1	2	1
State	22	0	2	1
Unknown	308	41	40	21
All asylums	975	204	147	50

Source: *Children Under Institutional Care, 1923.*

Table A9. Mean number of children placed in homes by asylums, by management style, in 1910.

Management	Total number of asylums that reported numbers	Number of asylums that placed children	Mean number of children placed by placing asylums
Catholic	241	106	50.9
Protestant	245	102	14.0
Jewish	20	5	78.2
Fraternal	18	5	16.2
County/City	93	75	27.1
State	16	11	137.5
Unknown	252	134	12.7
All asylums	885	438	28.6

Source: *Benevolent Institutions, 1910.*

Notes

Abbreviations

Angel Guardian	*Annual Report of the Ketteler Manual Training School for Boys and the Catharina Kasper Industrial School for Girls at the Angel Guardian Orphanage*
Brooklyn Hebrew O.A.	*Proceedings of the Annual Meeting of the Hebrew Orphan Asylum Society of the City of Brooklyn*
Brooklyn Industrial	*Annual Report of the Brooklyn Industrial School Association and Home for Destitute Children*
California CCC	*California Conference of Charities and Correction*
Chicago O.A.	*Annual Report of the Chicago Orphan Asylum*
Church Home	*Annual Report of the Church Home for Orphans and Destitute Children in Boston*
Colored O.A. of N.Y.C.	*Annual Report of the Association for the Benefit of Colored Orphans*
Colored Orphan Industrial Home	*Annual Report of the Colored Orphan Industrial Home, Lexington, Kentucky*
Dept. of Public Welfare, Connecticut	*Report of the Department of Public Welfare (Connecticut)*
Dept. of Public Welfare, Indiana	*Annual Report of the Department of Public Welfare (Indiana)*
Dept. of Public Welfare, Louisiana	*Annual Report of the State of Louisiana Department of Public Welfare*
Dept. of Social Welfare, California	*Biennial Report of the Department of Social Welfare in the State of California*

Duke Endowment	Annual Report of the Duke Endowment Orphans' Section
Eleventh Census: 1890	Report on Crime, Pauperism, and Benevolence in the United States at the Eleventh Census: 1890, Part 2, General Tables
Maria Kip	Annual Report of the Maria Kip Orphanage
Michigan State Public	Biennial Report of the Board of Control of the State Public School for Dependent Children (Michigan)
Minnesota State Public	Biennial Report of the Board of Control and Superintendent of the Minnesota State Public School for Dependent and Neglected Children
Montana State Home	Annual Report of the Superintendent of the State Orphans' Home of the State of Montana
NC Catholic	National Conference of Catholic Charities
NCCC	Proceedings of the National Conference of Charities and Correction
NCJC	National Conference of Jewish Charities
NC Jewish Social Services	National Conference of Jewish Social Services
NCSW	Proceedings of the National Conference of Social Work
New York CCC	New York Conference of Charities and Correction
Orphans' Home	Annual Report of the Orphans' Home and Asylum of the Protestant Episcopal Church in New York
Pacific Hebrew O.A.	Annual Report of the Pacific Hebrew Orphan Asylum and Home Society
Rochester O.A.	Annual Report of the Rochester Orphan Asylum
Roman Catholic O.A.s of N.Y.C	Report of the Roman Catholic Orphan Asylums of the City of New York
S.F. Presbyterian Orphanage	Annual Report of the San Francisco Presbyterian Orphanage and Farm
S.F. Protestant	Annual Report of the San Francisco Protestant Orphanage Society
State Board, Connecticut	Report of the State Board of Charities of the State of Connecticut

St. Mary's Home	*Report of St. Mary's Home for Children and Free Dispensary*
St. Mary's/Providence	*Report of St. Mary's Orphanage of Providence, Rhode Island*
White House Conference, 1909	*Proceedings of the Conference on the Care of Dependent Children* (Washington, D.C.: Government Printing Office, 1909)

Introduction

1. Of course, the majority of poor children have always lived with their own parents. And most poor children whose parents were temporarily or permanently unable to raise them have been cared for by their extended families, which in some cases included people not related by blood.
2. Michael B. Katz, *In the Shadow of the Poorhouse: A Social History of Welfare in America* (New York: Basic Books, 1987), pp. ix–xiv; Carole Haber, *Beyond Sixty-Five: The Dilemma of Old Age in America's Past* (New York: Cambridge University Press, 1983), pp. 98–99; Charles E. Rosenberg, *The Care of Strangers: The Rise of America's Hospital System* (New York: Basic Books, 1987), pp. 4–10; Ellen Dwyer, *Homes for the Mad: Life Inside Two Nineteenth-Century Asylums* (New Brunswick, N.J.: Rutgers University Press, 1987), pp. 1–2, 116.
3. Gerald N. Grob, *Mental Illness and American Society, 1875–1940* (Princeton: Princeton University Press, 1983), pp. x–xi.
4. David J. Rothman, *The Discovery of the Asylum: Social Order and Disorder in the New Republic* (Boston: Little, Brown, 1971), p. 237; Barbara M. Brenzel, *Daughters of the State: A Social Portrait of the First Reform School for Girls in North America, 1856–1905* (Cambridge: MIT University Press, 1983), pp. 5, 70; Eric M. Schneider, *In the Web of Class: Delinquents and Reformers in Boston, 1810s–1930s* (New York: New York University Press, 1992), pp. 1–33; Michael B. Katz, Michael J. Doucet, and Mark J. Stern, *The Social Organization of Early Industrial Capitalism* (Cambridge: Harvard University Press, 1982), pp. 354–355; Estelle B. Freedman, *Their Sisters' Keepers: Women's Prison Reform in America, 1830–1930* (Ann Arbor: University of Michigan Press, 1981), pp. 8–9; Rosenberg, *Care of Strangers*, pp. 290–291; Katz, *Shadow of the Poorhouse*, pp. xi–xii.
5. Schneider, *Web of Class*, p. 44.
6. Haber, *Beyond Sixty-Five*, pp. 64–93.
7. Susan Tiffin has argued that dependent children became "the subject of widespread and intensive concern toward the end of the nineteenth

century." Susan Tiffin, *In Whose Best Interest?: Child Welfare Reform in the Progressive Era* (Westport, Conn.: Greenwood Press, 1982), p. 7. While there is some truth to this, reformers hoping to improve groups or communities they found fault with—often poor immigrant communities—had been focusing on children for decades before 1900. Perhaps more importantly, communities concerned with their own future always focused on children; the surge in the building of new orphan asylums in immigrant communities in the 1830s in response to the cholera epidemic is just one example. In the late nineteenth century, state governments were becoming increasingly involved in regulating various kinds of institutions, and private organizations such as the Charity Organization Societies were becoming more centralized. Children were just one of the groups that received increased attention from government around the turn of the twentieth century.

8. Mark J. Stern, *Society and Family Strategy: Erie County, New York, 1850–1920* (Albany: State University of New York Press, 1987), pp. 136–138.
9. The literature on poverty, charity, and welfare is far too extensive to list here; some of it is cited in this work.
10. Gary Edward Polster, *Inside Looking Out: The Cleveland Jewish Orphan Asylum, 1868–1924* (Kent, Ohio: Kent State University Press, 1990) provides quite a bit of evidence about life inside that asylum, as well as detailing the influence of a succession of superintendents. Reena Sigman Friedman, *These Are Our Children: Jewish Orphanages in the United States, 1880–1925* (Hanover, N.H.: Brandeis University Press, 1994) focuses on three institutions: the same Cleveland Jewish Orphan Asylum studied by Polster, the Hebrew Orphan Asylum of New York, and the Jewish Foster Home of Philadelphia. Nurith Zmora, *Orphanages Reconsidered: Child Care Institutions in Progressive Era Baltimore* (Philadelphia: Temple University Press, 1994) focuses largely on that city's Hebrew Orphan Asylum and also has considerable evidence on the Samuel Ready School, a Protestant boarding school for poor but academically solid children of "worthy" parents, and the Dolan Home, a small Catholic institution. Kenneth Cmiel, *A Home of Another Kind: One Chicago Orphanage and the Tangle of Child Welfare* (Chicago: University of Chicago Press, 1995) examines the Chicago Nursery and Half-Orphan Asylum, later known as Chapin Hall. Cmiel focuses on the asylum's managers and their relationship with both child welfare organizations in the city and broad national trends; this study is particularly valuable in that it follows Chapin Hall's evolution into a residential treatment center in the years following World War II.
11. The works by Polster, Friedman, and Zmora cited in the previous note all began as dissertations. There are a number of useful dissertations still

out there, some of which are currently being revised for publication, that focus either fully or partially on orphanages. See Susan Lynne Porter, "The Benevolent Asylum—Image and Reality: The Care and Training of Female Orphans in Boston, 1800–1840" (Ph.D. dissertation, Boston University, 1984); Gail S. Murray, "Poverty and Its Relief in the Antebellum South. Perceptions and Realities in Three Selected Cities: Charleston, Nashville, and New Orleans" (Ph.D. dissertation, Memphis State University, 1991); Steven Edward Anders, "The History of Child Welfare in Cincinnati, 1790–1930" (Ph.D. dissertation, Miami University, 1981); Judith Ann Dulberger, "Refuge or Repressor: The Role of the Orphan Asylum in the Lives of Poor Children and Their Families in Late-Nineteenth-Century America" (Ph.D. dissertation, Carnegie-Mellon University, 1988); Catherine J. Ross, "Society's Children: The Care of Indigent Youngsters in New York City, 1875–1903" (Ph.D. dissertation, Yale University, 1977); Bernadine Courtright Barr, "Spare Children, 1900–1945: Inmates of Orphanages as Subjects of Research in Medicine and in the Social Sciences in America" (Ph.D. dissertation, Stanford University, 1992); Ruth Shackelford, "'To Shield Them from Temptation': Child-Saving Institutions and the Children of the Underclass in San Francisco, 1850–1910" (Ph.D. dissertation, Harvard University, 1991).

12. Priscilla Ferguson Clement, "Children and Charity: Orphanages in New Orleans, 1817–1914," *Louisiana History* 27, no. 4 (fall 1986), pp. 337–351; Marian J. Morton, "Homes for Poverty's Children: Cleveland's Orphanages, 1851–1933," *Ohio History* 98 (winter-spring 1989), pp. 5–22; Arthur E. Fink, "Changing Philosophies and Practices in North Carolina Orphanages," *North Carolina Historical Review* 48, no. 4 (October 1971), pp. 333–358; Marshall B. Jones, "Crisis of the American Orphanage, 1931–1940," *Social Service Review* 63, no. 4 (December 1989), pp. 613–629; Peter L. Tyor and Jamil S. Zainaldin, "Asylum and Society: An Approach to Institutional Change," *Journal of Social History* 13 (fall 1979), pp. 23–48; Susan Whitelaw Downs and Michael Sherraden, "The Orphan Asylum in the Nineteenth Century," *Social Service Review* 57 (June 1983), pp. 272–290; Jeanne Abrams, "'For a Child's Sake': The Denver Sheltering Home for Jewish Children in the Progressive Era," *American Jewish History* 79, no. 2 (winter 1989–1990), pp. 181–202; Nurith Zmora, "A Rediscovery of the Asylum: The Hebrew Orphan Asylum Through the Lives of Its First Fifty Orphans," *American Jewish History* 77, no. 3 (March 1988), pp. 452–475; Nancy J. Witmer, "The Mennonite Children's Home, 1909–1972," *Pennsylvania Mennonite Heritage* 8, no. 4, pp. 2–12; Bruce Bellingham, "Institution and Family: An Alternative View of Nineteenth-Century Child Saving," *Social Problems* 33, no. 6 (December 1986), pp. S33–S57; Gary C. Jenkins, "Almira S.

Steele and the Steele Home for Needy Children," *Tennessee Historical Quarterly* 48, no. 1 (spring 1989), pp. 29–36.

13. Tiffin, *In Whose Best Interest?*; Joan Gittens, *Poor Relations: The Children of the State in Illinois, 1818–1990* (Urbana: University of Illinois Press, 1994); and Peter C. Holloran, *Boston's Wayward Children: Social Services for Homeless Children, 1830–1930* (Cranbury, N.J.: Associated University Presses, 1989) all contain useful information on a variety of kinds of child welfare, but all misread or underestimate the role and nature of orphan asylums. Barbara L. Bellows, *Benevolence Among Slaveholders: Assisting the Poor in Charleston, 1670–1860* (Baton Rouge: Louisiana State University Press, 1993) contains a very nice chapter on the Charleston Orphan House in the first half of the nineteenth century. Probably the most insightful study of children's institutions broadly conceived is LeRoy Ashby, *Saving the Waifs: Reformers and Dependent Children, 1890–1917* (Philadelphia: Temple University Press, 1984). Ashby focuses on the Progressive Era and examines a home placement society, a national Christian agency, a newsboys' home, the almost unique Ford Republic, and the Good Will Farm—all Protestant institutions, none of which, except the last, has much in common with the thousand-plus orphan asylums spread across the nation.

14. Charles E. Rosenberg has found that Catholic and Jewish hospitals were founded in the late nineteenth century partly out of the "isolating and defensive character" of their immigrant populations. Hospital advocates did not want their Catholic or Jewish communities to have to depend on Protestant hospitals. See Rosenberg, *Care of Strangers*, p. 111.

15. One of the best examples of this argument can be found in Harold L. Wilensky, *The Welfare State and Equality: Structural and Ideological Roots of Public Expenditures* (Berkeley: University of California Press, 1975).

16. See Gaston Rimlinger, *Welfare Policy and Industrialization in Europe, America, and Russia* (New York: Wiley Press, 1971); Kirsten Gronbjerg, David Street, and Gerald D. Suttles, *Poverty and Social Change* (Chicago: University of Chicago Press, 1978).

17. Edward D. Berkowitz and Kim McQuaid, *Creating the Welfare State: The Political Economy of 20th-Century Reform*, revised edition (Lawrence: University Press of Kansas, 1992), pp. 1–9.

18. Walter Korpi, *The Democratic Class Struggle* (Boston: Routledge & Kegan Paul, 1983); John Myles, *Old Age in the Welfare State: The Political Economy of Public Pensions*, revised edition (Lawrence: University Press of Kansas, 1989).

19. Margaret Weir, Ann Shola Orloff, and Theda Skocpol, editors, *The Politics*

of *Social Policy in the United States* (Princeton: Princeton University Press, 1988), pp. 16–17; Theda Skocpol, *Protecting Soldiers and Mothers: The Political Origins of Social Policy in the United States* (Cambridge, Mass.: Belknap Press, 1992), p. 527.
20. For an excellent introduction to this literature, see Linda Gordon, editor, *Women, the State, and Welfare* (Madison: University of Wisconsin Press, 1990).
21. Katz, *Shadow of the Poorhouse*, p. xiii.
22. Ann Shola Orloff, "The Political Origins of America's Belated Welfare State," in Weir, Orloff, and Skocpol, *Politics of Social Policy*, p. 79.

1. The Growth and Triumph of an Institution

1. Michael B. Katz, *The Undeserving Poor: From the War on Poverty to the War on Welfare* (New York: Pantheon, 1989), pp. 11–12; Rothman, *Discovery of the Asylum*, pp. 5–7; Robert H. Bremner, *American Philanthropy* (Chicago: University of Chicago Press, 1960), pp. 8–15.
2. Katz, *Shadow of the Poorhouse*, pp. 13–14; Robert E. Cray Jr., *Paupers and Poor Relief in New York City and Its Environs, 1700–1830* (Philadelphia: Temple University Press, 1988), pp. 6–51; James Leiby, *Charity and Correction in New Jersey: A History of State Welfare Institutions* (New Brunswick, N.J.: Rutgers University Press, 1967), p. 10.
3. June Axinn and Herman Levin, *Social Welfare: A History of the American Response to Need* (New York: Harper & Row, 1975), p. 31; Katz, *Undeserving Poor*, pp. 12–14; Rothman, *Discovery of the Asylum*, pp. 156–157; Porter, "Benevolent Asylum," pp. 41–44; Murray, "Poverty and Its Relief in the Antebellum South," pp. 12–14; Priscilla Ferguson Clement, *Welfare and the Poor in the Nineteenth-Century City: Philadelphia, 1800–1854* (Cranbury, N.J.: Associated University Presses, 1985), p. 60; David Ward, *Poverty, Ethnicity, and the American City, 1840–1925: Changing Conceptions of the Slum and the Ghetto* (New York: Cambridge University Press, 1989), pp. 20–21.
4. Cray, *Paupers and Poor Relief*, p. 66; Katz, *Undeserving Poor*, pp. 12–15; Murray, "Poverty and Its Relief in the Antebellum South," pp. 25–29; Ronald G. Walters, *American Reformers, 1815–1860* (New York: Hill & Wang, 1978), pp. 173–176; Mary P. Ryan, *Cradle of the Middle Class: The Family in Oneida County, New York, 1790–1865* (New York: Cambridge University Press, 1981), pp. 52–53.
5. Cray, *Paupers and Poor Relief*, p. 43; Jack Larkin, *The Reshaping of Everyday Life, 1790–1840* (New York: Harper & Row, 1988), p. 14; Elizabeth Wisner, *Social Welfare in the South: From Colonial Times to World War I*

(Baton Rouge: Louisiana State University Press, 1970), pp. 12–13; Rothman, *Discovery of the Asylum,* p. 14.

6. Anders, "History of Child Welfare in Cincinnati," pp. 31–44; Porter, "Benevolent Asylum," pp. 4–5; David M. Schneider, *The History of Public Welfare in New York State, 1609–1866* (Chicago: University of Chicago Press, 1938), p. 180; Axinn and Levin, *Social Welfare,* pp. 12–13; Gittens, *Poor Relations,* p. 16; 28th *Proceedings of the National Conference of Charities and Correction* (hereafter *NCCC*) (1901), pp. 205–206.
7. Rothman, *Discovery of the Asylum,* p. 41; Schneider, *History of Public Welfare in New York State, 1609–1866,* p. 185.
8. Carl N. Degler, *At Odds: Women and the Family in America from the Revolution to the Present* (New York: Oxford University Press, 1980), pp. 66–67; Anders, "History of Child Welfare in Cincinnati," pp. 70–71; Susan Mintz and Steven Kellogg, *Domestic Revolutions: A Social History of American Family Life* (New York: The Free Press, 1988), pp. 17–21.
9. Homer Folks, *The Care of Destitute, Neglected, and Delinquent Children* (Albany: J. B. Lyon, 1900), p. 10; John O'Grady, *Catholic Charities in the United States* (Washington, D.C.: Conference of Catholic Charities, 1931), pp. 18–19.
10. Roger S. Kluttz, *The Lutheran Children's Home of the South: Seventy-Five Years of Service, 1888–1963* (Columbia, S.C.: State Printing, 1963), pp. 7–8; Folks, *Destitute, Neglected, and Delinquent Children,* p. 10; Wisner, *Social Welfare in the South,* pp. 19–21; Bremner, *American Philanthropy,* pp. 22–23.
11. Folks, *Destitute, Neglected, and Delinquent Children,* pp. 8–9; Murray, "Poverty and Its Relief in the Antebellum South," p. 144.
12. Folks, *Destitute, Neglected, and Delinquent Children,* p. 10.
13. O'Grady, *Catholic Charities in the United States,* pp. 8–21; Clement, *Welfare and the Poor,* p. 119.
14. John O'Grady has argued that asylums begun before 1840 "were largely educational, with the care of the orphan as an incident in their work." For O'Grady, it was only after 1840 that the care of orphan and half-orphan children became more central to Catholic charity. See O'Grady, *Catholic Charities in the United States,* p. 88. While education was certainly at the forefront of Catholic child welfare in the early part of the nineteenth century, caring for orphans and half-orphans was more important than O'Grady recognized. The rapid expansion of Catholic asylums in response to cholera in the early and mid-1830s was, first and foremost, an effort to provide shelter for children.
15. Hasia R. Diner, *Erin's Daughters in America: Irish Immigrant Women in the Nineteenth Century* (Baltimore: Johns Hopkins University Press, 1983),

pp. 132–133; Anders, "History of Child Welfare in Cincinnati," pp. 74–76.
16. Barbara J. Berg, *The Remembered Gate: Origins of American Feminism. The Woman and the City, 1800–1860* (New York: Oxford University Press, 1978), p. 159; Clement, *Welfare and the Poor,* p. 119; Clement, "Children and Charity," p. 340; Lori D. Ginzberg, *Women and the Work of Benevolence: Morality, Politics, and Class in the 19th-Century United States* (New Haven: Yale University Press, 1990), p. 39.
17. Anne Firor Scott, *Natural Allies: Women's Associations in American History* (Urbana: University of Illinois Press, 1991), p. 12.
18. The explosive growth of Catholic asylums mirrored the rapid growth of the nation's Catholic population. Spurred mainly by heavy immigration, the Catholic population grew dramatically before the Civil War; in the 1840s alone, the number of Catholics in the United States rose from 700,000 to 1,600,000. See Rev. Daniel T. McColgan, *A Century of Charity: The First One Hundred Years of the Society of St. Vincent de Paul in the United States,* volume 1 (Milwaukee: Bruce Publishing, 1951), p. 100.
19. Brenzel, *Daughters of the State,* pp. 22–25; Degler, *At Odds,* pp. 8–9; Bremner, *American Philanthropy,* p. 47; Ward, *Poverty, Ethnicity, and the American City,* p. 24.
20. Michael B. Katz, *Poverty and Policy in American History* (New York: Academic Press, 1983), p. 200.
21. Ira Katznelson and Margaret Weir, *Schooling for All: Class, Race, and the Decline of the Democratic Ideal* (New York: Basic Books, 1985), p. 24.
22. United States Bureau of the Census, *The Statistical History of the United States, from Colonial Times to the Present* (New York: Basic Books, 1976), p. 8; Carl F. Kaestle, *Pillars of the Republic: Common Schools and American Society, 1780–1860* (New York: Hill & Wang, 1983), p. 63; Ward, *Poverty, Ethnicity, and the American City,* p. 193.
23. Katz, Doucet, and Stern, *Social Organization,* pp. 102–103; Berg, *Remembered Gate,* p. 41; Charles E. Rosenberg, *The Cholera Years: The United States in 1832, 1849, and 1866* (Chicago: University of Chicago Press, 1962), pp. 36–37; Kathleen D. McCarthy, *Noblesse Oblige: Charity and Cultural Philanthropy in Chicago, 1849–1929* (Chicago: University of Chicago Press, 1982), p. 7; Stuart M. Blumin, *The Emergence of the Middle Class: Social Experience in the American City, 1760–1900* (Cambridge: Cambridge University Press, 1989), pp. 66–110.
24. United States Bureau of the Census, *Statistical History of the United States,* p. 12.
25. Catholic asylums were not the only ones that began as schools for poor children. Suzanne Lebsock found that the founders of the Female Orphan

Asylum of Petersburg, Virginia, first opened a school in 1812, while in the process of raising money for an asylum. See Suzanne Lebsock, *The Free Women of Petersburg: Status and Culture in a Southern Town, 1784–1860* (New York: W. W. Norton, 1984), p. 199; O'Grady, *Catholic Charities in the United States*, pp. 26–72.

26. Larkin, *Reshaping of Everyday Life*, p. 85.
27. McColgan, *Century of Charity*, volume 1, pp. 222–223; Holloran, *Boston's Wayward Children*, p. 67.
28. O'Grady, *Catholic Charities in the United States*, pp. 78–82; McColgan, *Century of Charity*, volume 1, pp. 103–105.
29. Clement, "Children and Charity," pp. 339–340; Wisner, *Social Welfare in the South*, pp. 88–89; Miriam Corcoran, "Catherine Spalding—Sister and Servant," *Filson Club History Quarterly* 62, no. 2 (April 1988), pp. 260–267; Robert L. Black, *The Cincinnati Orphan Asylum* (1952), pp. 13–17.
30. Larkin, *Reshaping of Everyday Life*, pp. 79–83.
31. Cholera first hit the United States from 1832 to 1834, then vanished until early 1849. It hit various cities until 1854, then vanished until 1866, by which time sanitation efforts in some cities had begun to dull its impact. See Rosenberg, *Cholera Years*.
32. 73rd *Annual Report of the San Francisco Protestant Orphanage Society* (hereafter *S.F. Protestant*) (1923), pp. 6–7; 80th *S.F. Protestant* (1930), p. 8; O'Grady, *Catholic Charities in the United States*, pp. 28–74; McColgan, *Century of Charity*, volume 1, pp. 123–124; Morton, "Homes for Poverty's Children," pp. 5–22; Rosenberg, *Cholera Years*, pp. 118–119; McCarthy, *Noblesse Oblige*, p. 8.
33. O'Grady, *Catholic Charities in the United States*, p. 22.
34. O'Grady, *Catholic Charities in the United States*, p. 76.
35. *History of Child Saving in the United States* (Montclair, N.J.: Paterson Smith, 1893), pp. 116–118; 1st *Annual Report of the Orphans' Home and Asylum of the Protestant Episcopal Church in New York* (hereafter *Orphans' Home*) (1852), pp. 6–7.
36. 2nd *National Conference of Jewish Charities* (hereafter *NCJC*) (1902), p. 109; Schneider, *History of Public Welfare in New York State, 1609–1866*, pp. 191, 337; *History of Child Saving*, pp. 162–165.
37. Morton, "Homes for Poverty's Children," p. 7.
38. This point is discussed at much greater length in Chapters 2 and 4.
39. William H. Slingerland, *Child Welfare Work in California: A Study of Agencies and Institutions* (New York: Russell Sage Foundation, 1915), pp. 30–109; 1st *Biennial Report of the Department of Social Welfare of the State of California* (hereafter *Dept. of Social Welfare, California*) (1927–1928), pp. 16–17.

40. Thomas Stritch, *The Catholic Church in Tennessee: The Sesquicentennial Story* (Nashville: The Catholic Center, 1987), pp. 113–116.
41. John W. Blassingame, *Black New Orleans, 1860–1880* (Chicago: University of Chicago Press, 1973), p. 13; Kathleen C. Berkeley, "'Colored Ladies Also Contributed': Black Women's Activities from Benevolence to Social Welfare, 1866–1896" in Walter J. Fraser Jr., R. Frank Saunders Jr., and Jon L. Wakelyn, editors, *The Web of Southern Social Relations: Women, Family, and Education* (Athens: University of Georgia Press, 1985), pp. 188–191.
42. Berg, *Remembered Gate*, p. 225; McColgan, *Century of Charity*, volume 1, p. 270.
43. Hospitals, which in the late nineteenth century were usually charitable institutions, also spread rapidly after the Civil War. More than most other institutions, charity hospitals shared several important traits with orphan asylums. They were run by a variety of religious groups; many were small but some were quite large; and though generally privately managed, there was considerable government involvement in their funding and management. See David Rosner, *A Once Charitable Enterprise: Hospitals and Health Care in Brooklyn and New York, 1885–1915* (New York: Cambridge University Press, 1982), pp. 16–18.
44. The Pearson correlation coefficient between the percentage of a state's population living in urban areas in 1890 and the percentage of that state's population in orphan asylums at the end of 1890 is 0.73, which shows a strong relationship between these two aspects of late-nineteenth-century life. If the five states where tax money supported a large number of asylum children—New York, California, Ohio, Connecticut, and Indiana—are removed from the equation, the correlation rises to 0.79.
45. Not all historians of urban development in the late nineteenth century have found that poverty grew concurrently. Eric Monkkonen's study of Columbus, Ohio, from 1860 to 1885 found "little or no evidence that urban growth or industrial growth affected the crime rates or poverty rates of Columbus." But Monkkonen admits that his poverty measure, the size of poorhouse populations, may not actually reveal the extent of poverty. See Eric H. Monkkonen, *The Dangerous Class: Crime and Poverty in Columbus, Ohio, 1860–1885* (Cambridge: Harvard University Press, 1975).
46. Olivier Zunz, *The Changing Face of Inequality: Urbanization, Industrial Development, and Immigrants in Detroit, 1880–1920* (Chicago: University of Chicago Press, 1982), pp. 3–5; Rosner, *Once Charitable Enterprise*, p. 27.
47. Rev. Francis Xavier Roth, *History of St. Vincent's Orphan Asylum, Tacony,*

Philadelphia: A Memoir of Its Diamond Jubilee, 1855–1933 (Philadelphia: "Nord-Amerika" Press, 1934), p. 43.
48. Jones, "Crisis of the American Orphanage," p. 615.
49. Gittens, *Poor Relations*, pp. 24–50.
50. Schneider, *History of Public Welfare in New York State, 1607–1866*, pp. 341–344; David M. Schneider and Albert Deutsch, *The History of Public Welfare in New York State, 1867–1940* (Chicago: University of Chicago Press, 1941), pp. 60–61; Katz, *Poverty and Policy*, p. 61; Bremner, *American Philanthropy*, pp. 95–96; Grob, *Mental Illness and American Society*, pp. 79–105.
51. Schneider and Deutsch, *History of Public Welfare in New York State, 1867–1940*, p. 65.
52. For example, see Dulberger, "Refuge or Repressor," pp. 21–22.
53. Leiby, *Charity and Correction in New Jersey*, p. 87.
54. 3rd NCJC (1904), pp. 64–65; 2nd *National Conference of Catholic Charities* (hereafter *NC Catholic*) (1912), pp. 50–53; George Paul Jacoby, *Catholic Child Care in Nineteenth Century New York* (1941), pp. 17–56.
55. *Report of the State Board of Charities of the State of Connecticut* (hereafter *State Board, Connecticut*) (1892), pp. 61–62.
56. Shackelford, "'To Shield Them from Temptation,'" pp. 220–221.
57. Wisner, *Social Welfare in the South*, pp. 92–93; 18th *NCCC* (1891), pp. 271–277; 19th *NCCC* (1892), p. 282.
58. 18th *NCCC* (1891), p. 274; 19th *NCCC* (1892), p. 278; Gittens, *Poor Relations*, p. 29.
59. *History of Child Saving*, pp. 204–217.
60. 14th *NCCC* (1887), p. 21; 18th *NCCC* (1891), pp. 269–273; 3rd *California Conference of Charities and Correction* (hereafter *California CCC*) (1904), p. 145; Shackelford, "'To Shield Them from Temptation,'" pp. 408–411.
61. 17th *NCCC* (1890), p. 213.
62. Dwyer, *Homes for the Mad*, p. 49.
63. If you add together the total number of asylums that Table 1.1 and Table 1.2 show as having been created by 1890, you would come to the conclusion there were 620 orphan asylums in the United States by that year. Throughout the tables for this book, however, the number given for 1890 is 563. The 1890 census shows 563, while the 1910 census, on which Tables 1.1 and 1.2 are based, claims the higher number of 620 already existed by 1890. The actual number was probably between 600 and 620; the 1890 census clearly missed some asylums. On the other hand, the founding date given in the 1910 census is sometimes misleading, as asylum managers reported the year in which an association was

formed as the date an asylum was created, when in fact the asylum may not have appeared for years.
64. McColgan, *Century of Charity,* volume 1, p. 270; Jenkins, "Almira Steele," pp. 29–31.
65. *Report on Crime, Pauperism, and Benevolence in the United States at the Eleventh Census: 1890, Part 2, General Tables* (Washington, D.C.: Government Printing Office, 1895), pp. 894–937.
66. *Eleventh Census: 1890.*
67. Witmer, "Mennonite Children's Home," pp. 2–4
68. *Eleventh Census: 1890; Benevolent Institutions, 1910* (Washington, D.C.: Government Printing Office, 1913); *Children Under Institutional Care, 1923* (Washington, D.C.: Government Printing Office, 1925); *Children Under Institutional Care and in Foster Homes, 1933* (Washington, D.C.: Government Printing Office, 1935).
69. For a related discussion of criticisms of orphan asylums and asylums' attempts to improve in response, see Chapter 5.
70. 3rd *NCJC* (1904), p. 91.
71. 4th *New York Conference of Charities and Correction* (hereafter *New York CCC*) (1903), p. 107.
72. During the same period, from the 1880s to the 1910s, "the reputation and public image of mental hospitals declined precipitously." See Grob, *Mental Illness and American Society,* pp. 4–5. As with orphan asylums, this change occurred even as the number of people within mental hospitals continued to rise. Some other institutions, such as women's prisons, continued to have reformers' support despite having failed to live up to "their founders' ideals, in large part because there were so few alternatives." See Freedman, *Their Sisters' Keepers,* p. 146.
73. *National Conference of Jewish Social Service* (hereafter *NC Jewish Social Services*) (1927), pp. 83–98. Dulberger makes the point that the wide variety of charges leveled against orphan asylums were "only somewhat diminished" by the lack of evidence to support them. See Dulberger, "Refuge or Repressor," p. 53.
74. *Proceedings of the Conference on the Care of Dependent Children* (hereafter *White House Conference, 1909*) (Washington, D.C.: Government Printing Office, 1909), pp. 6–9; Jones, "Crisis of the American Orphanage," p. 621; Skocpol, *Protecting Soldiers and Mothers,* p. 425.
75. 1st *NC Catholic* (1910), pp. 285–332.
76. Shackelford, "'To Shield Them from Temptation,'" pp. 261–263; Friedman, *These Are Our Children,* p. 56.
77. Though some historians see the 1909 conference as a major turning point, others have more accurately noted that it did not lead directly to

the closing of orphan asylums. For example, see Dulberger, "Refuge or Repressor," p. 45; 2nd *Annual Report of the Duke Endowment Orphans' Section* (hereafter *Duke Endowment*) (1926), pp. 29–34.
78. 1st *NC Catholic* (1910), p. 338; Axinn and Levin, *Social Welfare,* p. 118.
79. 3rd *NCJC* (1904), p. 205; 6th *NCJC* (1910), pp. 220–225; Shackelford, "'To Shield Them from Temptation,'" p. 184; 49th *Proceedings of the National Conference of Social Work* (hereafter *NCSW*) (1922), p. 28; 51st *NCSW* (1924), p. 130.
80. 28th *NCCC* (1901), pp. 224–226.
81. 7th *Annual Report of the Superintendent of State Orphans' Home of the State of Montana* (hereafter *Montana State Home*) (1900), p. 4.
82. *Children Under Institutional Care, 1923.*
83. Schneider, *History of Public Welfare in New York State, 1609–1866,* pp. 187–188; Katz, *Poverty and Policy,* p. 123. Bruce Bellingham, in a study of Charles Loring Brace and other child savers, has argued that their chosen course, "family destruction, was not seriously challenged until the Mothers' Pension movement of the early twentieth century." See Bruce Bellingham, "The 'Unspeakable Blessing': Street Children, Reform Rhetoric, and Misery in Early Industrial Capitalism," *Politics and Society* 12 (1983), pp. 303–330. While some orphan asylums also sought to break up families, many others directly challenged—or simply ignored—the idea of family breakup throughout the nineteenth century by seeking eventual family reconciliation. And orphan asylums dealt with far more children than groups such as the Children's Aid Society.
84. 2nd *NCJC* (1902), pp. 121–127; 7th *New York CCC* (1906), pp. 64–65.
85. June Axinn and Mark J. Stern, *Dependency and Poverty: Old Problems in a New World* (Lexington, Mass.: Lexington Books, 1988), p. 60; Linda Gordon, *Pitied But Not Entitled: Single Mothers and the History of Welfare, 1890–1935* (New York: The Free Press, 1994), p. 37; Skocpol, *Protecting Soldiers and Mothers,* p. 425.
86. Katz, *Shadow of the Poorhouse,* p. 124.
87. Shackelford, "'To Shield Them from Temptation,'" pp. 589–595; Axinn and Levin, *Social Welfare,* p. 131. Two recent, important works provide somewhat different accounts of the creation of mothers' pensions. Theda Skocpol contrasts them with pensions for Civil War veterans in Skocpol, *Protecting Soldiers and Mothers.* Linda Gordon tells the story of the fight for relief for poor women and their children from mothers' pensions to ADC in Gordon, *Pitied But Not Entitled.*
88. Katz, *Shadow of the Poorhouse,* pp. 128–129.
89. James T. Patterson, *America's Struggle Against Poverty, 1900–1980* (Cambridge: Harvard University Press, 1981), p. 27.

Notes to Pages 44–49   245

90. Skocpol, *Protecting Soldiers and Mothers,* pp. 467–472; Gordon, *Pitied But Not Entitled,* pp. 48–49.
91. 4th *NC Catholic* (1916), p. 194.
92. Schneider and Deutsch, *History of Public Welfare in New York State, 1867–1940,* pp. 256–265; Dulberger, "Refuge or Repressor," pp. 30–31; Axinn and Levin, *Social Welfare,* p. 134; Skocpol, *Protecting Soldiers and Mothers,* p. 466; Abbott, *Child and the State,* volume 2, p. 237; also see Table 1.3.
93. Michael B. Katz, "The History of an Impudent Poor Woman in New York City from 1918 to 1923" in Peter Mandler, editor, *The Uses of Charity: The Poor on Relief in the Nineteenth-Century Metropolis* (Philadelphia: University of Pennsylvania Press, 1990), pp. 242–243; Wiley Britton Sanders, *Negro Child Welfare in North Carolina* (Chapel Hill: University of North Carolina Press, 1933), pp. 162–169.
94. Kluttz, *Lutheran Children's Home,* p. 55; 84th *Annual Report of the Chicago Orphan Asylum* (hereafter *Chicago O.A.*) (1933), pp. 14–20; Jones, "Crisis of the American Orphanage," p. 624.
95. Morton, "Homes for Poverty's Children," p. 15; Anders, "History of Child Welfare in Cincinnati," pp. 206–208; Schneider, *Web of Class,* pp. 151–171; Rosner, *Once Charitable Enterprise,* pp. 94–95; McCarthy, *Noblesse Oblige,* pp. 138–139; Ward, *Poverty, Ethnicity, and the American City,* p. 123.
96. Morton, "Homes for Poverty's Children," p. 15; Polster, *Inside Looking Out,* pp. 185–196.
97. Cmiel, *Home of Another Kind,* pp. 122–125; Abrams, "'For a Child's Sake,'" p. 201; Witmer, "Mennonite Children's Home," pp. 7–8.
98. 64th *Annual Report of the Church Home for Orphan and Destitute Children in Boston* (hereafter *Church Home*) (1922), p. 6; 81st *Chicago O.A.* (1930), p. 11; Abbott, *Child and the State,* volume 2, p. 13; *Report of St. Mary's Home for Children and Free Dispensary* (hereafter *St. Mary's Home*) (1944–1946), pp. 7–11; Fink, "Changing Philosophies and Practices," p. 357.
99. This is a very different pattern than occurred with other Progressive Era innovations, which, as David Rothman writes, "often became add-ons to the system, not replacements." See David J. Rothman, *Conscience and Convenience: The Asylum and Its Alternatives in Progressive America* (Boston: Little, Brown, 1980), p. 12.
100. *Annual Report of the Department of Public Welfare* (hereafter *Dept. of Public Welfare, Indiana*) (1948), p. 914; 23rd *Annual Report of the State of Louisiana Department of Public Welfare* (hereafter *Dept. of Public Welfare, Louisiana*) (1960), pp. 12–33; 29th *Dept. of Public Welfare, Louisiana* (1966), pp. 9–10.
101. Hospitals had undergone a similar shift from religious institutions to

secular ones, though in the case of hospitals, unlike that of orphan asylums, institutional care remained a central forum. See Rosenberg, *Care of Strangers,* pp. 8–9.

102. Katz, *Shadow of the Poorhouse,* pp. 58–66; Paul Boyer, *Urban Masses and Moral Order in America, 1820–1920* (Cambridge: Harvard University Press, 1978), p. 84; United States Bureau of the Census, *Statistical History of the United States,* p. 8; Table 1.1 in this volume; Ginzberg, *Women and the Work of Benevolence,* p. 192.
103. United States Bureau of the Census, *Statistical History of the United States,* p. 8. As Table 1.1 in this chapter shows, according to the 1910 orphanage census there were 195 asylums in 1860. Table 1.2 shows that, according to the same census, another 425 asylums were built between 1860 and 1890, which would give a total of 620 asylums in 1890. But as Table 1.3 shows, according to the 1890 orphanage census, there were only 563 asylums in 1890. The actual number was somewhere between 563 and 620, though exactly where is impossible to reconstruct in the 1990s. The actual number was certainly within a few dozen of 600, and thus represented a tripling of asylums from 1860. Please see note 63.
104. United States Bureau of the Census, *Statistical History of the United States,* p. 8; Table 1.3.
105. Skocpol, *Protecting Soldiers and Mothers,* p. 472.
106. Cmiel, *Home of Another Kind,* pp. 121–131.
107. Gittens, *Poor Relations,* pp. 57–58.

2. The Changing Nature of Orphan Asylums

1. Katz, *Shadow of the Poorhouse,* p. 25.
2. Rothman, *Discovery of the Asylum,* p. 206.
3. Porter, "Benevolent Asylum," pp. 11–64, 116.
4. Porter, "Benevolent Asylum," pp. 116–117; Murray, "Poverty and Its Relief in the Antebellum South," p. 227.
5. O'Grady, *Catholic Charities in the United States,* p. 37.
6. 5th *Annual Report of the Association for the Benefit of Colored Orphans* (hereafter *Colored O.A. of N.Y.C.*) (1841), p. 5; Downs and Sherraden, "Orphan Asylum in the Nineteenth Century," pp. 277–282.
7. Anders, "History of Child Welfare in Cincinnati," p. 88; Porter, "Benevolent Asylum," pp. 110–111; Dwyer, *Homes for the Mad,* pp. 1–57.
8. Berg, *Remembered Gate,* p. 66.
9. Clement, *Welfare and the Poor,* p. 123.
10. David Rothman has detailed the Jacksonian period's shift toward institutions as the solution to crime, poverty, and insanity. He also describes the

failure of these reforms; by the Civil War era poorhouses had become even more degraded than they had been earlier in the century, and both mental hospitals and prisons had become primarily custodial institutions with little expectation of reforming their inmates. See Rothman, *Discovery of the Asylum*.

11. 6th *Orphans' Home* (1857), p. 6.
12. Bellows, *Benevolence Among Slaveholders*, pp. 132–134; 8th *Orphans' Home* (1859), p. 8.
13. As Michael Katz writes, the institutions "on which historians have focused most sharply treated deviance: mental hospitals, poorhouses, reformatories, penitentiaries." Orphan asylums had a simpler task to perform, at least partly because their task was widely seen as worthwhile. They were, like other institutions, "character-building," but that was far easier to do with children than with adults. For a discussion of institutions in the nineteenth century, see Michael B. Katz, "Origins of the Institutional State," *Marxist Perspectives* (winter 1978), pp. 6–22. For poorhouse policies, see Katz, *Shadow of the Poorhouse*, pp. xi–xii.
14. Grob, *Mental Illness and American Society*, p. 167; 18th *NCCC* (1891), p. 151; Katz, *Shadow of the Poorhouse*, p. 55.
15. Katz, *Poverty and Policy*, p. 132.
16. 9th Annual Report of the Brooklyn Industrial School Association and Home for Destitute Children (hereafter *Brooklyn Industrial*) (1863), p. 6.
17. 13th *Brooklyn Industrial* (1867), p. 12; Dulberger, "Refuge or Repressor," pp. 47–48; Clement, "Children and Charity," p. 145.
18. 16th *Orphans' Home* (1867), p. 9; Jacoby, *Catholic Child Care*, pp. 110–111.
19. 25th *Chicago O.A.* (1874), p. 4; 1st Annual Report of the Maria Kip Orphanage (hereafter *Maria Kip*) (1890), p. 13; 2nd *NCJC* (1902), pp. 120–121; Jacoby, *Catholic Child Care*, pp. 202–238.
20. 20th *Brooklyn Industrial* (1874), p. 21.
21. 10th *Orphans' Home* (1861), pp. 9–10.
22. Grob, *Mental Illness and American Society*, p. 246; 6th *Maria Kip* (1895), p. 5.
23. Blassingame, *Black New Orleans*, pp. 168–171; Katz, *Shadow of the Poorhouse*, p. 61; Polster, *Inside Looking Out*, p. 85; Friedman, *These Are Our Children*, p. 149; Ross, "Society's Children," p. 149.
24. 36th *Orphans' Home* (1887), p. 9. Emphasis is in the original.
25. Michael Katz writes that "only in the 1870s, when environmentally based policy seemed to have failed, did hereditarian theory begin to dominate explanations of deviance and dependency." See Katz, *Poverty and Policy*, p. 177. By and large, however, reformers continued to see poor children

as needing to be saved. It was the belief that children, unlike their parents, could become self-supporting, honest citizens that caused the argument between institution advocates and placing-out advocates to last for decades.

26. Cmiel, *Home of Another Kind*, pp. 14–15.
27. Of course, many poor children worked much of the time, often in place of attending school.
28. Friedman, *These Are Our Children*, p. 8.
29. 14th *NCCC* (1887), p. 237.
30. For discussions of how the shift to integrative asylums played out in several arenas, see Chapters 5, 6, and 7.
31. Brenzel, *Daughters of the State*, p. 5.
32. Katz, Doucet, and Stern, *Social Organization*, p. 355.
33. Roy Lubove, *The Professional Altruist: The Emergence of Social Work as a Career, 1880–1930* (Cambridge: Harvard University Press, 1965), pp. 55–84; McCarthy, *Noblesse Oblige*, pp. 138–139.
34. The first need cited by the speaker, Elsa Ueland, was for a home, and the second was for a measure of success. See 51st *NCSW* (1924), pp. 128–129.
35. Cmiel, *Home of Another Kind*, pp. 50–53.
36. 5th *Annual Report of the San Francisco Presbyterian Orphanage and Farm* (hereafter *Presbyterian Orphanage*) (1900), p. 30; Kluttz, *Lutheran Children's Home*, p. 37; 11th *Montana State Home* (1904), p. 9.
37. *St. Mary's Home* (1924), p. 4; 27th *NCCC* (1900), p. 228; 15th *Montana State Home* (1908), pp. 6–9.
38. The committee argued that Jewish children in institutions were almost always there because of poverty rather than neglect or abandonment, a sharp contrast with the harsh view usually expressed toward parents of institutionalized children at the National Conference of Charities and Corrections. 2nd *NCJC* (1902), p. 120; 3rd *NCJC* (1904), p. 89; 6th *NCJC* (1910), p. 230; 51st *NCSW* (1924), pp. 139–141; 2nd *NC Catholic* (1912), p. 198.
39. 5th *Presbyterian Orphanage* (1900), p. 20.
40. 73rd *S.F. Protestant* (1923), p. 17.
41. 33rd *Presbyterian Orphanage* (1928), p. 30; 66th *Annual Report of the Ketteler Manual Training School for Boys and the Catharina Kasper Industrial School for Girls at the Angel Guardian Orphanage* (hereafter *Angel Guardian*) (1930).
42. 1st *NC Catholic* (1910), p. 307; 2nd *NC Catholic* (1912), pp. 248–250.
43. 74th *S.F. Protestant* (1924), p. 25; 2nd *NC Catholic* (1912), pp. 194–242; Morton, "Homes for Poverty's Children," p. 17.

44. Abrams, "For a Child's Sake," p. 186.
45. 84th *Chicago O.A.* (1933), p. 24.
46. Porter, "Benevolent Asylum," p. 123.
47. 22nd *Brooklyn Industrial* (1876), p. 17.
48. Dulberger, "Refuge or Repressor," p. 83.
49. 9th *NC Catholic* (1923), p. 112.
50. 48th *NCSW* (1921), pp. 81–82.

3. Managers and Funding

1. McCarthy, *Noblesse Oblige*, p. 4.
2. Berg, *Remembered Gate*, pp. 147–154.
3. Schneider, *History of Public Welfare in New York State, 1607–1866*, p. 189; Lebsock, *Free Women of Petersburg*, pp. 200–201; Berg, *Remembered Gate*, p. 164.
4. Lebsock, *Free Women of Petersburg*, p. 210; see also Berg, *Remembered Gate*, pp. 145–161.
5. Nancy A. Hewitt, *Women's Activism and Social Change: Rochester, New York, 1822–1872* (Ithaca: Cornell University Press, 1984), p. 40.
6. Hewitt, *Women's Activism*, pp. 88–94.
7. Degler, *At Odds*, pp. 298–301; McCarthy, *Noblesse Oblige*, pp. 4–5; Ginzberg, *Women and the Work of Benevolence*, p. 1; Lebsock, *Free Women of Petersburg*, pp. 200–210; Katz, *Shadow of the Poorhouse*, pp. 64–65.
8. Berg, *Remembered Gate*, p. 68.
9. Ann Firor Scott, "Women's Voluntary Associations: From Reform to Charity" in Kathleen D. McCarthy, *Lady Bountiful Revisited: Women, Philanthropy, and Power* (New Brunswick, N.J.: Rutgers University Press, 1990), pp. 35–54.
10. Murray, "Poverty and Its Relief in the Antebellum South," pp. 210–216.
11. O'Grady, *Catholic Charities in the United States*, p. 23; Roth, *History of St. Vincent's*, pp. 29–30.
12. O'Grady, *Catholic Charities in the United States*, pp. 30–83; Roth, *History of St. Vincent's*, p. 17.
13. Anders, "History of Child Welfare in Cincinnati," pp. 82–83; 5th *Colored O.A. of N.Y.C.* (1841); 13th *Colored O.A. of N.Y.C.* (1849); 2nd *Orphans' Home* (1853), pp. 10–11.
14. 3rd *Orphans' Home* (1854), pp. 6–7.
15. 3rd *Church Home* (1860); Hewitt, *Women's Activism and Social Change*, p. 155; Porter, "Benevolent Asylum," pp. 78–104. See also Ginzberg, *Women and the Work of Benevolence*, p. 127.
16. Lebsock, *Free Women of Petersburg*, p. 198.

17. Rachel B. Marks, "Institutions for Dependent and Delinquent Children: Histories, Nineteenth-Century Statistics, and Recurring Goals" in Donnell M. Pappenfort, Dee Morgan Kilpatrick, and Robert W. Roberts, editors, *Child Caring: Social Policy and the Institution* (Chicago: Aldine Publishing, 1973), p. 51; McCarthy, *Noblesse Oblige*, p. 8.
18. 2nd *Orphans' Home* (1853), p. 3; Black, *Cincinnati Orphan Asylum*, p. 133.
19. Barbara L. Bellows, "'My Children, Gentlemen, Are My Own': Poor Women, the Urban Elite, and the Bonds of Obligation in Antebellum Charleston" in Fraser, Saunders, and Wakelyn, *Web of Southern Social Relations*, pp. 52–71.
20. *Report of St. Mary's Orphanage of Providence, Rhode Island* (hereafter *St. Mary's/Providence*) (1897), p. 12; Cmiel, *Home of Another Kind*, pp. 17–30.
21. 25th *Chicago O.A.* (1874), pp. 3–11; 37th *Chicago O.A.* (1886).
22. Roth, *History of St. Vincent's*, pp. 30–35; *Report of the Roman Catholic Orphan Asylums of the City of New York* (hereafter *Roman Catholic O.A.s of N.Y.C.*) (1874); Kluttz, *Lutheran Children's Home*, p. 17.
23. 16th *Proceedings of the Annual Meeting of the Hebrew Orphan Asylum Society of the City of Brooklyn* (hereafter *Brooklyn Hebrew O.A.*) (1894).
24. Zmora, *Orphanages Reconsidered*, p. 23.
25. 16th *Brooklyn Hebrew O.A.* (1894), pp. 15–21.
26. Friedman, *These Are Our Children*, pp. 11–12.
27. 44th *Chicago O.A.* (1893), pp. 23–24; 45th *Chicago O.A.* (1894), p. 22; Roth, *History of St. Vincent's*, p. 97.
28. Zmora, *Orphanages Reconsidered*, p. 25; Gittens, *Poor Relations*, p. 25.
29. 17th *Brooklyn Hebrew O.A.* (1895), p. 17.
30. Freedman, *Their Sisters' Keepers*, pp. 77–78.
31. 27th *Orphans' Home* (1878), pp. 8–9; 25th *Chicago O.A.* (1874).
32. Ross, "Society's Children," p. 71.
33. 58th *Chicago O.A.* (1907), pp. 7–8; 71st *Brooklyn Industrial* (1924), p. 3.
34. *State Board, Connecticut* (1904), p. 352.
35. 52nd *Angel Guardian* (1916), pp. 6–9; 68th *Angel Guardian* (1932).
36. 73rd *S.F. Protestant* (1923), pp. 2–4; 74th *S.F. Protestant* (1924), p. 32; *St. Mary's Home* (1905); Sanders, *Negro Child Welfare*, pp. 72–75.
37. Bremner, *American Philanthropy*, p. 115; McCarthy, *Noblesse Oblige*, pp. 10–11.
38. 80th *S.F. Protestant* (1930), p. 21; Cmiel, *Home of Another Kind*, p. 90; Sanders, *Negro Child Welfare*, pp. 131–132; McCarthy, *Noblesse Oblige*, p. 142; 33rd *Presbyterian Orphanage* (1928), pp. 30–42.
39. Sanders, *Negro Child Welfare*, p. 76.
40. Witmer, "Mennonite Children's Home," p. 9.
41. Fink, "Changing Philosophies and Practices," p. 355.

42. Cmiel, *Home of Another Kind*, p. 112.
43. O'Grady, *Catholic Charities in the United States*, p. 22; Black, *Cincinnati Orphan Asylum*, p. 30; Hewitt, *Women's Activism and Social Change*, p. 115.
44. 1st *Orphans' Home* (1852), p. 11.
45. Blassingame, *Black New Orleans*, pp. 169–170.
46. Both asylums had begun by accepting both boys and girls, despite the fact that the Sisters of Charity in France "did not accept boys." As the two asylums became crowded, however, they changed their admissions policies so that they accepted only girls, thus helping to create the need for the founding of St. Vincent's Male Orphan Asylum in 1836. See Roth, *History of St. Vincent's*, p. 15.
47. Roth, *History of St. Vincent's*, p. 15.
48. 9th *Orphans' Home* (1860), pp. 8–9.
49. Folks, *Destitute, Neglected, and Delinquent Children*, p. 23; Murray, "Poverty and Its Relief in the Antebellum South," p. 168. Orphan asylums were not the only institutions that mixed private and public funding, nor did this only occur in predominantly "private" institutions. For example, the State Industrial School for Girls in Lancaster, Massachusetts, a "public" reform school, was founded in the 1850s with both public and private money. See Brenzel, *Daughters of the State*, pp. 42–43.
50. Black, *Cincinnati Orphan Asylum*, pp. 30–43.
51. Wisner, *Social Welfare in the South*, p. 92.
52. Schneider, *History of Public Welfare in New York State, 1607–1866*, pp. 338–339; 1st *New York CCC* (1900), pp. 132–133.
53. Similarly, before the 1890s, "charity hospitals traditionally depended upon a number of diverse sources for their financial support." See Rosner, *Once Charitable Enterprise*, pp. 36–43.
54. 1st *Maria Kip* (1890), p. 7; 2nd *Maria Kip* (1891), p. 6; 7th *Maria Kip* (1896), p. 6.
55. *Roman Catholic O.A.s of N.Y.C.* (1876), p. 12; 16th *Brooklyn Hebrew O.A.* (1894), p. 23; 21st *Brooklyn Hebrew O.A.* (1899), p. 21.
56. 3rd *Annual Report of the Colored Orphan Industrial Home, Lexington, Kentucky* (hereafter *Colored Orphan Industrial Home*) (1896), p. 7.
57. 2nd *Maria Kip* (1891); Cmiel, *Home of Another Kind*, p. 21.
58. 2nd *Maria Kip* (1891); 3rd *Maria Kip* (1892), p. 7; 20th *Brooklyn Industrial* (1874), p. 26; 22nd *Orphans' Home* (1873), p. 8; Jacoby, *Catholic Child Care*, p. 216; Roth, *History of St. Vincent's*, p. 37. See also Cmiel, *Home of Another Kind*, p. 21.
59. 38th *Chicago O.A.* (1887), p. 29.
60. 31st *Chicago O.A.* (1881), p. 20.
61. 9th *Maria Kip* (1898), p. 9; 20th *Orphans' Home* (1871), p. 7.

62. Cmiel, *Home of Another Kind*, pp. 32–33.
63. 38th *Brooklyn Industrial* (1892), pp. 36–55; *Roman Catholic O.A.s of N.Y.C.* (1876), p. 12; Roth, *History of St. Vincent's*, pp. 26–60.
64. 28th *Chicago O.A.* (1877), p. 15.
65. 16th *Brooklyn Hebrew O.A.* (1894), p. 10; 17th *Brooklyn Hebrew O.A.* (1895), p. 12; 19th *Brooklyn Hebrew O.A.* (1897), p. 11.
66. 3rd *Maria Kip* (1892), p. 4.
67. 19th *Brooklyn Hebrew O.A.* (1897), pp. 11–71; Roth, *History of St. Vincent's*, pp. 53–59; Stritch, *Catholic Church in Tennessee*, pp. 114–116; Michael E. Engh, S.J., *Frontier Faiths: Church, Temple, and Synagogue in Los Angeles, 1846–1888* (Albuquerque: University of New Mexico Press, 1992), p. 83.
68. 2nd *Maria Kip* (1891), pp. 11–12; 39th *Chicago O.A.* (1888), p. 20.
69. 2nd *Maria Kip* (1891), pp. 4–8.
70. 1st *Maria Kip* (1890), pp. 4–7; 2nd *Maria Kip* (1891), p. 8.
71. Rosner, *Once Charitable Enterprise*, p. 46; 5th *Maria Kip* (1894), pp. 3–4; 7th *Maria Kip* (1896), pp. 3–5.
72. 5th *Presbyterian Orphanage* (1900), p. 34; *St. Mary's Home* (1923), pp. 21–26.
73. 80th *S.F. Protestant* (1930), pp. 25–26; 33rd *Presbyterian Orphanage* (1928), p. 25; 61st *Angel Guardian* (1925), p. 34; *St. Mary's Home* (1906), pp. 20–21.
74. Zmora, *Orphanages Reconsidered*, p. 28.
75. Lubove, *Professional Altruist*, pp. 183–219; Patterson, *America's Struggle Against Poverty*, pp. 25–26.
76. Anders, "History of Child Welfare in Cincinnati," p. 204.
77. 1st *Duke Endowment* (1925), p. 37.
78. Roth, *History of St. Vincent's*, pp. 54–91.
79. 28th *NCCC* (1901), pp. 214–215; Shackelford, "'To Shield Them from Temptation,'" pp. 483–593.
80. 47th *NCSW* (1920), pp. 133–135; 48th *NCSW* (1921), p. 222.
81. 33rd *Presbyterian Orphanage* (1928), p. 27.
82. Katz, "History of an Impudent Poor Woman" in Mandler, *Uses of Charity*, p. 227; 2nd *NC Catholic* (1912), pp. 222–223.
83. 17th *NCCC* (1890), pp. 202–205; 19th *NCCC* (1892), pp. 200–201.
84. Jacoby, *Catholic Child Care*, pp. 50–51.

4. Through the Asylum Doors

1. For a superb discussion of the impact of, and changing views about, unemployment, see Alexander Keyssar, *Out of Work: The First Century of Unemployment in Massachusetts* (Cambridge: Cambridge University Press,

1986). Also see Blumin, *Emergence of the Middle Class*, pp. 109–110. Illness was also a constant threat to working-class families' ability to remain financially independent. More than half of the inmates of poorhouses in New York from 1875 to 1894 were institutionalized due to illness. See Katz, *Poverty and Policy*, p. 126. Middle-class families also resorted to institutions when they were no longer able to handle the problems of family members. Ellen Dwyer has found that patients were brought to insane asylums by their relatives as a last resort. See Dwyer, *Homes for the Mad*, pp. 87–91.
2. Katz, *Shadow of the Poorhouse*, p. 9; Katz, Doucet, and Stern, *Social Organization*, pp. 6–7; Ross, "Society's Children," p. 46; Schlereth, *Victorian America*, p. 77.
3. 26th *Brooklyn Industrial* (1880), pp. 15–16.
4. 26th *Brooklyn Industrial* (1880), pp. 15–16; Cmiel, *Home of Another Kind*, p. 20. Among the unusual characteristics of the Chicago Nursery and Half-Orphan Asylum were its insistence that parents pay a relatively high board rate for their children, its focus on children of preschool age (the average age of its children was five and a half, several years younger than that of most asylums), and the relatively short stays of most of its children. It is a good example of the variety of orphan asylums in the late nineteenth century; there was no one "typical" asylum, but instead several general kinds of asylums, each of which was by no means a hard-and-fast box into which hundreds of asylums fit.
5. Eric Monkkonen writes about entrants to Columbus, Ohio's poorhouse in the late nineteenth century that "A skilled job, moderate income, and small amount of property may not have been enough to preserve a person from the threat of destitution, as it may be today." Monkkonen hits on a basic fact of life for the working class that few middle-class Americans have understood over the past century or more: a willingness to work, and even some success at holding a job or series of jobs, may not be enough to prevent a slide into poverty. See Monkkonen, *Dangerous Class*, p. 144.
6. Keyssar, *Out of Work*, p. 153; Friedman, *These Are Our Children*, p. 159.
7. Michael Katz argues that in the early twentieth century, the "sources of relief were landmarks on a complex topographical map that poor people had to learn to read to survive. The rules for the journey were as important as the locations of the aid." See Katz, "History of an Impudent Poor Woman" in Mandler, *Uses of Charity*, p. 228. In the middle of the nineteenth century, the map was certainly less complex, but poor people already understood its importance.
8. Bellingham, "Institution and Family," pp. 43–46; Bruce Bellingham, "Waifs and Strays: Child Abandonment, Foster Care, and Families in

Mid-Nineteenth-Century New York" in Mandler, *Uses of Charity,* pp. 123–160.

9. Brenzel, *Daughters of the State,* p. 7.
10. Lynn Hollen Lees, "The Survival of the Unfit: Welfare Policies and Family Maintenance in Nineteenth-Century London" in Mandler, *Uses of Charity,* pp. 68–91.
11. 33rd *Presbyterian Orphanage* (1928), p. 21; 80th *S.F. Protestant* (1930), p. 24; Gordon, *Pitied But Not Entitled,* p. 20; Elaine Tyler May, *Great Expectations: Marriage and Divorce in Post-Victorian America* (Chicago: University of Chicago Press, 1980), p. 2; Schlereth, *Victorian America,* p. 288; Holloran, *Boston's Wayward Children,* p. 77.
12. Elias L. Trotzkey, *Institutional Care and Placing Out: The Place of Each in the Care of Dependent Children* (Chicago: Marks Nathan Jewish Orphan Home, 1930), p. 86.
13. At the same time, many of the children in state-managed institutions for "delinquent" girls were also court placements. Courts were involved in placing children in institutions long before the creation of juvenile courts in the Progressive Era. See Brenzel, *Daughters of the State,* p. 12; Rothman, *Conscience and Convenience,* pp. 205–235; Black, *Cincinnati Orphan Asylum,* pp. 103–105; Jacoby, *Catholic Child Care,* p. 222.
14. Jacoby, *Catholic Child Care,* pp. 222–234; Ross, "Society's Children," p. 26.
15. Catholic children were accepted by a nearby Catholic orphan asylum, which also received county payments. See 22nd *Brooklyn Industrial* (1876), pp. 19–20; 23rd *Brooklyn Industrial* (1877), p. 13.
16. 49th *NCSW* (1922), pp. 145–147.
17. 55th *Angel Guardian* (1919), p. 25.
18. Porter, "Benevolent Asylum," pp. 138–139.
19. How closely the New York Orphan Asylum actually followed its stated policy of sending children with living parents to the almshouse is difficult to say. At the same time it had this rule, the asylum also announced proudly that it had never denied admission to a destitute child. Jacoby, *Catholic Child Care,* pp. 60–114.
20. This may have been more true of Protestant and "nonsectarian" asylums than of southern Catholic asylums, most of which almost certainly accepted at least some half-orphans.
21. Kluttz, *Lutheran Children's Home,* pp. 23–24; 4th *Colored Orphan Industrial Home* (1897), p. 23; Fink, "Changing Philosophies and Practices," p. 340.
22. 1st *Orphans' Home* (1852), p. 7.
23. Priscilla Ferguson Clement found a similar pattern in her study of several New Orleans asylums, where "only in the antebellum era were many" of

the children accepted into asylums full orphans. See Clement, "Children and Charity," p. 344; 16th *Brooklyn Hebrew O.A.* (1894), p. 11. Admissions standards also fluctuated in response to economic conditions and to an asylum's fortunes. For example, after the Civil War ended the Cincinnati Orphan Asylum gave priority to orphans, with "the merely destitute to fill in the vacancies." But in the depression of the 1870s, the asylum's managers "were forced again to open wide the doors" just as they had done during the war. See Black, *Cincinnati Orphan Asylum*, pp. 118–119.

24. *Roman Catholic O.A.s of N.Y.C.* (1874).
25. 4th *Colored Orphan Industrial Home* (1897); 50th *Brooklyn Industrial* (1904), p. 72; Hewitt, *Women's Activism and Social Change*, p. 204.
26. John H. Ehrenreich, *The Altruistic Imagination: A History of Social Work and Social Policy in the United States* (Ithaca: Cornell University Press, 1985), p. 43.
27. Ehrenreich, *Altruistic Imagination*, p. 62.
28. Downs and Sherraden, "Orphan Asylum in the Nineteenth Century," p. 280; Keyssar, *Out of Work*, p. 40; Jacoby, *Catholic Child Care*, pp. 229–230; Fink, "Changing Philosophies and Practices," p. 336.
29. *State Board, Connecticut* (1892), pp. 55, 142.
30. 7th *Montana State Home* (1900), p. 6.
31. Polster, *Inside Looking Out*, p. 185.
32. *State Board, Connecticut* (1904), pp. 343–352.
33. *St. Mary's/Providence* (1903), pp. 11–13.
34. 46th *Chicago O.A.* (1895), p. 24.
35. Ashby, *Saving the Waifs*, p. 133; Cmiel, *Home of Another Kind*, p. 1; *Report of the Department of Public Welfare* (hereafter *Dept. of Public Welfare, Connecticut*) (1930), p. 194.
36. Porter, "Benevolent Asylum," p. 63.
37. 2nd *NCJC* (1902), p. 110; 52nd *Angel Guardian* (1916), p. 3; Clement, "Children and Charity," p. 342; 10th *Brooklyn Industrial* (1864); 9th *Orphans' Home* (1860), p. 10; 5th *Presbyterian Orphanage* (1900), p. 43; 4th *Colored Orphan Industrial Home* (1897); 1st *Duke Endowment* (1926), p. 48. Around the turn of the century, placing agencies may have focused on slightly older children. The median age of children placed by the New York Children's Aid Society was thirteen, with only 15 percent of their children being ten or younger. See Bellingham, "Institution and Family," p. S47.
38. *St. Mary's Home* (1907), p. 5; *St. Mary's Home* (1914), p. 7.
39. Many recipients of welfare and charity used the relief system quite actively. For example, see Katz, *Poverty and Policy*, pp. 41–42.
40. 33rd *Presbyterian Orphanage* (1928), p. 41.

41. 80th *S.F. Protestant* (1930), p. 23.
42. Roth, *History of St. Vincent's*, p. 63; 2nd *Orphans' Home* (1853), p. 8.
43. 55th *Angel Guardian* (1919), p. 25; 56th *Angel Guardian* (1920), p. 25; 66th *Angel Guardian* (1930).
44. Holloran, *Boston's Wayward Children*, p. 46; Morton, "Homes for Poverty's Children," p. 18; Ward, *Poverty, Ethnicity, and the American City*, p. 199. This kind of extensive racism existed in child placement as well. As Marilyn Holt writes, "For 'colored children,' as well as the Chinese, American Indian, Spanish, Turkish, and Slavic children, there was virtually no placing out." Holt, *Orphan Trains*, p. 71.
45. Hewitt, *Women's Activism and Social Change*, pp. 175–239.
46. The asylums listed as caring for "all ethnic and racial types" actually split into two categories. Some were public asylums, mainly in Ohio and Connecticut, that seem to have genuinely accepted children of both races as regular policy; many of these asylums held more than just one or two black children. The other asylums listed as accepting all races held just one or two black children at the time of the census. These latter institutions were mostly Catholic asylums where, apparently, desperate enough cases were accepted regardless of race, at least temporarily.
47. Cmiel, *Home of Another Kind*, p. 126.
48. Diner, *Erin's Daughters*, p. 133.
49. Jacoby, *Catholic Child Care*, pp. 91–112; Porter, "Benevolent Asylum," p. 88.
50. Jacoby, *Catholic Child Care*, pp. 91–112.
51. 1st *Maria Kip* (1890), pp. 18–19.
52. 4th *NC Catholic* (1916), p. 173.
53. 52nd *NCSW* (1925), p. 88.
54. Trotzkey, *Institutional Care and Placing-Out*, p. 82; 81st *S.F. Protestant* (1931), p. 15.
55. Lebsock, *Free Women of Petersburg*, pp. 200–201.
56. Bellows, *Benevolence Among Slaveholders*, p. 127; 25th *Chicago O.A.* (1874), p. 5.
57. 25th *Chicago O.A.* (1874), pp. 11–12.
58. 25th *Chicago O.A.* (1874), pp. 11–12; 10th *Brooklyn Industrial* (1864); 2nd *Church Home* (1859); 18th *Church Home* (1875), p. 27; Roth, *History of St. Vincent's*, p. 63.
59. *State Board, Connecticut* (1912), pp. 108–109; 51st *NCSW* (1924), pp. 142–143. David Rothman has argued that child-care organizations supported the creation of juvenile courts and sought greater legal control over children through such courts. While some orphan asylums may have done so, Rothman's argument fits child-placing agencies and homes for

delinquent children far better than it fits institutions for dependent children, which usually tried to maintain control over their own admission policies. See Rothman, *Conscience and Convenience,* pp. 226–229.
60. Porter, "Benevolent Asylum," pp. 168–170; 10th *Brooklyn Industrial* (1864); Black, *Cincinnati Orphan Asylum,* p. 146; 18th *Church Home* (1875), p. 28; 46th *Chicago O.A.* (1895), p. 26.
61. 13th *New York CCC* (1912), p. 63.
62. 33rd *Presbyterian Orphanage* (1928).
63. 3rd *Maria Kip* (1892), p. 3; Roth, *History of St. Vincent's,* p. 64.
64. Schlereth, *Victorian America,* p. 277.
65. Porter, "Benevolent Asylum," pp. 281–282.
66. Clement, "Children and Charity," pp. 146–147; Dulberger, "Refuge or Repressor," pp. 160–162; Downs and Sherraden, "Orphan Asylum in the Nineteenth Century," p. 281.
67. Ross, "Society's Children," pp. 89–90.
68. 80th *S.F. Protestant* (1930), p. 26; Jones, "Crisis of the American Orphanage," pp. 618–623; Polster, *Inside Looking Out,* p. 86.
69. 82nd *S.F. Protestant* (1932), p. 21; Dulberger, "Refuge or Repressor," pp. 168–172.
70. Dulberger, "Refuge or Repressor," pp. 139–141.
71. Katz, *Poverty and Policy,* pp. 83–84.
72. Walters, *American Reformers,* p. 205.
73. Holt, *Orphan Trains,* pp. 33, 178–179.
74. Wisner, *Social Welfare in the South,* pp. 12–15; Jacoby, *Catholic Child Care,* p. 92; Murray, "Poverty and Its Relief," p. 232; Porter, "Benevolent Asylum," pp. 172–282; Lebsock, *Free Women of Petersburg,* p. 201.
75. Porter, "Benevolent Asylum," pp. 231–249; Polster, *Inside Looking Out,* pp. 114–115.
76. Porter, "Benevolent Asylum," pp. 269–282.
77. 25th *Chicago O.A.* (1874), pp. 5–10; Dulberger, "Refuge or Repressor," pp. 112–113. Other nineteenth-century institutions for children used indenture even more frequently than did orphan asylums. See Brenzel, *Daughters of the State,* pp. 72–73.
78. Anders, "History of Child Welfare in Cincinnati," p. 84.
79. Murray, "Poverty and Its Relief in the Antebellum South," pp. 212–217.
80. Jacoby, *Catholic Child Care,* p. 119; 1st *Maria Kip* (1890), p. 19; Roth, *History of St. Vincent's,* pp. 64–65.
81. Jacoby, *Catholic Child Care,* pp. 115–117; Anders, "History of Child Welfare in Cincinnati," p. 195; Downs and Sherraden, "Orphan Asylum in the Nineteenth Century," pp. 272–290; Schneider, *Web of Class,* pp. 82–83.

82. Engh, *Frontier Faiths*, pp. 158–160; Katz, Doucet, and Stern, *Social Organization*, pp. 97–101.
83. Zmora, *Orphanages Reconsidered*, p. 161; 4th *NC Catholic* (1916), p. 198.
84. Viviana A. Zelizer, *Pricing the Priceless Child: The Changing Social Value of Children* (New York: Basic Books, 1985).
85. *State Board, Connecticut* (1892), p. 60.
86. 47th *Chicago O.A.* (1896), p. 16; 55th *Chicago O.A.* (1904), p. 14; Jacoby, *Catholic Child Care*, p. 217.
87. 13th *NCCC* (1886), pp. 158–161.
88. 13th *NCCC* (1886), p. 129; Friedman, *These Are Our Children*, p. 52.
89. 51st *NCSW* (1924), pp. 122–123; 4th *NC Catholic* (1916), pp. 184–185.
90. Porter, "Benevolent Asylum," pp. 197–198; 41st *Annual Report of the Rochester Orphan Asylum* (hereafter *Rochester O.A.*) (1879), p. 9; *St. Mary's/Providence* (1903), p. 19.
91. 38th *Presbyterian Orphanage* (1928), pp. 30–31; 81st *Chicago O.A.* (1930), p. 9.
92. 9th *NC Catholic* (1923), pp. 148–154.
93. *St. Mary's Home* (1944–1946), pp. 7–10; 94th *Chicago O.A.* (1944), pp. 8–10; Witmer, "Mennonite Children's Home," pp. 4–5.
94. Porter, "Benevolent Asylum," pp. 195–197.
95. 15th *Orphans' Home* (1866), p. 8; 29th *Orphans' Home* (1880), p. 8; 36th *Orphans' Home* (1887), p. 7; Jacoby, *Catholic Child Care*, p. 120; 2nd *Maria Kip* (1891), p. 4; 10th *Maria Kip* (1899), p. 61; Dulberger, "Refuge or Repressor," pp. 150–151; 47th *Chicago O.A.* (1896), p. 31; 52nd *Angel Guardian* (1916), p. 13; 53rd *Angel Guardian* (1917), pp. 2–7.
96. Katz, Doucet, and Stern, *Social Organization*, pp. 244–284.
97. 7th *State Board, California* (1916), pp. 118–119.
98. 81st *S.F. Protestant* (1931), p. 15.

5. Routine, Discipline, and Improvement in Asylum Life

1. Porter, "Benevolent Asylum," pp. 135–136.
2. Polster, *Inside Looking Out*, pp. 21–22.
3. Roth, *History of St. Vincent's*, p. 65.
4. Kluttz, *Lutheran Children's Home*, pp. 38–43.
5. Schneider, *Web of Class*, p. 48. Girls in reformatories faced similarly restricted schedules. In the 1850s, the children of the State Industrial School for Girls in Lancaster, Massachusetts, had this daily agenda: wake at 6:00 A.M., clean and dress, clean their rooms, have breakfast at 7:00, do housework until 9:00, have a religious service, work (either at "labor" or domestic duties) until noon, eat dinner, school from 1:30 P.M. until 4:30, supper at 5:00, followed by sewing, knitting, and reading in the

workroom until 8:00, say prayers, then bedtime. At some point in the midst of this schedule, time was allowed for exercise outside. See Brenzel, *Daughters of the State,* pp. 74–75.
6. Polster, *Inside Looking Out,* p. 12; Ross, "Society's Children," pp. 76–77; Cmiel, *Home of Another Kind,* p. 27.
7. Porter, "Benevolent Asylum," pp. 134–135; Black, *Cincinnati Orphan Asylum,* pp. 26–27; 26th *Chicago O.A.* (1875); *Biennial Report of the Board of Control of the State Public School for Dependent Children* (hereafter *Michigan State Public*) (1881–1882), p. 33; 8th *Biennial Report of the Board of Control and Superintendent of the Minnesota State Public School for Dependent and Neglected Children* (hereafter *Minnesota State Public*) (1889–1900), p. 16; Friedman, *These Are Our Children,* p. 41.
8. 3rd *Church Home* (1860); *St. Mary's Home* (1906).
9. 6th *Colored O.A. of N.Y.C.* (1842), pp. 5–6; 11th *Colored O.A. of N.Y.C.* (1847), p. 5; 13th *Colored O.A. of N.Y.C.* (1849), p. 14.
10. Cmiel, *Home of Another Kind,* p. 25.
11. *St. Mary's Home* (1907), p. 9.
12. *Michigan State Public* (1881–1882), pp. 35–36; 47th *Chicago O.A.* (1896), pp. 24–25; 49th *Chicago O.A.* (1898), pp. 24–33.
13. 50th *Chicago O.A.* (1899), p. 20.
14. *Michigan State Public* (1883–1884), p. 72.
15. 81st *Chicago O.A.* (1930), p. 18; 54th *Angel Guardian* (1918), p. 3.
16. Polster, *Inside Looking Out,* p. 99.
17. Ross, "Society's Children," pp. 75–76; Stuart and Stuart, *Fred Finch Children's Home,* p. 21.
18. Ross, "Society's Children," p. 74; 4th *Chicago Home for Jewish Orphans* (1899), p. 10; Polster, *Inside Looking Out,* p. 178.
19. Polster, *Inside Looking Out,* pp. 12–14; Ross, "Society's Children," pp. 71–72.
20. Ross, "Society's Children," pp. 71–72; Dwyer, *Homes for the Mad,* p. 25; Polster, *Inside Looking Out,* pp. 147–151; Zmora, *Orphanages Reconsidered,* p. 132.
21. Polster, *Inside Looking Out,* pp. 141–142; Ross, "Society's Children," pp. 88–89.
22. Bellows, *Benevolence Among Slaveholders,* p. 147.
23. Polster, *Inside Looking Out,* pp. 12, 143–174.
24. 26th *Brooklyn Industrial* (1880), p. 17.
25. *Michigan State Public* (1881–1882), pp. 37–38.
26. Ross, "Society's Children," pp. 86–88.
27. Polster, *Inside Looking Out,* p. 135; Stuart and Stuart, *Fred Finch Children's Home,* p. 15.
28. Four children also died within the asylum that year, and six were "sent

out West," which was probably, in at least a few cases, another way of dealing with children who were deemed to have behavioral problems. 7th *Orphans' Home* (1858), p. 7.
29. Bellows, *Benevolence Among Slaveholders*, pp. 139–140.
30. Bellows, *Benevolence Among Slaveholders*, p. 147; Polster, *Inside Looking Out*, pp. 144–145.
31. Selma Cantor Berrol, *Growing Up American: Immigrant Children in America, Then and Now* (New York: Twayne Publishers, 1995), p. 74.
32. Polster, *Inside Looking Out*, pp. 137–153; Ross, "Society's Children," pp. 84–85; Zmora, *Orphanages Reconsidered*, p. 133; Friedman, *These Are Our Children*, p. 46.
33. 7th *Montana State Home* (1900), pp. 10–11.
34. 11th *Montana State Home* (1904), p. 9.
35. Schneider, *Web of Class*, pp. 102–105.
36. Ross, "Society's Children," pp. 144–146; Marilyn Irvin Holt, *The Orphan Trains: Placing Out in America* (Lincoln: University of Nebraska Press, 1992), pp. 120–144.
37. 17th *NCCC* (1890), pp. 202–205; 19th *NCCC* (1892), pp. 200–201.
38. 13th *NCCC* (1886), p. 144.
39. Dwyer, *Homes for the Mad*, pp. 24–25.
40. Jacoby, *Catholic Child Care*, pp. 50–51.
41. Leiby, *Charity and Correction in New Jersey*, pp. 88–89.
42. 22nd *Brooklyn Industrial* (1876), p. 17.
43. Dulberger, "Refuge or Repressor," p. 83.
44. 1st *Maria Kip* (1890), p. 3; 2nd *Maria Kip* (1891), p. 4.
45. 8th *Orphans' Home* (1859), p. 12.
46. Bellows, *Benevolence Among Slaveholders*, p. 141.
47. Roth, *History of St. Vincent's*, pp. 71–115; 39th *Chicago O.A.* (1888); 43rd *Chicago O.A.* (1892), p. 20; 75th *Angel Guardian* (1939), p. 6; Stuart and Stuart, *Fred Finch Children's Home*, pp. 20–30; Polster, *Inside Looking Out*, p. 177; Zmora, *Orphanages Reconsidered*, p. 72.
48. 4th *Chicago Home for Jewish Orphans* (1899), pp. 9–10; 32nd *Chicago Home for Jewish Orphans* (1926), p. 4; Roth, *History of St. Vincent's*, pp. 97–113; Kluttz, *Lutheran Children's Home*, pp. 43–53; 73rd *S.F. Protestant* (1923), pp. 9–10; 74th *S.F. Protestant* (1924), p. 9.
49. 37th *Chicago O.A.* (1886); 38th *Chicago O.A.* (1887), p. 27.
50. 20th *Brooklyn Industrial* (1874), p. 21; Roth, *History of St. Vincent's*, p. 115.
51. 20th *Brooklyn Industrial* (1874), pp. 76–77.
52. 23rd *Brooklyn Industrial* (1877), p. 15.
53. Polster, *Inside Looking Out*, p. 179.

54. Polster, *Inside Looking Out*, p. 185.
55. Dulberger, "Refuge or Repressor," pp. 120–123; Schneider, *Web of Class*, pp. 78–79; Dwyer, *Homes for the Mad*, p. 137; 7th *New York CC* (1906), pp. 71–73; Rothman, *Conscience and Convenience*, p. 265; Walters, *American Reformers*, p. 199; Shackelford, "To Shield Them from Temptation," pp. 181–184.
56. Dulberger, "Refuge or Repressor," pp. 119–121; Kluttz, *Lutheran Children's Home*, pp. 43–51; 71st *Angel Guardian* (1935); 81st *Chicago O.A.* (1930), p. 22.
57. 73rd *S.F. Protestant* (1923), pp. 9–10.
58. 74th *S.F. Protestant* (1924), p. 17; 75th *S.F. Protestant* (1925), p. 14; 81st *Chicago O.A.* (1930), p. 22.
59. 33rd *Presbyterian Orphanage* (1928), p. 41; 15th *Montana State Home* (1908), pp. 6–7.
60. 52nd *Angel Guardian* (1916), p. 2; 56th *Angel Guardian* (1920), p. 4; 58th *Angel Guardian* (1922), p. 2; 60th *Angel Guardian* (1924).
61. 9th *NC Catholic* (1923), pp. 112–113; Roth, *History of St. Vincent's*, p. 125.
62. 2nd *NCJC* (1902), p. 121.
63. 74th *S.F. Protestant* (1924), p. 7.
64. Roth, *History of St. Vincent's*, p. 81.
65. Rothman, *Conscience and Convenience*, p. 9.

6. Education and Building Character

1. These goals were the same as in many middle-class families. By the 1830s, child rearing in America had shifted from earlier attempts to break children's wills to "the internalization of moral prohibitions, behavioral standards, and a capacity for self-government that would prepare a child for the outside world." See Mintz and Kellogg, *Domestic Revolutions*, p. 58; Michael B. Katz, *Reconstructing American Education* (Cambridge: Harvard University Press, 1987), pp. 22–23; Kaestle, *Pillars of the Republic*, pp. 88–89; David Nasaw, *Schooled to Order: A Social History of Public Schooling in the United States* (New York: Oxford University Press, 1979), pp. 24–25.
2. By contrast, the first statewide compulsory education law was not passed until 1851 in Massachusetts. Furthermore, compulsory attendance laws were not very effective during the nineteenth century, whereas asylum managers could ensure that their children did attend school. See Katz, *Reconstructing American Education*, pp. 51–52.
3. Anders, "History of Child Welfare in Cincinnati," pp. 88–90.

4. Nasaw, *Schooled to Order*, p. 69.
5. Porter, "The Benevolent Asylum," pp. 31–32, 111–193; Larkin, *Reshaping of Everyday Life*, p. 35.
6. 5th *Colored O.A. of N.Y.C.* (1841), p. 5; Kaestle, *Pillars of the Republic*, pp. 92–96.
7. 1st *Orphans' Home* (1852), pp. 8–9.
8. Katznelson and Weir, *Schooling for All*, p. 37.
9. 10th *Orphans' Home* (1861), pp. 10–11.
10. 1st *Maria Kip* (1890), pp. 5–19; *St. Mary's Home* (1915), p. 7.
11. *St. Mary's Home* (1923), p. 5; Dulberger, "Refuge or Repressor," pp. 96–97; Jacoby, *Catholic Child Care*, p. 57.
12. 1st *Maria Kip* (1890), pp. 4–5; Roth, *History of St. Vincent's*, pp. 64–65, 108; 11th *Orphans' Home* (1862), p. 11.
13. 11th *Church Home* (1868), p. 6; 3rd *Maria Kip* (1892), pp. 5–6; 8th *Maria Kip* (1897), p. 4.
14. 15th *Orphans' Home* (1866), p. 10; 25th *Orphans' Home* (1876), p. 12.
15. 36th *Orphans' Home* (1887), p. 7; 50th *Chicago O.A.* (1899), p. 21; 33rd *Presbyterian Orphanage* (1928), p. 17; 75th *S.F. Protestant* (1925), p. 7; Kluttz, *Lutheran Children's Home*, p. 38.
16. *State Board, Connecticut* (1904), pp. 202–204.
17. 9th *State Board, California* (1920), pp. 64–65.
18. Clement, "Children and Charity," p. 142; *State Board, Connecticut* (1904), p. 357.
19. Morton, "Homes for Poverty's Children," p. 11.
20. Black, *Cincinnati Orphan Asylum*, p. 28.
21. Inmates in nineteenth-century institutions often performed most of the housecleaning duties, and occasionally did even more than that. Poorhouse inmates cooked, cleaned, cared for the ill, and "virtually ran the larger poorhouses." See Katz, *Shadow of the Poorhouse*, p. 28. Similarly, Ellen Dwyer has shown that New York State's insane asylums worked their inmates as part of their treatment, for the asylums' economies, and to develop their work ethics. See Dwyer, *Homes for the Mad*, pp. 131–136.
22. 9th *Orphans' Home* (1860), pp. 10–11; 33rd *Chicago O.A.* (1882), p. 14; Stuart and Stuart, *Fred Finch Children's Home*, p. 16; 80th *S.F. Protestant* (1930), p. 10; Kluttz, *Lutheran Children's Home*, pp. 37–38; Fink, "Changing Philosophies and Practices," pp. 348–349.
23. Jacoby, *Catholic Child Care*, pp. 239–240; Roth, *History of St. Vincent's*, pp. 69–70.
24. 19th *Brooklyn Hebrew O.A.* (1897), p. 75; 37th *Annual Report of the Pacific Hebrew Orphan Asylum and Home Society* (hereafter *Pacific Hebrew O.A.*) (1908), pp. 29–30; Zmora, "Baltimore Hebrew Orphan Asylum," p. 464.

25. 84th *Chicago O.A.* (1933), p. 20.
26. Inmates of virtually all nineteenth-century institutions were required to perform considerable amounts of housework. However, the rationale for this varied from one institution to another. For example, mental hospitals justified work performed by inmates on the theory that inactivity was harmful even to healthy minds; performing chores was part of therapy. See Grob, *Mental Illness and American Society*, pp. 23–24.
27. Black, *Cincinnati Orphan Asylum*, p. 28; 15th *Orphans' Home* (1866), p. 8; 9th *Brooklyn Industrial* (1863), p. 7.
28. This was true in homes as well as in institutions. One of the most obvious problems with attacks by child-placing advocates was their refusal to acknowledge that parents, like institution managers, sought submission and obedience. See Daniel T. Rodgers, "Socializing Middle-Class Children: Institutions, Fables, and Work Values in Nineteenth-Century America" in *Growing Up in America: Children in Historical Perspective*, N. Ray Hiner and Joseph M. Hawes, editors (Urbana: University of Illinois Press, 1985), pp. 119–134.
29. Rodgers, "Socializing Middle-Class Children," p. 122.
30. 13th *NCCC* (1886), pp. 133–134.
31. 13th *NCCC* (1886), pp. 133–134; Kluttz, *Lutheran Children's Home*, p. 38; 7th *Montana State Home* (1900), p. 11.
32. 50th *Brooklyn Industrial* (1904), p. 28; 71st *Brooklyn Industrial* (1925), p. 19; 13th *NCCC* (1886), p. 134.
33. 5th *Presbyterian Orphanage* (1900), p. 30; 81st *S.F. Protestant* (1931), p. 15.
34. 33rd *Presbyterian Orphanage* (1928), pp. 32–33.
35. Degler, *At Odds*, p. 98.
36. Lawrence A. Cremin, *The Transformation of the School: Progressivism in American Education, 1876–1957* (New York: Alfred A. Knopf, 1961), pp. 32–33; Katznelson and Weir, *Schooling for All*, pp. 81–82.
37. Dulberger, "Refuge or Repressor," pp. 104–105; 30th *Church Home* (1887); Roth, *History of St. Vincent's*, p. 64.
38. Polster, *Inside Looking Out*, p. 33; Kluttz, *Lutheran Children's Home*, p. 34.
39. Diner, *Erin's Daughters*, pp. 136–137.
40. Brenzel, *Daughters of the State*, pp. 72–74; Freedman, *Their Sisters' Keepers*, pp. 90–91; Diner, *Erin's Daughters*, pp. 76–89.
41. *St. Mary's Home* (1913), p. 5; *St. Mary's Home* (1914), p. 6; 66th *Chicago O.A.* (1915), p. 11.
42. 36th *Orphans' Home* (1887), p. 7; 7th *Montana State Home* (1900), p. 12.
43. Sanders, *Negro Child Welfare*, pp. 84–85.
44. 80th *S.F. Protestant* (1930), p. 10.

45. 33rd *Orphans' Home* (1884), pp. 10–11.
46. 27th *Orphans' Home* (1878), pp. 8–9; 48th *Chicago O.A.* (1897), p. 30.
47. 37th *Chicago O.A.* (1886), p. 23; 48th *Chicago O.A.* (1897), p. 24; 45th *Chicago O.A.* (1894), p. 31.
48. 48th *Chicago O.A.* (1897), p. 30; David B. Tyack, *The One Best System: A History of American Urban Education* (Cambridge: Harvard University Press, 1974), p. 230.
49. *State Board, Connecticut* (1904), pp. 202–204, 343.
50. 2nd *Orphans' Home* (1853), p. 3; 12th *Orphans' Home* (1863), pp. 9–10; 50th *Chicago O.A.* (1899), p. 29; Tyack, *One Best System,* pp. 61–62.
51. 27th *Chicago O.A.* (1875), p. 13.
52. Tyack, *One Best System,* p. 232.
53. Tyack, *One Best System,* pp. 178–181.
54. Cremin, *Transformation of the School,* pp. 12–14.
55. 20th *Orphans' Home* (1871), p. 9; 1st *Maria Kip* (1890), p. 5.
56. 43rd *Chicago O.A.* (1892), pp. 20–21; Kluttz, *Lutheran Children's Home,* p. 57.
57. Clement, "Children and Charity," pp. 143–144; 6th *Church Home* (1863), p. 6; *Dept. of Public Welfare, Connecticut* (1922), pp. 192–193.
58. Fink, "Changing Philosophies and Practices," p. 345.
59. 5th *Presbyterian Orphanage* (1900), pp. 20–30.
60. Roth, *History of St. Vincent's,* pp. 60–61; Clement, "Children and Charity," pp. 344–351; 4th *NC Catholic* (1916), p. 175; 9th *State Board, California* (1920), pp. 98–101.
61. Tyack, *One Best System,* pp. 56–57; Stern, *Society and Family Strategy,* pp. 99–106; 75th *S.F. Protestant* (1925), p. 16.
62. Zmora, *Orphanages Reconsidered,* p. 99; 15th *Montana State Home* (1908), p. 5.
63. 33rd *Presbyterian Orphanage* (1928), pp. 3, 32; Sanders, *Negro Child Welfare,* p. 84; Fink, "Changing Philosophies and Practices," p. 348.
64. Roth, *History of St. Vincent's,* pp. 118–119.
65. Dulberger, "Refuge or Repressor," pp. 137–149.

7. Play, Holidays, and Vacations

1. 9th *Orphans' Home* (1860), p. 9; 25th *Orphans' Home* (1876), p. 13.
2. 23rd *NCCC* (1896), p. 323.
3. At the same time, inmates of a women's prison were losing their recreation time because it was deemed harmful to their moral character and discipline. Freedman, *Their Sisters' Keepers,* p. 97. In this, as in many other ways, orphan asylums, designed to raise children, were different

than institutions designed to reform character, no matter how much asylum managers might talk about shaping or reforming their children's characters.
4. 6th *New York CCC* (1905), pp. 141–142; Rodgers, "Socializing Middle-Class Children" in Hiner and Hawes, *Growing Up in America*, pp. 126–127; 38th *Pacific Hebrew O.A.* (1909), p. 44.
5. 39th *Pacific Hebrew O.A.* (1910), p. 40.
6. 2nd *NC Catholic* (1912), p. 283; 4th *NC Catholic* (1916), p. 175; 34th *Chicago Home for Jewish Orphans* (1928), p. 12; Jacoby, *Catholic Child Care*, p. 120.
7. Hastings H. Hart, *Cottage and Congregate Institutions for Children* (New York: Charities Publication Committee, 1910), pp. 38–69.
8. Roth, *History of St. Vincent's*, p. 90.
9. 6th *State Board, California* (1914), p. 197.
10. 40th *Pacific Hebrew O.A.* (1911), p. 18; 3rd *S.F. Protestant* (1923), p. 10; 7th *State Board, California* (1916), p. 27.
11. Paul Boyer argues that the strategies and goals of the playground movement had much in common with the earlier Sunday school movement. See Boyer, *Urban Masses and Moral Order*, pp. 242–245.
12. 34th *Chicago Home for Jewish Orphans* (1928), pp. 11–12; 19th *Brooklyn Hebrew O.A.* (1897), p. 19; 23rd *Brooklyn Hebrew O.A.* (1901), p. 15; 4th *NC Catholic* (1916), p. 198; 52nd *Angel Guardian* (1916), p. 4.
13. 19th *Brooklyn Industrial* (1897), pp. 10–14.
14. Black, *Cincinnati Orphan Asylum*, p. 145; 3rd *Church Home* (1860), p. 5.
15. 11th *Brooklyn Industrial* (1865), p. 15.
16. 32nd *Chicago O.A.* (1881), p. 15; 37th *Chicago O.A.* (1886), p. 20; 33rd *Orphans' Home* (1884), p. 12.
17. 16th *Brooklyn Hebrew O.A.* (1894), p. 14; 12th *Brooklyn Industrial* (1866), p. 15.
18. Schlereth, *Victorian America*, p. 209; 19th *Church Home* (1876), p. 8; 43rd *Chicago O.A.* (1892), p. 27; 44th *Chicago O.A.* (1893), p. 32; 47th *Chicago O.A.* (1896), p. 25.
19. Friedman, *These Are Our Children*, pp. 44–45.
20. Roth, *History of St. Vincent's*, p. 102; 19th *Brooklyn Hebrew O.A.* (1897), p. 14; 21st *Brooklyn Hebrew O.A.* (1899), p. 20.
21. *St. Mary's/Providence* (1897), p. 11.
22. 61st *Chicago O.A.* (1910), p. 11; 39th *Pacific Hebrew O.A.* (1910), p. 49.
23. 73rd *S.F. Protestant* (1923), p. 20.
24. 51st *NCSW* (1924), p. 142; 81st *Chicago O.A.* (1930), p. 17; 73rd *S.F. Protestant* (1923), p. 17.
25. 66th *Chicago O.A.* (1915), pp. 10–11.

26. 62nd *Angel Guardian* (1926); 63rd *Angel Guardian* (1927).
27. 82nd *S.F. Protestant* (1932), p. 23.
28. 82nd *S.F. Protestant* (1932), p. 23; Boyer, *Urban Masses and Moral Order,* pp. 179–181; Friedman, *These Are Our Children,* p. 129; 9th *New York CCC* (1908), pp. 148–149.
29. Schlereth, *Victorian America,* p. 278; 33rd *Presbyterian Orphanage* (1928), pp. 31–33.
30. Schlereth, *Victorian America,* pp. 224–225; 73rd *S.F. Protestant* (1923), p. 21; 74th *S.F. Protestant* (1924), pp. 8–18; 77th *S.F. Protestant* (1927), pp. 24–25; Roth, *History of St. Vincent's,* p. 118.
31. Mintz and Kellogg, *Domestic Revolutions,* p. 118.
32. 3rd *Church Home* (1860), p. 5.
33. 8th *Maria Kip* (1897), pp. 6–7; 54th *Chicago O.A.* (1903), p. 15; 54th *Angel Guardian* (1918), p. 4; 73rd *S.F. Protestant* (1923), p. 18; 75th *S.F. Protestant* (1925), p. 18.
34. 13th *New York CCC* (1912), p. 63.
35. Schlereth, *Victorian America,* p. 53; 33rd *Chicago O.A.* (1882), p. 15; 55th *Chicago O.A.* (1904), p. 17; 12th *Brooklyn Industrial* (1866), p. 15.
36. 48th *Chicago O.A.* (1898), p. 22.
37. 73rd *Chicago O.A.* (1922), p. 8.
38. 75th *S.F. Protestant* (1925), p. 17.
39. 48th *Chicago O.A.* (1898), p. 22; 12th *Brooklyn Industrial* (1866), p. 15; Degler, *At Odds,* p. 71.
40. Thomas Bender, *Toward an Urban Vision: Ideas and Institutions in Nineteenth Century America* (Lexington: University Press of Kentucky, 1975), p. 91.
41. Schlereth, *Victorian America,* p. 19.
42. 39th *Orphans' Home* (1890), p. 7.
43. 49th *Orphans' Home* (1900), p. 11; 53rd *Orphans' Home* (1904).
44. Fink, "Changing Philosophies and Practices," p. 345.
45. 71st *Brooklyn Industrial* (1925), p. 19; 79th *Chicago O.A.* (1928), p. 8.
46. 75th *S.F. Protestant* (1925), pp. 18–19; 82nd *S.F. Protestant* (1932), p. 14.

Conclusion

1. Stern, *Society and Family Strategy,* pp. 74–77.
2. Similarly, Bruce Bellingham has found that in the mid–nineteenth century, families used "child-saving agencies as a resource in forming survival strategies." See Bellingham, "Waifs and Strays," p. 145. Unlike the agencies he studied, however, orphan asylums often recognized and accepted that they were being used in this way.

3. Porter, "Benevolent Asylum," pp. 267–268.
4. Katz, *Poverty and Policy*, pp. 2–3.
5. As Michael Katz writes, there is a "discrepancy between the structural roots of dependence and the perception of it in social thought." See Katz, *Poverty and Policy*, p. 183. Similarly, Estelle B. Freedman has argued that progressives "and other liberals since" have tried to reduce "crime by ameliorating the symptoms of class or sex exploitation, rather than by attacking the source of the problem." See Freedman, *Their Sisters' Keepers*, p. 115.
6. Katz, Doucet, and Stern, *Social Organization of Early Industrial Capitalism*, p. 357.
7. Some other institutions underwent a similar change in clientele. For example, hospitals, which had been charity institutions in the nineteenth century, began to care for increasing numbers of middle-class patients in the early twentieth century. See Rosenberg, *Care of Strangers*, pp. 237–261.
8. Haber, *Beyond Sixty-Five*, p. 107.
9. John Myles, *Old Age in the Welfare State: The Political Economy of Public Pensions*, revised edition (Lawrence: University Press of Kansas, 1989), p. 33.
10. Skocpol, *Protecting Soldiers and Mothers*, p. 477.
11. Haber, *Beyond Sixty-Five*, pp. 127–128; Schneider, *Web of Class*, p. 70; Katz, Doucet, and Stern, *Social Organization of Early Industrial Capitalism*, p. 385; Rothman, *Conscience and Convenience*, p. 5.
12. Axinn and Stern, *Dependency and Poverty*, pp. 16–69.
13. Weir, Orloff, and Skocpol, *Politics of Social Policy*, p. 5.
14. William J. Bennett, "The Best Welfare Reform: End It," *The Washington Post*, March 30, 1994, p. A19.

Bibliography

The most important sources for this book were the annual reports of several dozen orphan asylums, referred to in the notes. A word may be in order as to the kind of information they contain and how it was used. Asylum reports generally start with a report from a superintendent or secretary, discussing that year's events. These short reports are a treasure well worth mining. They discuss such matters as where asylum children attended school, how many children entered or left the asylum that year, where they came from and where they went, changes made in the asylum's physical plant, its management, and even its goals. They also often have extensive information on the donations the asylum received and other sources of funding, whether the children were allowed outside the asylum, and if so in what manner, and attitudes toward parents. Of course, not everything in these reports is trustworthy. When a manager writes that all the children are "cheerful and happy," or that the principal at the local public school says that asylum children are "among the school's best students," it may have little or no truth to it. But when a report says that "27 children departed the asylum that year, 19 returning to relatives or friends," that seems to be fairly reliable information.

Most of the tables in this volume were constructed from a large database created from the four censuses of institutional care in the United States, for 1890, 1910, 1923, and 1933. Information on each individual institution was entered into a computer database designed to match that year's set of questions. Only institutions whose primary function was the care of school-age, nondelinquent children were included in the database; infant asylums, nurseries, day care institutions, and reformatories were excluded. This allowed for construction of much more accurate tables than those provided in the various censuses, since their composite tables include information on these other institutions as well as orphan asylums. The data for 1890 were drawn from a lengthy table in the *Eleventh Census*; for 1910, from Table 1 in *Benevolent Institutions, 1910*; for 1923, from *Children Under Institutional Care, 1923*; and for 1933, from *Children Under Institutional Care and in Foster Homes in 1933*. (*Benevolent Institutions, 1904* and various incomplete sources from before 1890 were not used.)

Primary Sources

Orphan asylum annual or biennial reports

Annual Report of the Association for the Benefit of Colored Orphans.
Annual Report of the Brooklyn Industrial School Association and Home for Destitute Children.
Annual Report of the Chicago Orphan Asylum.
Annual Report of the Church Home for Orphans and Destitute Children in Boston.
Annual Report of the Colored Orphan Industrial Home, Lexington, Kentucky.
Annual Report of the Ketteler Manual Training School for Boys and the Catharina Kasper Industrial School for Girls at the Angel Guardian Orphanage.
Annual Report of the Maria Kip Orphanage.
Annual Report of the Orphans' Home and Asylum of the Protestant Episcopal Church in New York.
Annual Report of the Pacific Hebrew Orphan Asylum and Home Society.
Annual Report of the Rochester Orphan Asylum.
Annual Report of the San Francisco Presbyterian Orphanage and Farm.
Annual Report of the San Francisco Protestant Orphanage Society.
Annual Report of the Superintendent of the State Orphans' Home of the State of Montana.
Biennial Report of the Board of Control and Superintendent of the Minnesota State Public School for Dependent and Neglected Children.
Biennial Report of the Board of Control of the State Public School for Dependent Children (Michigan).
Proceedings of the Annual Meeting of the Hebrew Orphan Asylum Society of the City of Brooklyn.
Report of St. Mary's Home for Children and Free Dispensary.
Report of the Roman Catholic Orphan Asylums of the City of New York.
Report of St. Mary's Orphanage of Providence, Rhode Island.

State board or other agency reports

Annual Report of the Department of Public Welfare (Indiana).
Annual Report of the Duke Endowment Orphans' Section.
Annual Report of the State of Louisiana Department of Public Welfare.
Biennial Report of the Department of Social Welfare in the State of California.
Report of the Department of Public Welfare (Connecticut).
Report of the State Board of Charities of the State of Connecticut.

Institutional censuses

Benevolent Institutions, 1910 (Washington, D.C.: Government Printing Office, 1913).
Children Under Institutional Care, 1923 (Washington, D.C.: Government Printing Office, 1925).
Children Under Institutional Care and in Foster Homes, 1933 (Washington, D.C.: Government Printing Office, 1935).
Report on Crime, Pauperism, and Benevolence in the United States at the Eleventh Census: 1890, Part 2, General Tables (Washington, D.C.: Government Printing Office, 1895).

National, state, or religious conferences

California Conference of Charities and Correction.
National Conference of Catholic Charities.
National Conference of Jewish Charities.
National Conference of Jewish Social Services.
New York Conference of Charities and Correction.
Proceedings of the Conference on the Care of Dependent Children (Washington, D.C.: Government Printing Office, 1909).
Proceedings of the National Conference of Charities and Correction.
Proceedings of the National Conference of Social Work.

Secondary Sources

Abbott, Grace. *The Child and the State.* Volume 2. 1938. Reprint, New York: Greenwood Press, 1968.

Abrams, Jeanne. "'For a Child's Sake': The Denver Sheltering Home for Jewish Children in the Progressive Era." *American Jewish History* 79, no. 2 (winter 1989–1990), pp. 181–202.

Abramovitz, Mimi. *Regulating the Lives of Women: Social Welfare Policy from Colonial Times to the Present.* Boston: South End Press, 1988.

Anders, Steven Edward. "The History of Child Welfare in Cincinnati, 1790–1930." Ph.D. dissertation, Miami University, 1981.

Anderson, James D. *The Education of Blacks in the South, 1860–1935.* Chapel Hill: University of North Carolina Press, 1988.

Ashby, LeRoy. *Saving the Waifs: Reformers and Dependent Children, 1890–1917.* Philadelphia: Temple University Press, 1984.

Ashford, Douglas E. *The Emergence of the Welfare States.* New York: Basil Blackwell, 1987.

Axinn, June, and Herman Levin. *Social Welfare: A History of the American Response to Need.* New York: Harper & Row, 1975.

Axinn, June, and Mark J. Stern. *Dependency and Poverty: Old Problems in a New World.* Lexington, Mass.: Lexington Books, 1988.

Barr, Bernadine Courtright. "Spare Children, 1900–1945: Inmates of Orphanages as Subjects of Research in Medicine and in the Social Sciences in America." Ph.D. dissertation, Stanford University, 1992.

Bellingham, Bruce. "The 'Unspeakable Blessing': Street Children, Reform Rhetoric, and Misery in Early Industrial Capitalism." *Politics and Society* 12 (Volume 12, No. 3, 1983), pp. 303–330.

———. "Institution and Family: An Alternative View of Nineteenth-Century Child Saving." *Social Problems* 33, no. 6, (December 1986), pp. S33–S57.

———. "Waifs and Strays: Child Abandonment, Foster Care, and Families in Mid-Nineteenth-Century New York." In *The Uses of Charity: The Poor on Relief in the Nineteenth-Century Metropolis,* pp. 123–160. Philadelphia: University of Pennsylvania Press, 1990.

Bellows, Barbara L. *Benevolence Among Slaveholders: Assisting the Poor in Charleston, 1670–1860.* Baton Rouge: Louisiana State University Press, 1993.

Bender, Thomas. *Toward an Urban Vision: Ideas and Institutions in Nineteenth Century America.* Lexington: University Press of Kentucky, 1975.

Berg, Barbara J. *The Remembered Gate: Origins of American Feminism. The Woman and the City, 1800–1860.* New York: Oxford University Press, 1978.

Berkeley, Kathleen C. "'Colored Ladies Also Contributed': Black Women's Activities from Benevolence to Social Welfare, 1866–1896." In *The Web of Southern Social Relations: Women, Family, and Education,* edited by Walter J. Fraser Jr., R. Frank Saunders Jr., and Jon L. Wakelyn, pp. 181–203. Athens: University of Georgia Press, 1985.

Berkowitz, Edward D. *America's Welfare State: From Roosevelt to Reagan.* Baltimore: Johns Hopkins University Press, 1991.

Berkowitz, Edward D., and Kim McQuaid. *Creating the Welfare State: The Political Economy of 20th-Century Reform.* Revised edition. Lawrence: University Press of Kansas, 1992.

Bernstein, Iver. *The New York City Draft Riots: Their Significance for American Society and Politics in the Age of the Civil War.* New York: Oxford University Press, 1990.
Berrol, Selma Cantor. *Growing Up American: Immigrant Children in America, Then and Now.* New York: Twayne Publishers, 1995.
Berry, Mary Frances. *The Politics of Parenthood: Child Care, Women's Rights, and the Myth of the Good Mother.* New York: Viking, 1993.
Billingsley, Andrew, and Jeanne M. Giovannoni. *Children of the Storm: Black Children and American Child Welfare.* New York: Harcourt Brace Jovanovich, 1972.
Black, Robert L. *The Cincinnati Orphan Asylum.* 1952.
Blassingame, John W. *Black New Orleans, 1860–1880.* Chicago: University of Chicago Press, 1973.
Blumin, Stuart M. *The Emergence of the Middle Class: Social Experience in the American City, 1760–1900.* New York: Cambridge University Press, 1989.
Bodnar, John. *The Transplanted: A History of Immigrants in Urban America.* Bloomington: Indiana University Press, 1985.
Boyer, Paul. *Urban Masses and Moral Order in America, 1820–1920.* Cambridge: Harvard University Press, 1978.
Boylan, Anne M. *Sunday School: The Formation of an American Institution, 1790–1880.* New Haven: Yale University Press, 1988.
Bremner, Robert H. *From the Depths: The Discovery of Poverty in the United States.* New York: New York University Press, 1956.
———. *American Philanthropy.* Chicago: University of Chicago Press, 1960.
Brenzel, Barbara M. *Daughters of the State: A Social Portrait of the First Reform School for Girls in North America, 1856–1905.* Cambridge: MIT Press, 1983.
Caputo, Richard K. *Welfare and Freedom American Style: The Role of the Federal Government, 1900–1940.* Lanham, Md.: University Press of America, 1991.
Cavallo, Dominick. *Muscles and Morals: Organized Playgrounds and Urban Reform, 1880–1920.* Philadelphia: University of Pennsylvania Press, 1981.
Clark, Dennis. *The Irish in Philadelphia: Ten Generations of Urban Experience.* Philadelphia: Temple University Press, 1973.
Clement, Priscilla Ferguson. *Welfare and the Poor in the Nineteenth-Century City: Philadelphia, 1800–1854.* Cranbury, N.J.: Associated University Presses, 1985.
———. "Children and Charity: Orphanages in New Orleans, 1817–1914." *Louisiana History,* 27 no. 4 (fall 1986), pp. 337–351.
Cmiel, Kenneth. *A Home of Another Kind: One Chicago Orphanage and the Tangle of Child Welfare.* Chicago: University of Chicago Press, 1995.
Corcoran, Miriam. "Catherine Spalding—Sister and Servant" *Filson Club History Quarterly,* 62 no. 2 (April 1988), pp. 260–267.

Cray, Robert E., Jr. *Paupers and Poor Relief in New York City and Its Rural Environs, 1700–1830*. Philadelphia: Temple University Press, 1988.

Cremin, Lawrence A. *The Transformation of the School: Progressivism in American Education, 1876–1957*. New York: Alfred A. Knopf, 1961.

Davis, Lawrence B. *Immigrants, Baptists, and the Protestant Mind in America*. Urbana: University of Illinois Press, 1973.

Dawley, Alan. *Class and Community: The Industrial Revolution in Lynn*. Cambridge: Harvard University Press, 1976.

Degler, Carl N. *At Odds: Women and the Family in America from the Revolution to the Present*. New York: Oxford University Press, 1980.

Diner, Hasia R. *Erin's Daughters in America: Irish Immigrant Women in the Nineteenth Century*. Baltimore: Johns Hopkins University Press, 1983.

Downs, Susan Whitelaw, and Michael W. Sherraden. "The Orphan Asylum in the Nineteenth Century." *Social Service Review* 57 (June 1983), pp. 272–290.

Dulberger, Judith A. "Refuge or Repressor: The Role of the Orphan Asylum in the Lives of Poor Children and Their Families in Late-Nineteenth-Century America." Ph.D. dissertation, Carnegie-Mellon University, 1988.

Dwyer, Ellen. *Homes for the Mad: Life Inside Two Nineteenth-Century Asylums*. New Brunswick, N.J.: Rutgers University Press, 1987.

Ehrenreich, John H. *The Altruistic Imagination: A History of Social Work and Social Policy in the United States*. Ithaca: Cornell University Press, 1985.

Engh, Michael E., S.J. *Frontier Faiths: Church, Temple, and Synagogue in Los Angeles, 1846–1888*. Albuquerque: University of New Mexico Press, 1992.

Fink, Arthur E. "Changing Philosophies and Practices in North Carolina Orphanages." *The North Carolina Historical Review* 48 (October 1971), pp. 333–358.

Folks, Homer. *The Care of Destitute, Neglected, and Delinquent Children*. Albany: J. B. Lyon, 1900.

Foy, Jessica, and Thomas J. Schlereth, editors. *American Home Life, 1880–1930: A Social History of Spaces and Services*. Knoxville: University of Tennessee Press, 1992.

Fraser, Walter J., Jr., R. Frank Saunders Jr., and Jon L. Wakelyn, editors. *The Web of Southern Social Relations: Women, Family, and Education*. Athens: University of Georgia Press, 1985.

Freedman, Estelle B. *Their Sisters' Keepers: Women's Prison Reform in America, 1830–1930*. Ann Arbor: University of Michigan Press, 1981.

Friedman, Reena Sigman. *These Are Our Children: Jewish Orphanages in the United States, 1880–1925*. Hanover, N.H.: Brandeis University Press, 1994.

Ginzberg, Lori D. *Women and the Work of Benevolence: Morality, Politics, and Class in the 19th-Century United States*. New Haven: Yale University Press, 1990.

Gittens, Joan. *Poor Relations: The Children of the State in Illinois, 1818–1990*. Urbana: University of Illinois Press, 1994.

Gordon, Linda. *Heroes of Their Own Lives: The Politics and History of Family Violence*. New York: Viking, 1988.

———, editor. *Women, the State, and Welfare*. Madison: University of Wisconsin Press, 1990.

———. *Pitied But Not Entitled: Single Mothers and the History of Welfare, 1890–1935*. New York: The Free Press, 1994.

Graebner, William. *A History of Retirement: The Meaning and Function of an American Institution, 1885–1978*. New Haven: Yale University Press, 1980.

Greven, Philip. *The Protestant Temperament: Patterns of Child-Rearing, Religious Experience, and the Self in Early America*. Chicago: University of Chicago Press, 1977.

Grob, Gerald N. *Mental Illness and American Society, 1875–1940*. Princeton: Princeton University Press, 1983.

Gronbjerg, Kirsten, David Street, and Gerald D. Suttles. *Poverty and Social Change*. Chicago: University of Chicago Press, 1978.

Gutmann, Amy, editor. *Democracy and the Welfare State*. Princeton: Princeton University Press, 1988.

Haber, Carole. *Beyond Sixty-Five: The Dilemma of Old Age in America's Past*. New York: Cambridge University Press, 1983.

Hart, Hastings H. *Cottage and Congregate Institutions for Children*. New York: Charities Publication Committee, 1910.

Hennesey, James, S.J. *American Catholics: A History of the Roman Catholic Community in the United States*. New York: Oxford University Press, 1981.

Hewitt, Nancy A. *Women's Activism and Social Change: Rochester, New York, 1822–1872*. Ithaca: Cornell University Press, 1984.

Higham, John. *Send These to Me: Immigrants in Urban America*. Revised edition. Baltimore: Johns Hopkins University Press, 1984.

Hiner, N. Ray, and Joseph M. Hawes, editors. *Growing Up in America: Children in Historical Perspective*. Urbana: University of Illinois Press, 1985.

History of Child Saving in the United States. Montclair, N.J.: Paterson Smith, 1893.

Hogan, David John. *Class and Reform: School and Society in Chicago, 1880–1930*. Philadelphia: University of Pennsylvania Press, 1985.

Holloran, Peter C. *Boston's Wayward Children: Social Services for Homeless Children, 1830–1930*. Cranbury, N.J.: Associated University Presses, 1989.

Holt, Marilyn Irvin. *The Orphan Trains: Placing Out in America*. Lincoln: University of Nebraska Press, 1992.

Horn, Margo. *Before It's Too Late: The Child Guidance Movement in the United States*. Philadelphia: Temple University Press, 1989.

Jacoby, George Paul. *Catholic Child Care in Nineteenth Century New York*. 1941.

Jenkins, Gary C. "Almira S. Steele and the Steele Home for Needy Children." *Tennessee Historical Quarterly,* 48 no. 1 (spring 1989), pp. 29–36.

Jones, Marshall B. "Crisis of the American Orphanage, 1931–1940." *Social Service Review,* 63 no. 4 (December 1989), pp. 613–629.

Kaestle, Carl F. *Pillars of the Republic: Common Schools and American Society, 1780–1860.* New York: Hill & Wang, 1983.

Kamerman, Sheila B., and Alfred J. Kahn, editors. *Privatization and the Welfare State.* Princeton: Princeton University Press, 1989.

Katz, Michael B. "Origins of the Institutional State." *Marxist Perspectives* (winter 1978), pp. 6–22.

———. *Poverty and Policy in American History.* New York: Academic Press, 1983.

———. *In the Shadow of the Poorhouse: A Social History of Welfare in America.* New York: Basic Books, 1986.

———. *Reconstructing American Education.* Cambridge: Harvard University Press, 1987.

———. *The Undeserving Poor: From the War on Poverty to the War on Welfare.* New York: Pantheon Books, 1989.

———. "The History of an Impudent Poor Woman in New York City from 1918 to 1923." In *The Uses of Charity: The Poor on Relief in the Nineteenth-Century Metropolis,* edited by Peter Mandler, pp. 227–246. Philadelphia: University of Pennsylvania Press, 1990.

———, editor. *The "Underclass" Debate: Views from History.* Princeton: Princeton University Press, 1993.

Katz, Michael B., Michael J. Doucet, and Mark J. Stern. *The Social Organization of Early Industrial Capitalism.* Cambridge: Harvard University Press, 1982.

Katznelson, Ira, and Margaret Weir. *Schooling for All: Class, Race, and the Decline of the Democratic Ideal.* New York: Basic Books, 1985.

Kessner, Thomas. *The Golden Door: Italian and Jewish Immigrant Mobility in New York City, 1880–1915.* New York: Oxford University Press, 1977.

Kett, Joseph F. *Rites of Passage: Adolescence in America, 1790 to the Present.* New York: Basic Books, 1977.

Keyssar, Alexander. *Out of Work: The First Century of Unemployment in Massachusetts.* New York: Cambridge University Press, 1986.

Kluttz, Roger S. *The Lutheran Children's Home of the South, Salem, Virginia: Seventy-Five Years of Service, 1888–1963.* Columbia, S.C.: State Printing, 1963.

Knobel, Dale T. *Paddy and the Republic: Ethnicity and Nationality in Antebellum America.* Middletown, Conn.: Wesleyan University Press, 1986.

Korpi, Walter. *The Democratic Class Struggle.* Boston: Routledge & Kegan Paul, 1983.

Koven, Seth, and Sonya Michel, editors. *Mothers of a New World: Maternalist Politics and the Origins of Welfare States.* New York: Routledge, 1993.

Kramer, Ralph M. *Voluntary Agencies in the Welfare State.* Berkeley: University of California Press, 1981.

Labaree, David F. *The Making of an American High School: The Credentials Market and the Central High School of Philadelphia, 1838–1939.* New Haven: Yale University Press, 1988.

Larkin, Jack. *The Reshaping of Everyday Life, 1790–1840.* New York: Harper & Row, 1988.

Lasch, Christopher. *Haven in a Heartless World: The Family Besieged.* New York: Basic Books, 1977.

Laurie, Bruce. *Artisans into Workers: Labor in Nineteenth-Century America.* New York: Hill & Wang, 1989.

Lebsock, Suzanne. *The Free Women of Petersburg: Status and Culture in a Southern Town, 1784–1860.* New York: W. W. Norton, 1984.

Lees, Lynn Hollen. "The Survival of the Unfit: Welfare Policy and Family Maintenance in Nineteenth-Century London." In *The Uses of Charity: The Poor on Relief in the Nineteenth-Century Metropolis,* edited by Peter Mandler, pp. 68–91. Philadelphia: University of Pennsylvania Press, 1990.

Leiby, James. *Charity and Correction in New Jersey: A History of State Welfare Institutions.* New Brunswick, N.J.: Rutgers University Press, 1967.

Levine, Daniel. *Poverty and Society: The Growth of the American Welfare State in International Comparison.* New Brunswick, N.J.: Rutgers University Press, 1988.

Lubove, Roy. *The Professional Altruist: The Emergence of Social Work as a Career, 1880–1930.* Cambridge: Harvard University Press, 1965.

———. *The Struggle for Social Security, 1900–1935.* Cambridge: Harvard University Press, 1968.

Mandler, Peter, editor. *The Uses of Charity: The Poor on Relief in the Nineteenth-Century Metropolis.* Philadelphia: University of Pennsylvania Press, 1990.

Marks, Rachel B. "Institutions for Dependent and Delinquent Children: Histories, Nineteenth Century Statistics, and Recurring Goals." In Donnel M. Pappenfort, Dee Morgan Kilpatrick and Robert W. Roberts, editors, *Child Caring: Social Policy and the Institution.* Chicago: Aldine Publishing, 1973.

May, Elaine Tyler. *Great Expectations: Marriage and Divorce in Post-Victorian America.* Chicago: University of Chicago Press, 1980.

McCarthy, Kathleen D. *Noblesse Oblige: Charity and Cultural Philanthropy in Chicago, 1849–1929.* Chicago: University of Chicago Press, 1982.

———, editor. *Lady Bountiful Revisited: Women, Philanthropy, and Power.* New Brunswick, N.J.: Rutgers University Press, 1990.

McColgan, Rev. Daniel T. *A Century of Charity: The First One Hundred Years of the Society of St. Vincent de Paul in the United States.* Volume 1. Milwaukee: Bruce Publishing, 1951.

McDowell, John Patrick. *The Social Gospel in the South: The Woman's Home Mission Movement in the Methodist Episcopal Church, South, 1886–1939.* Baton Rouge: Louisiana State University Press, 1982.

Meyerowitz, Joanne J. *Women Adrift: Independent Wage Earners in Chicago, 1880–1930.* Chicago: University of Chicago Press, 1988.

Mintz, Steven, and Susan Kellogg. *Domestic Revolutions: A Social History of American Family Life.* New York: The Free Press, 1988.

Modell, John. *Into One's Own: From Youth to Adulthood in the United States, 1920–1975.* Berkeley: University of California Press, 1989.

Monkkonen, Eric H. *The Dangerous Class: Crime and Poverty in Columbus, Ohio, 1860–1885.* Cambridge: Harvard University Press, 1975.

Moody, J. Carroll, and Alice Kessler-Harris, editors. *Perspectives on American Labor History: The Problems of Synthesis.* DeKalb: Northern Illinois University Press, 1989.

Morton, Marian J. "Homes for Poverty's Children: Cleveland's Orphanages, 1851–1933." *Ohio History* 98 (winter-spring 1989), pp. 5–22.

Murray, Gail S. "Poverty and Its Relief in the Antebellum South. Perceptions and Realities in Three Selected Cities: Charleston, Nashville, and New Orleans." Ph.D. dissertation, Memphis State University, 1991.

Myles, John. *Old Age in the Welfare State: The Political Economy of Public Pensions.* Revised edition. Lawrence: University Press of Kansas, 1989.

Nasaw, David. *Schooled to Order: A Social History of Public Schooling in the United States.* New York: Oxford University Press, 1979.

O'Grady, John. *Catholic Charities in the United States.* Washington, D.C.: National Conference of Catholic Charities, 1931.

Patterson, James T. *America's Struggle Against Poverty, 1900–1980.* Cambridge: Harvard University Press, 1981.

Perlmann, Joel. *Ethnic Differences: Schooling and Social Structure Among the Irish, Italians, Jews, and Blacks in an American City, 1880–1935.* New York: Cambridge University Press, 1988.

Platt, Anthony M. *The Child Savers: The Invention of Delinquency.* Second edition. Chicago: University of Chicago Press, 1977.

Polster, Gary Edward. *Inside Looking Out: The Cleveland Jewish Orphan Asylum, 1868–1924.* Kent, Ohio: Kent State University Press, 1990.

Porter, Susan Lynne. "The Benevolent Asylum—Image and Reality: The Care and Training of Female Orphans in Boston, 1800–1840." Ph.D. dissertation, Boston University, 1984.

Rimlinger, Gaston. *Welfare Policy and Industrialization in Europe, America, and Russia.* New York: Wiley Press, 1971.

Rodgers, Daniel T. *The Work Ethic in Industrial America, 1850–1920.* Chicago: University of Chicago Press, 1978.

———. "Socializing Middle-Class Children: Institutions, Fables, and Work Values in Nineteenth-Century America." In *Growing Up in America: Children in Historical Perspective*, edited by N. Ray Hiner and Joseph M. Hawes, pp. 119–134. Urbana: University of Illinois Press, 1985.

Rosenberg, Charles E. *The Cholera Years: The United States in 1832, 1849, and 1866*. Chicago: University of Chicago Press, 1962.

———. *The Care of Strangers: The Rise of America's Hospital System*. New York: Basic Books, 1987.

Rosner, David. *A Once Charitable Enterprise: Hospitals and Health Care in Brooklyn and New York, 1885–1915*. New York: Cambridge University Press, 1982.

Ross, Catherine J. "Society's Children: The Care of Indigent Youngsters in New York City, 1875–1903." Ph.D. dissertation, Yale University, 1977.

Roth, Rev. Francis Xavier, O.S.A. *History of St. Vincent's Orphan Asylum, Tacony, Philadelphia: A Memoir of Its Diamond Jubilee, 1855–1933*. Philadelphia: "Nord-Amerika" Press, 1934.

Rothman, David J. *The Discovery of the Asylum: Social Order and Disorder in the New Republic*. Boston: Little, Brown, 1971.

———. *Conscience and Convenience: The Asylum and Its Alternatives in Progressive America*. Boston: Little, Brown, 1980.

Ryan, Mary P. *Cradle of the Middle Class: The Family in Oneida County, New York, 1790–1865*. New York: Cambridge University Press, 1981.

———. *Women in Public: Between Banners and Ballots, 1825–1880*. Baltimore: Johns Hopkins University Press, 1990.

Sanders, Wiley Britton. *Negro Child Welfare in North Carolina*. Chapel Hill: University of North Carolina Press, 1933.

Schlereth, Thomas J. *Victorian America: Transformations in Everyday Life, 1876–1915*. New York: Harper Collins, 1991.

Schneider, David M. *The History of Public Welfare in New York State, 1609–1866*. Chicago: University of Chicago Press, 1938.

Schneider, David M., and Albert Deutsch. *The History of Public Welfare in New York State, 1867–1940*. Chicago: University of Chicago Press, 1941.

Schneider, Eric C. *In the Web of Class: Delinquents and Reformers in Boston, 1810s–1930s*. New York: New York University Press, 1992.

Scott, Anne Firor. *Natural Allies: Women's Associations in American History*. Urbana: University of Illinois Press, 1991.

———. "Women's Voluntary Associations: From Charity to Reform." In *Lady Bountiful Revisited: Women, Philanthropy, and Power*, edited by Kathleen D. McCarthy, pp. 35–54. New Brunswick, N.J.: Rutgers University Press, 1990.

Shackelford, Ruth. "'To Shield Them from Temptation': Child-Saving Institutions and the Children of the Underclass in San Francisco, 1850–1910." Ph.D. dissertation, Harvard University, 1991.

Skocpol, Theda. *Protecting Soldiers and Mothers: The Political Origins of Social Policy in the United States.* Cambridge: Harvard University Press, 1992.

Slingerland, William H. *Child Welfare Work in California: A Study of Agencies and Institutions.* New York: Russell Sage Foundation, 1915.

Stern, Mark J. *Society and Family Strategy: Erie County, New York, 1850–1920.* Albany: State University of New York Press, 1987.

Stritch, Thomas. *The Catholic Church in Tennessee: The Sesquicentennial Story.* Nashville: The Catholic Center, 1987.

Stuart, Reginald R., and Grace D. Stuart. *A History of the Fred Finch Children's Home: Oldest Methodist Home for Children in California, 1891–1955.* Oakland, Calif.: Fred Finch Children's Home, 1955.

Sutherland, Neil. *Children in English-Canadian Society: Framing the Twentieth-Century Consensus.* Toronto: University of Toronto Press, 1976.

Sutton, John R. *Stubborn Children: Controlling Delinquency in the United States, 1640–1981.* Berkeley: University of California Press, 1988.

Thernstrom, Stephan. *Poverty and Progress: Social Mobility in a Nineteenth Century City.* Cambridge: Harvard University Press, 1964.

———. *The Other Bostonians: Poverty and Progress in the American Metropolis, 1880–1970.* Cambridge: Harvard University Press, 1973.

Tiffin, Susan. *In Whose Best Interest?: Child Welfare Reform in the Progressive Era.* Westport, Conn.: Greenwood Press, 1982.

Trattner, Walter I. *Crusade for the Children: A History of the National Child Labor Committee and Child Labor Reform in America.* Chicago: Quadrangle Books, 1970.

———. *From Poor Law to Welfare State: A History of Social Welfare in America.* Third edition. New York: The Free Press, 1984.

Trotzkey, Elias L. *Institutional Care and Placing Out: The Place of Each in the Care of Dependent Children.* Chicago: Marks Nathan Jewish Orphans Home, 1930.

Tyack, David B. *The One Best System: A History of American Urban Education.* Cambridge: Harvard University Press, 1974.

Tyack, David B., and Elisabeth Hansot. *Learning Together: A History of Coeducation in American Public Schools.* New Haven: Yale University Press, 1990.

Tyor, Peter L., and Jamil S. Zainaldin. "Asylum and Society: An Approach to Institutional Change." *Journal of Social History* 13 (fall 1979), pp. 23–48.

Ueda, Reed. *Avenues to Adulthood: The Origins of the High School and Social Mobility in an American Suburb.* New York: Cambridge University Press, 1987.

United States Bureau of the Census. *The Statistical History of the United States, from Colonial Times to the Present.* New York: Basic Books, 1976.

Vinovskis, Maris A. *Education, Society, and Economic Opportunity: A Historical Perspective on Persistent Issues.* New Haven: Yale University Press, 1995.

Walters, Ronald G. *American Reformers, 1815–1860.* New York: Hill & Wang, 1978.

Ward, David. *Poverty, Ethnicity, and the American City, 1840–1925: Changing Conceptions of the Slum and the Ghetto.* New York: Cambridge University Press, 1989.

Weatherford, Doris. *Foreign and Female: Immigrant Women in America, 1840–1930.* New York: Schocken Books, 1986.

Weir, Margaret, Ann Shola Orloff, and Theda Skocpol, editors. *The Politics of Social Policy in the United States.* Princeton: Princeton University Press, 1988.

West, Elliott, and Paula Petrik, editors. *Small Worlds: Children and Adolescents in America, 1850–1950.* Lawrence: University Press of Kansas, 1992.

Wilensky, Harold L. *The Welfare State and Equality: Structural and Ideological Roots of Public Expenditures.* Berkeley: University of California Press, 1975.

Wilentz, Sean. *Chants Democratic: New York City and the Rise of the American Working Class, 1788–1850.* New York: Oxford University Press, 1984.

Wishy, Bernard. *The Child and the Republic: The Dawn of Modern American Child Nurture.* Philadelphia: University of Pennsylvania Press, 1968.

Wisner, Elizabeth. *Social Welfare in the South: From Colonial Times to World War I.* Baton Rouge: Louisiana State University Press, 1970.

Witmer, Nancy J. "The Mennonite Children's Home, 1909–1972." *Pennsylvania Mennonite Heritage* 8, no. 4, pp. 2–12.

Yans-McLaughlin, Virginia. *Family and Community: Italian Immigrants in Buffalo, 1880–1930.* Ithaca: Cornell University Press, 1977.

———, editor. *Immigration Reconsidered: History, Sociology, and Politics.* New York: Oxford University Press, 1990.

Youcha, Geraldine. *Minding the Children: Child Care in America from Colonial Times to the Present.* New York: Scribner, 1995.

Zelizer, Viviana A. *Pricing the Priceless Child: The Changing Social Value of Children.* New York: Basic Books, 1985.

Zmora, Nurith. "The Baltimore Hebrew Orphan Asylum Through the Lives of Its First Fifty Orphans." *American Jewish History* 77 (March 1988), pp. 452–475.

———. *Orphanages Reconsidered: Child Care Institutions in Progressive Era Baltimore.* Philadelphia: Temple University Press, 1994.

Zunz, Olivier. *The Changing Face of Inequality: Urbanization, Industrial Development, and Immigrants in Detroit, 1880–1920.* Chicago: University of Chicago Press, 1982.

Index

Abrams, Jeanne, 71
Admission policies, 104–147; religious training and, 71; social agencies and, 104–105, 110–113; reasons for entry and, 106–110; social agencies and, 110–113; rules governing, 113–120; age of children and, 118–119; ethnicity and, 120–121; race and, 121–123, 147; gender and, 123–124, 147; decision-making in, 124–126; parental rights and, 126–129; length of stay and, 129–133; medical examinations and, 153–154; behavioral problems and, 166
Adolescents: admission policies for, 119; length of stay and, 130
Adoption, 67, 139; shift from orphan asylums to, 47, 140–141
African American children: in New York City, 25; community organizations and, 26–27; mothers' pensions and, 44, 45; protection of a child's heritage and, 65; staffing and, 85; social workers and, 87; child-staff ratio and, 88; donors and, 90; admission policies for, 121–123; manual training for, 186–187
Age of children: admission policies and, 118–119; length of stay and, 129, 130; boarding out and, 139; return to parents and, 142
Aid to Dependent Children (ADC), 4, 5, 45; development of welfare state and, 9; decline of institutions for dependent children and, 40, 48, 50–51; asylum philosophies and, 64; Catholic orphan asylums and, 74
Aid to Families with Dependent Children (AFDC), 218–220, 221–222
Alabama State Child Welfare Department, 100
Albany, New York, 20, 79, 131, 132, 134–135, 142, 167, 185
Almshouses, 15, 16–17, 25, 76, 107
American Revolution, 11
Angel Guardian Orphanage, Chicago, 33, 68, 86, 98, 112, 119, 120–121, 142, 153–154, 163, 167, 168, 169, 201, 204
Antebellum period, 54–55; institutional innovations during, 49; isolating asylums during, 56, 59; integrative asylums during, 57; goals of, 58–61; protective asylums during, 59; asylum management in, 76–81; funding in, 89–92; discharge from asylums during, 105; admission policies during, 123, 124, 126; indenture during, 133; education in, 174–177
Apprenticeships, 15, 16, 133–134, 136
Arkansas, 22
Ashby, LeRoy, 118
Association for the Benefit of Colored Orphans, New York City, 25, 27
Asylum for Destitute Boys, 131
Athletic leagues, 57

283

Babies, in orphan asylums, 118, 153, 164
Baltimore, 18, 20, 22, 23, 35, 83, 84, 98, 136, 163, 181, 193
Baptist orphan asylums, 19, 96, 114. *See also* Protestant orphan asylums
Bath nights, 154, 163
Behavioral problems, children with, 46–47, 118, 166
Bellefaire, Cleveland, 47. *See also* Jewish Orphan Asylum, Cleveland
Bellingham, Bruce, 244n83, 266n2
Bellows, Barbara, 157
Bennett, William, 220
Bequests, 95, 97, 98, 99
Berg, Barbara, 60
Bethesda, Georgia, 18
Binding out, 16. *See also* Indenture
Bishop Armitage Orphanage, California, 161
Black orphans. *See* African American orphans
Blassingame, John, 90
Boarding homes, 105; state support for, 43, 45, 48; discharge to, 136–137
Boarding out, 137–141
Board payments, 94–95, 98, 99, 127
Boards of trustees. *See* Trustees
Bohemian Club, 96
Boston, 121; before the 1830s, 18, 19, 20, 22–23; Church Home for Orphan and Destitute Children of, 47, 80, 127, 152, 178, 185, 191, 201, 202, 207; Children's Aid Society of, 217
Boston Female Asylum (BFA), 72, 80, 175–176; goals of, 58, 60; admission policies of, 113, 119, 124; visitation rights in, 128; length of stay in, 130; indenture and, 133–134, 141; adoption and, 139; return of children to their families by, 142; daily schedule in, 149; diet at, 151
Boyer, Paul, 200, 204
Boys: focus of reformatories on, 3; segregation of, in asylums, 154–155, 168, 170; chores in asylums and, 183; manual training for, 185
Boys Clubs of America, 206

Boy Scouts of America, 57, 68, 206
Brace, Charles Loring, 9, 159, 160, 244n83
Brenzel, Barbara M., 108
Briggs, Robert, 112, 125
Brooklyn, New York: Catholic Charities in, 37; Hebrew Orphan Asylum of, 83, 84, 94, 96, 114–115, 181, 200, 201, 202, 203; Home for Children of, 86, 210; Home for Destitute Children of, 107, 111, 115, 119, 127, 128, 156, 183, 202, 210
Brooklyn Industrial School Association's Home, 62, 64, 72, 94–95, 95–96, 161, 165
Buffalo, New York, 20, 23, 24
Building funds, 90–91, 163–164
Business schools, 193–194

California, 22, 87, 98; government support for orphan asylums in, 12; religious organizations in, 26; public funding of orphan asylums in, 43, 49, 92, 93, 100; mothers' pensions in, 43, 100; "mixed" asylums in, 122; return of children to parents in, 142–143; Fred Finch Children's Home of, 154, 157, 163; Bishop Armitage Orphanage of, 161; growth of asylums in, 161, 164; play and recreation in asylums in, 199–200
California State Board of Charities and Corrections, 100, 179
Camp Fire Girls, 206
Carson College for Orphan Girls, 68
Catholic Charities, 37, 125
Catholic orphan asylums, 52, 53, 217; focus on poor children by, 4; as protective institutions, 7; cholera epidemics and founding of, 12, 22, 23–24; religious groups and founding of, 17; before the 1830s, 18–20; care of dependent children and, 22–23; ethnicity and, 23; in California, 26; in the South, 26; mothers' pensions and, 44; isolating asylums and, 56; protective asylums and, 56; during the antebellum period,

58, 59; religious training in, 59, 71, 177, 179; asylum philosophies and, 63; protection of a child's religious heritage by, 65; isolation of children in, 66; education and, 68, 191–192, 193–194, 238n14; return of children to parents as goal of, 69, 70, 74; individualized treatment of each child in, 71; "small group system" in, 73; foster care and, 74; male and female roles in, 75; women as founders of, 79; men's and women's roles in, 80–81; management structure of, 82–83, 86; child-staff ratio in, 87, 88, 103; funding of, 89, 90, 96, 99, 101, 103, 160; donors and, 95, 96; placement of children in, 110, 112; admission policies of, 113–114, 117, 120–121, 123, 125, 127; boarding out and, 139–140; daily schedule in, 150; criticism of, 160; cottage system and, 167, 168–169; chores in, 174, 181; play and recreation in, 199, 203; growth of Catholic population and growth of, 239n18

Census of asylums: boarding out and, 139; cottage system on, 168, 172; number of children in asylums in, 242n63, 246n103

Chapin Hall (Nursery and Half-Orphans Asylum), Chicago, 47, 50, 66, 68, 82, 87, 89, 94, 95, 107, 118, 122, 151, 152

Character building: asylum philosophies on, 66; isolation of asylum children as a means to, 67; Progressive Era asylums and, 71–72; play and, 198

Charitable organizations, 4, 120

Charity Organization Society, 160

Charleston, South Carolina, 18, 20, 25, 60, 81, 91, 126, 133, 135, 155, 157, 163

Chattanooga, Tennessee, 35

Chicago, 24, 81, 112, 122; Angel Guardian Orphanage of, 33, 68, 86, 98, 112, 119, 120–121, 142, 153–154, 163, 167, 168, 169, 201, 204; Nursery and Half-Orphan Asylum (Chapin Hall) of, 47, 50, 66, 68, 82, 87, 89, 94, 95, 107, 118, 122, 151, 152; St. Mary's Home for Children of, 47, 69, 98, 119, 141, 152, 153, 177, 186; Marks Nathan Jewish Orphan Home of, 70; Home for Jewish Orphans of, 154, 163, 199, 200

Chicago Orphan Asylum, 46, 63, 72, 142, 163, 164; founding of, 24; foster care and, 47; management and matrons of, 82, 84, 85, 86, 87; funding of, 95, 96, 97; categories of children in, 117–118; guardianship and parental rights at, 126, 127, 128; indenture and, 134; boarding out and, 138, 140, 141; meals at, 151; medical care at, 153, 154; cottage system at, 167; religious training and, 179; chores at, 180, 181; education at, 186, 188, 189, 190; play and recreation at, 203, 204, 210–211; holidays at, 207, 208–209

Chicken pox, 153

Childhood, beliefs about, 20

Children's Act (1875), New York State, 29–30

Children's Aid Society: of New York, 66, 111, 159, 160, 255n37; of Boston, 217

Children's Bureau of Philadelphia, 111–112, 139

Children's Home, Millersville, Pennsylvania, 36, 47

Child welfare reformers, 13

Chinese children, 122

Cholera, 21, 26, 152, 240n31; founding of Catholic institutions and, 12, 22, 23–24; urban growth and, 22

Chores, 158, 173–174, 180–181, 194–195; daily schedule and, 149; rationale for, 181–184

Christmas, 207–208

Churches: establishment of asylums and, 19, 24, 25, 77–78; integrative asylums and, 57; funding of asylums and, 90, 95–96, 98; placement of children in asylums and, 106. *See also* Religious organizations

Church Home for Orphan and Destitute Children, Boston, 47, 80, 127, 152, 178, 185, 191, 201, 202, 207

Cincinnati, Ohio, 19, 22, 23, 79, 81, 89, 91, 99, 110, 128, 135, 136, 151, 175, 180, 201, 255n23
Cities: growth of orphan asylums in, 12, 76; need for aid in colonial America in, 14–15; poverty and development of, 15, 21, 240n35; before the 1830s, 20; nineteenth-century growth of, 21–22
City government: support for institutions for dependent children from, 75; outdoor relief from, 76; building of orphan asylums and, 91; funding of orphan asylums by, 93; public welfare departments of, 104; placement of children in asylums by, 110, 113. *See also* Local government
Civil War: institutions for the poor after, 2; growth of orphan asylums after, 11–12
Class structure, 21
Clement, Priscilla, 23, 60, 130, 192, 254n23
Cleveland, 46–47, 117, 121, 131, 134, 149–150, 151, 154, 155, 156, 157, 163, 165–166, 179, 185
Clubs, 205–207
Cmiel, Ken, 47, 50, 66, 68, 82, 89, 118, 122, 234n10
Colleges, asylum children at, 193
Colonial America, 13–17; care of poor children in, 11; indenture in, 11, 15, 16–17, 133; attitudes toward the poor in, 13–14; need for aid in, 14–15
Colored Orphanage, Oxford, North Carolina, 187, 193
Colored Orphan Asylum, New York City, 59, 79, 85, 152, 156, 176
Colored Orphan Asylum, North Carolina, 86, 88
Colored Orphan Industrial Home, Lexington, Kentucky, 94, 114, 115, 119
Commission on Defective, Delinquent, and Dependent Children, New Jersey, 160–161
Community: isolation of asylum children from, 66–67; integrative asylums and, 68; funding of asylums and, 90; orphan asylums and, 221
Community-based orphan asylums, 5, 6, 55, 73
Community chests, 98, 100
Congregational Church, 179
Connecticut, 49; county homes of, 12, 76, 113, 188; admission policies in, 116, 117, 118; guardianship in, 127–128
Connecticut State Board of Charities, 31–32
Connolly, Bishop John, 79
Cooks, 84
Corporal punishment, 156, 158
Cottage system, 148–149, 166–170; child-staff ratio in, 88; living conditions in, 167–168; census of, 168, 172; Catholic institutions and, 168–169; Jewish institutions and, 169–170
Council of Social Agencies, 99
County government: widows' pensions and, 43; placement of children in asylums by, 110, 113
County-managed asylums, 12, 52, 53, 67, 76, 137, 188; superintendents and, 100; placement of children in, 113
Courts, and placement in orphan asylums, 104, 105, 106, 110–111, 112, 125, 146, 254n13
Cultural values: orphan asylums and preservation of, 5, 71; welfare state and, 7

Daily routing, 149–155
Day trips, 201–205
Degler, Carl, 20
Delaware, 100
Delinquent children, 3; admission policies and, 118; discipline and, 157; placement by courts of, 254n13
Denver, 47, 71
Dependent children: Catholic asylums and, 22–23; mothers' pensions and, 42–45; asylum philosophies on, 61; ad-

mission policies on, 63; asylum philosophies on, 63–64; admission policies and, 104, 118; placing out of, 137; discipline and, 157. *See also* Orphan asylums

Depression: decline of orphan asylums and, 45; fund-raising and, 97; admission policies and, 115, 117; length of stay and, 131–132

Destitute children, admission policies for, 63, 106, 117–118

Detroit, 20

Diet, 148, 151–152, 165–166

Diphtheria, 153

Disadvantaged groups. *See* African American orphans; Mexican American orphans

Discharge from asylums, 105–106; return of children to their own families in, 106; length of stay and, 130; boarding houses and, 136–137

Discipline of asylum children, 73, 148, 155–159, 161

District of Columbia, 18, 20, 22, 100

Divorce, 109

Domestic service: indenture in, 134, 136, 141; training for, 185–186

Donors: staffing and, 88; funding and, 89–90, 95, 96–97; play and, 201, 202

Duke Endowment, 39, 47

East European Jews, 65

Ebenezer Colony, 17–18

Economic conditions: decline of orphan asylums and, 45; fund-raising and, 97; admission policies and, 104, 115–116

Education outside the asylum. *See* Colleges; High school; Public schools

Education within the asylum, 105, 173–195; as mission of orphan asylums, 5, 6; creation of public schools and, 21; integrative asylums and, 57; staff of, 86; length of stay and, 130; indenture and, 134; daily schedule and, 149; in the antebellum period, 174–177; religion and, 174–175; manual training and, 184–187; from the Civil War to the Progressive Era, 187–190; teachers in, 188–189; musical training in, 200; Catholic asylums and, 238n14

Ehrenreich, John, 115–116

Emmitsburg, Maryland, St. Joseph's Academy, 18–19

Emotional problems, children with, 46–47

Environment, and a child's character, 66

Epidemics: founding of orphan asylums and, 21, 23–24; medical care and, 152–153, 164–165

Episcopalian orphan asylums, 19, 120; funding of, 95, 96, 98; education and, 176. *See also* Orphans' Home and Asylum, New York City; Protestant orphan asylums

Ethnicity: staffing of orphan asylums and, 85; admission policies and, 120–121

Ethnic organizations: focus on orphan asylums by, 4–5, 21; Catholic orphan asylums and, 23; protection of a child's heritage by, 65; fund-raising events and, 96. *See also specific groups*

Exceptional Children's Act, Louisiana, 48

Fairs, for fund-raising, 96

Families: child savers and breakup of, 3, 244n83; White House Conference on Dependent Children (1909) on need to maintain, 4; attitudes toward the poor and policies regarding, 9–10; nineteenth-century orphan asylums and, 12–13; indenture of children and, 16; middle-class attitudes about, and founding of asylums, 20; epidemics and disease and, 26; protective asylums and, 57; integrative asylums and, 57; admission policies and investigation of, 124–126. *See also* Mothers' pensions; Parents

Family, asylum setting seen as, 60

Federal government, and welfare state, 7–9

Female Asylum, Boston. *See* Boston Female Asylum
Female Beneficent Society, Hartford, Connecticut, 24–25
Female Charitable Society, Rochester, New York, 77
Female Orphan Asylum, Petersburg, Virginia, 76, 80–81, 126, 239n25
Fink, Arthur E., 180, 191, 210
Flogging, 158
Florida, 22
Folks, Homer, 42
Ford Republic, 118
Foster care, 2; White House Conference on Dependent Children (1909) on, 4; during the early twentieth century, 13; shift from orphan asylums to, 47–48, 50, 140–141; Catholic orphan asylums and, 74
Franklin County (Ohio) Children's Home, 67
Fraternal orphan asylums: child-staff ratio in, 87, 103; funding and, 99, 103; placement of children in, 113, 121, 123; boarding out and, 140
Fraternal societies, 4; orphan asylums founded by, 12, 52, 53
Fred Finch Children's Home, California, 154, 157, 163
Free blacks, 26–27
Friedman, Reena Sigman, 67, 108, 138–139, 234n10
Funding: public, of private orphan asylums, 43, 49; depression and, 46; government support for, 75–76, 91–92; men's and women's roles in asylum management and, 79–80, 83; in the antebellum period, 89–92; donors and, 89–90, 95, 97; building and, 90–91, 163–164; after the Civil War, 92–98; board payments and, 94–95; bequests and, 95; churches and, 95–96; state involvement and, 98–101; sources of, 103; placement of children in asylums and, 111; criticism of, 160; cottage system and, 167

Fund-raising, 92–93; managers and approaches to, 75–76, 102; parents and, 94; churches and, 95–96; concerts and performances and, 96, 99

Gender: male and female roles within religious asylums and, 75; Catholic orphan asylums and, 79, 82–83; admission policies and, 123, 147; segregation of asylum populations by, 154–155, 168, 170; chores in asylums and, 183
Geo. C. Shreve & Co., 97
Georgia, 18, 100
German Catholic children, 23, 59, 79, 120–121, 150, 178, 192
German Jewish children, 65, 85, 98
Gingrich, Newt, 219
Ginzberg, Lori, 49, 78
Girls: focus of orphan asylums of, 3; institutions for, before 1830, 18, 19; segregation of, in asylums, 154–155, 168, 170; chores in asylums and, 183; manual training for, 185–186
Girl Scouts of America, 57, 68, 206
Good Will Farm, 118
Gordon, Linda, 109, 244n87
Government: focus on orphan asylums by, 4, 5; welfare state and, 7–9; in the last decades of the nineteenth century, 12. *See also* Federal government; Local government; State government
Grob, Gerald, 2
Guardianships, 126–129, 138

Haber, Carole, 3–4
Half-orphans: in colonial America, 11; admission policies on, 63, 104, 113–115, 117–118; length of stay for, 162
Hart, Hastings, 199
Hartford, Connecticut, 24–25, 117, 138, 188
Hartford County Home, Connecticut, 188
Hastings-on-the-Hudson, New York, Orphan Asylum Society, 129
Health of parents, 109

Hebrew Benevolent and Orphan Asylum Society, New York City, 25
Hebrew Orphan Asylum, Baltimore, 83, 84, 98, 114–115, 136, 163, 181, 193
Hebrew Orphan Asylum, Brooklyn, 83, 84, 94, 96, 181, 200, 201, 202, 203
Hebrew Orphan Asylum, New York, 108, 155, 158
Hebrew Orphan Asylum, San Francisco, 206
Heredity, and a child's character, 66
Hewitt, Nancy, 77–78, 122
High school, 57, 192–194. See also Public schools
Holidays, 207–209
Holloran, Peter, 121
Home, asylum setting seen as, 60, 65–66, 68–69, 73, 161, 221
Home for Children, Brooklyn, 86, 210
Home for Destitute Children, Brooklyn, 107, 111, 115, 119, 127, 128, 156, 183, 202, 210
Home for Jewish Orphans, Chicago, 154, 163, 199, 200
Hospitals, 54, 240n31; orphan asylums with, 22, 26, 164–165
Hungarian children, 121

Illegitimate children, admission policies for, 117
Illinois, 16, 43, 84, 133
Immigrants, 20, 105; urban growth and, 21; ethnicity and Catholic orphan asylums and, 23; admission policies and, 121
Indenture, 60, 105, 133–137, 141; in the colonial era, 11, 15, 16–17; length of stay and, 130, 131–132; rules for protecting children in, 135–136; shift to placing out rather than, 137
Indiana, 12, 48, 76
Indoor relief, 76
Industrialism, 7
Industrialization, 21
Insane asylums: role of inmates in, 60; duties of inmates of, 262n21, 263n26

Integrative asylums, 6, 55, 57, 68, 73
Iowa, 22
Irish Catholic children, 22, 23, 59, 65, 85, 121
Isolating asylums, 6, 54–55; description of, 55–56; during the antebellum period, 59
Italian Catholic children, 65, 121

Japanese children, 122
Jewish Foster Home, Philadelphia, 83–84
Jewish orphanages, 5, 12, 52, 53, 198, 203; as protective institutions, 7; first, 25; mothers' pensions and, 42; during the antebellum period, 58; asylum philosophies and, 63; protection of a child's religious heritage by, 65; return of children to parents as goal of, 69; religious training in, 71, 177; male and female roles in, 75, 83; management structure of, 83–84, 86; child-staff ratio in, 87, 88, 103; donors and, 95; funding of, 98, 103; admission policies of, 120, 123; boarding out and, 138–139, 140; daily schedule in, 149–150; cottage system and, 169–170; chores in, 174, 181
Jewish Orphan Asylum, Cleveland, 47, 117, 131, 134, 149–150, 151, 154, 155, 156, 157, 163, 165–166, 185
Jones, Marshall, 131
Josephite Fathers, 35
Juvenile courts, and placement in orphan asylums, 104, 111, 125, 256n59
Juvenile reformatories, 3

Kaestle, Carl, 176
Katz, Michael, 8, 43, 175, 215, 247n13, 247n25, 253n7, 267n5
Katznelson, Ira, 21
Kentucky, 100
Keyssar, Alexander, 107–108
Knights of Columbus, 207

Labor: poverty in the nineteenth century and, 15; indenture and, 16

Ladies of Isabella, 207
Ladies Society for the Relief of the Poor Widows with Small Children, New York, 42
Lancaster, Massachusetts, State Industrial School for Girls, 108, 166, 258n5
Laws and legislation: indenture of children under, 16; Children's Act, New York State, 29–30; mothers' pensions and, 43–44, 45; Mothers' Aid Law, North Carolina, 45; Exceptional Children's Act, Louisiana, 48; guardianship under, 126
Lebsock, Suzanne, 77, 78, 80–81, 126, 239n25
Lees, Lynn, 108
Length of stay, 129–133, 160, 161, 189, 214–215
Letchworth, William, 160
Lexington, Kentucky, Colored Orphan Industrial Home, 94, 114, 115, 119
Literary societies, 200–201
Living conditions: isolation of asylum children and, 66–67; diet and, 148, 151–152, 165–166; uniforms and, 148, 154; daily routing in, 149–155; medical care and, 152–153; bath nights in, 154, 163; beds in, 154, 163; discipline and, 155–159; violence from older children and, 157–158; chores and, 158, 173–174; overcrowding in, 161–162; cottage system and, 167–168
Local government: focus on orphan asylums by, 4; county-managed asylums and, 12, 188; methods for aiding dependent people in colonial America and, 14; placement of children in asylums by, 125. *See also* City government
London, 108
Los Angeles, 26
Louisiana, 48, 91–92
Louisville, Kentucky, 23
Lutheran Children's Home of the South, 83, 185
Lutheran Children's Home of Virginia, 114, 150, 164, 167, 179, 180, 183, 190
Lutheran orphan asylums, 17–18

Mallon, Patrick, 44
Management: men's and women's roles in, 79–80; in Protestant orphan asylums, 79–80, 82, 86; in Catholic orphan asylums, 80, 82–83, 86; hiring of former inmates by, 81, 85; in Jewish orphan asylums, 83–84, 86; in the Progressive Era, 85–89; placement in orphan asylums and, 105, 127; visitation rights and, 128–129; length of stay and, 130
Managers: asylum setting seen as home by, 60, 65–66; women as, 75; fund-raising and, 75–76, 97, 102; in the antebellum period, 76–81; placement of children in asylums and, 107; return of children to parents and, 141; discipline and, 155, 161; length of stay and, 162; cottage system and, 166–167; education and, 173, 176, 193; chores and, 181–182; manual training and, 187; play and, 197–198, 201, 202–203
Manual training, 184–187
Maria Kip Orphanage, San Francisco, 63, 64, 161, 177, 178, 190; funding of, 93, 94, 95, 97; admission policies of, 124; length of stay at, 130; indenture and, 135, 136; return of children to their families by, 142; holidays at, 207
Marks, Rachel, 81
Marks Nathan Jewish Orphan Home, Chicago, 70
Maryland, 18–19
Masons, 32, 99, 116, 217
Massachusetts, 16, 133, 158; shift to placing out and foster care in, 47; State Industrial School for Girls of, 108; boarding out in, 138; State Reform School for Boys of, 150–151
Matrons, 81, 84, 88, 159; parental role of, 60, 83; asylum management and, 81, 84; employment of families of, 81; cottage system and, 149; discipline and, 155, 156; as teachers, 188
McCarthy, Kathleen, 76, 81
Mealtime, 151

Measles, 153
Medical care, 152–153, 164–165
Medical examinations, 153–154
Memphis, Tennessee, 20, 26
Men: in Catholic orphan asylums, 79, 82–83, 86; asylum management and, 79–80; staffing after the Civil War and, 81–85; in Jewish orphan asylums, 83–84, 86. *See also* Gender
Mennonite Children's Home, Millersville, Pennsylvania, 36, 47, 88, 141
Mental hospitals, 54, 243n72; "reform" approach of, 56; release from, 133; duties of inmates of, 262n21, 263n26
Mental retardation, 118
Mercantile capitalism, 20–21
Methodist orphan asylums, 19, 96, 180, 217. *See also* Protestant orphan asylums
Mexican American children, 44, 121, 122
Michigan, 12, 76, 133, 137
Michigan State Public School, 66, 151–152, 153, 156
Michigan State School, 47
Middle-class women, and founding of asylums, 77–78
Middlesex County Home, Connecticut, 188
Millersville, Pennsylvania, Mennonite Children's Home, 36, 47, 141
Milwaukee, 20, 24
Ministers, and management of asylums, 79
Minnesota State Public Schools, 152
Minority orphans. *See* African American children; Mexican American children
Missouri, 44
Mixed asylums, 122–123, 147
Monkkonen, Eric, 253n5
Montana State Orphans' Home, 41, 69, 116, 158, 168, 183, 186, 193
Moral education, 5. *See also* Religious training
Mortality rates, for children, 152–153
Morton, Marian J., 25, 121, 179
Mothers' Aid Law (1923), North Carolina, 45

Mother Seton's Sisters, 79
Mothers' pensions, 2, 4, 104, 107; development of welfare state and, 9; state support for, 42–45, 50, 100; asylum philosophies and, 64; creation of, 244n87
Murray, Charles, 219, 220
Murray, Gail S., 78, 234–235n11
Musical training, 200
Myles, John, 216

Nasaw, David, 175
Nashville, 26, 96, 133
National Conference of Catholic Charities, 38–39, 140
National Conference of Charities and Correction, 39, 61, 69, 93, 101, 138, 159, 160, 182–183, 197–198, 248n38
National Conference of Jewish Charities, 37, 42, 69, 169–170
National Conference of Social Work, 74, 139
Newburyport, Massachusetts, 19
New Deal, 50
New Hampshire, 22
New Haven, Connecticut, 24, 86, 117
New Jersey, 15
New Jersey Commission on Defective, Delinquent, and Dependent Children, 160–161
New Orleans, 19, 25, 79, 130; Poydras Orphan Asylum of, 17, 91, 130, 135, 179; before the 1830s, 20, 22; black orphanages in, 26, 65, 90; public funding for orphan asylums in, 91–92; education in, 191
New York Children's Act (1875), 29–30
New York City, 131; growth of orphan asylums in, 12, 113–114; first orphan asylum in, 16; private associations in, 18; before the 1830s, 19, 20, 23; black orphans in, 25; mothers' pensions and, 42; Irish Catholics in, 65; placement of children in asylums in, 110–111, 112
New York City Board of Education, 94

New York City institutions: Hebrew Benevolent and Orphan Asylum Society of, 25; Association for the Benefit of Colored Orphans of, 25, 27; Thomas Asylum for Orphans and Destitute Indian Children of, 25; Ladies Society for the Relief of the Poor Widows with Small Children of, 42; Colored Orphan Asylum of, 59, 79, 85, 152, 156, 176; St. Joseph's Asylum of, 63; St. Stephen's Home for Children of, 63; Roman Catholic Orphan Asylum of, 63, 83, 94, 96, 113, 114, 124, 133, 135, 136, 142, 199; Children's Aid Society of, 66, 111, 159, 160, 255n37; Orphan Asylum Society of, 76, 115, 129, 165; Orphan Asylum of, 92, 113, 254n19; Hebrew Orphan Asylum of, 108, 155, 158; St. Agnes Home of, 110; St. Benedict's Home of, 116; St. Vincent de Paul Orphan Asylum, of, 138. *See also* Orphans' Home and Asylum, New York City

New York Orphan Asylum Society, 76

New York State, 79, 98, 154; government support for orphan asylums in, 12; poor law (1788) in, 16; public funding of orphan asylums in, 43, 49, 92, 93–94, 102; mothers' pensions in, 44–45; St. Ann's Home for Destitute Children of, 63; Society for the Prevention of Cruelty to Children (SPCC) of, 110, 165; turnover rate of asylum populations in, 132; indenture in, 133; growth of asylums in, 161, 164; St. James' Home of, 181

New York State Board of Charities, 156

New York State Board of Public Charities, 29

New York State Conference of Charities (1906), 42

New York State Constitutional Convention (1894), 31

Nonsectarian asylums: isolation of children in, 66; management structure of, 82; funding from churches and, 95–96

North Carolina: orphan asylums in, 22, 87, 88, 99, 114, 119, 180; mothers' pensions in, 45; foster care in, 47; regulation by, 100; public schools in, 193

North Carolina State Board of Public Welfare, 100

Northern states: attitudes toward poverty in, 15; almshouses in, 17; private associations in, before the 1830s, 18–19; admission policies in, 114

Norwich, Connecticut, Rock Nook Home, 179

Nursery and Half-Orphan Asylum (Chapin Hall), Chicago, 47, 50, 66, 68, 82, 87, 89, 94, 95, 107, 118, 122, 151, 152

Nurses, 84

Odd Fellows, 99

O'Grady, John, 59, 238n14

Ohio, 12, 25, 49, 67, 76, 91, 113, 133, 137

Ohio Bureau of Health, 165–166

Old-age homes, 3–4

Order of Free Masons, and Oxford Orphan Asylum, North Carolina, 32, 116

Oregon, 22

Orloff, Ann Shola, 8, 9, 218

Orphan Asylum, Albany, 131, 132, 134–135, 142, 167, 185

Orphan Asylum, Chicago. *See* Chicago Orphan Asylum

Orphan Asylum, Cincinnati, 79, 81, 89, 91, 99, 110, 128, 135, 136, 151, 175, 180, 201, 255n23

Orphan Asylum, New Haven, Connecticut, 25, 117

Orphan Asylum, New York, 92, 113, 254n19

Orphan Asylum Association (O. A. A.), Rochester, New York, 77, 89, 122

Orphan asylums: compared with other institutions for the poor, 2; differences and similarities among the variety of, 2–3; compared with prisons and reformatories, 3; mission of, 5; common features of, 6; ideal types of, 6–7; development of the welfare state and, 7–9; attitudes toward the poor and, 9–10; types of, 55–58; number of, by census, 242n63, 246n103

Orphan Asylum Society, New York, 76, 115, 129, 165

Orphan Guardian Society, Philadelphia, 42

Orphan House, Charleston, South Carolina, 18, 60, 81, 91, 126, 133, 135, 155, 157, 163

Orphans' Home and Asylum, New York City, 25, 141, 180; goals of, 60; asylum philosophies and, 63, 64, 65–66; managers of, 79–80, 85; funding for, 89–90, 91, 95; admissions policy and, 114, 119, 120; discipline in, 157; length of stay at, 162; education at, 176–177, 178, 179, 186, 187, 188–189; play and recreation at, 197, 202, 210–211

Orphan Society, Nashville, 133

Outdoor relief, 104, 107; mothers' pensions and, 42, 43, 44; city government and, 76

Outings, 201–205

Oxford, North Carolina, 32, 116, 187, 193

Pacific Union Club, 96

Parents: return of asylum children to, 1–2, 62, 63–64, 69–70, 73–74, 106, 141–143, 144–145; state government and direct aid to, 48; isolating asylums and, 56; superintendents and matrons serving as, 60; goals of orphan asylums and poverty of, 60–61; asylum philosophies and, 61–64; board payments by, 94–95, 98, 99, 127; reasons for entry of children to asylums and, 106–109; death of, 106, 109; as immoral or unworthy, for placing children in asylums, 107, 108, 109–110, 143–144; admission policies and, 112, 116–117, 119–120, 146; guardianship and, 126–128; visitation rights of, 128–129; criticisms of asylums and, 162; education and, 175. *See also* Families; Mothers' pensions

Pastors, and admission policies, 112, 146

Patterson, James, 44

Paupers, 15, 25

Peekskill, New York, St. Joseph's Asylum, 111

Pennsylvania, 20

Petersburg, Virginia, Female Orphan Asylum, 76, 80–81, 126, 239n25

Philadelphia, 18, 20, 22, 23, 24, 25, 60, 111–112; St. Vincent's Orphan Asylum of, 23, 82, 84, 96, 99, 120, 127, 130, 135–136, 150, 163–164, 165, 170, 178, 181, 185, 192, 194, 199, 203; St. John's Orphan Asylum of, 24, 90; St. Joseph's Orphan Asylum of, 24, 90; Orphan Guardian Society of, 42; Jewish Foster Home of, 83–84; St. John's Church of, 89; Children's Bureau of, 111–112

Physicians, 151, 152

Pittsburgh, 23, 24, 79

Placing out, 137–141, 159; state shift from orphan asylums to, 47; asylum philosophies on, 61, 64, 66, 74, 144

Play: in daily schedule, 149; opportunities for, 196–197; inside the asylum, 197–201; day trips outside the asylum and, 201–205

Pneumonia, 153

Political factors, and welfare state, 8

Polster, Gary, 157, 166, 234n10

Poor, attitudes toward: policies regarding poor children and, 9–10, 17; in colonial America, 13–14, 15; in the nineteenth century, 15, 25–26; goals of orphan asylums and, 60–61; asylum philosophies and, 61–68; founding of asylums and, 77–78. *See also* Poverty

Poor children: orphan asylums and institutions for, 2–3; Catholic orphan asylums for, 4, 24; attitudes toward the poor and policies regarding, 9–10, 17; in colonial America, 11, 13–17; nineteenth-century orphan asylums and, 12–13, 25–26; Protestant orphan

Poor children (*continued*)
    asylums for, 24–25; placement in orphan asylums for, 105, 106. *See also* Poverty
Poor Clares, 18
Poorhouses, 2, 4, 54, 56, 61, 253n5, 262n21
Poor laws, 16
Population growth: growth of asylums and, 13; nineteenth-century urban growth and, 21–22
Porter, Susan Lynne, 58, 72, 134, 234–235n11
Portsmouth, New Hampshire, 19
Poverty: in colonial America, and need for aid, 14–15; urban development and, 15, 21–22, 76, 240n35; public relief in the nineteenth century to remedy, 15–16, 21; response of black communities to, 26–27; mothers' pensions and, 44; isolating asylums and, 56; asylum philosophies and views on, 61–62; parental immorality as cause of, 107. *See also* Poor, attitudes toward; Poor children
Poydras Orphan Asylum, 17, 91, 130, 135, 179
Prayer, in daily schedule, 149, 150, 178
Presbyterian orphan asylums, 24, 96, 184, 217. *See also* Protestant orphan asylums
Presbyterian Orphanage and Farm, San Francisco, 70, 100, 119, 120, 129, 168, 184, 191, 193, 206
Prisons, 3, 54, 56
Private charity organizations: orphan asylums and, 9, 76, 76–77; in the nineteenth century, 16; mothers' pensions and, 42–43; funding from, 101; placement of children in asylums by, 110–111
Private orphan asylums: early examples of, in northern cities, 18; public funding of, 43, 76, 160–161; goals of, 60; admission policies of, 117
Program for Catholic Child-Caring Homes, 70
Progressive Era, 158, 245n99; asylum philosophies in, 68–72; management in, 85–89; admission policies in, 115
Protective asylums, 6, 7, 54–55; description of, 56–57; during the antebellum period, 59
Protestant Orphanage, San Francisco, 120, 125, 131, 143–144, 164, 167–168, 211
Protestant Orphanage Society, San Francisco, 167, 203, 204, 206, 211
Protestant Orphan Asylum, Cleveland, 46–47
Protestant Orphan Asylum, Hartford, Connecticut, 188
Protestant Orphan Asylum, Rochester, New York, 115, 139
Protestant Orphan Asylum, St. Louis, 59, 116, 131, 136
Protestant orphan asylums, 12, 52, 217; before the 1830s, 18, 19–20; institutions for the poor and, 24–25; in California, 26; as isolating asylums, 56; during the antebellum period, 58; protection of a child's religious heritage by, 65; isolation of children in, 66–67; religious training in, 71, 177, 178, 179; foster care and, 74; male and female roles in, 75; women as founders of, 76–78; management structure of, 79–80, 82, 86; child-staff ratio in, 87, 88, 103; donors and, 95, 96; funding of, 98, 99, 101, 103; placement of children in, 111, 112; admission policies in, 120, 121, 123; boarding out and, 139–140; chores in, 174
Providence, St. Mary's Orphanage, 82, 117, 139, 203
Psychiatrists, 166
Psychological problems, children with, 46–47, 166
Publicly managed orphan asylums: during the antebellum period, 58; male and female roles in, 75; child-staff ratio in, 87, 88, 103; funding of, 103; admission policies and, 116, 123
Public schools, 21, 54, 175; integrative asylums and, 55, 57, 68; Catholic asylums and, 68; clothing of asylum chil-

dren in, 154; asylum education similar to, 188; shift toward enrollment of asylum children in, 190–192. *See also* High school
Public welfare departments, 104
Punishment, 155–157

Quakers, 27

Race: admission policies and, 121–123, 147. *See also* African American children; Mexican American children
Recreation, 151, 196, 201–205
Reformatories, 54, 133
Reformers and reform organizations: criticism of asylums by, during the 1890s, 13; concern about immigrants by, 20; resistance to mothers' pensions from, 43; asylum philosophies and, 62
Reform schools, 3, 136, 138, 150–151, 158
Regulation of orphan asylums, 100
Relief, and unemployment, 107–108. *See also* Outdoor relief
Religion: asylum philosophies and, 64–65; as part of asylums' programs, 71; founders of asylums and, 77–78; admission policies and, 120–121; education and, 174–175
Religious organizations asylums: institutions for the poor and, 2, 24; focus on orphan asylums by, 4–5, 21; first orphanage founded by, 17; before the 1830s, 18–19; epidemics and, 23–24; in California, 26; aid to black orphans from, 27; protection of a child's religious heritage and, 65; male and female roles with, 75; funding of orphan asylums and, 99; religious training and, 177–180; Sunday schools and, 178–179. *See also* Catholic orphan asylums; Lutheran orphan asylums; Protestant orphan asylums
Religious training, 173, 177–180; protective asylums and, 56; in antebellum asylums, 59; Progressive Era asylums and, 71. *See also* Moral education
Rewards, and discipline, 156–157

Rights of parents, 126–129
Rochester, New York, 20, 77; Female Charitable Society of, 77; Orphan Asylum Association (O. A. A.) of, 77, 89, 122; Protestant Orphan Asylum of, 115, 139
Rock Nook Home, Norwich, Connecticut, 179
Rodgers, Daniel, 182
Roman Catholic Benevolent Society, 133
Roman Catholic Orphan Asylum, New York City, 63, 83, 94, 96, 113, 114, 124, 133, 135, 136, 142, 199
Roosevelt, Theodore, 38
Rosenberg, Charles E., 236n14
Ross, Catherine J., 131, 154, 156, 234–235n11
Rothman, David, 58, 245n99, 246n10, 256n59
Runaways, 155, 157
Russian Jewish children, 85

St. Agnes Academy, Memphis, 26
St. Agnes Home, New York, 110
St. Aloysious Orphan Society, Cincinnati, 23
St. Ann's Home for Destitute Children, New York State, 63
St. Benedict's Home, New York City, 116
St. Francis' Orphan Asylum, New Haven, Connecticut, 86, 117
St. Francis School and Colored Orphanage, Baltimore, 35
St. James Asylum, Hartford, Connecticut, 117
St. James' Home, New York State, 181
St. John's Church, Philadelphia, 24, 89
St. John's Orphan Asylum, Philadelphia, 24, 90
St. Joseph's Academy, Emmitsburg, Maryland, 18–19
St. Joseph's Asylum, Peekskill, New York, 111
St. Joseph's Asylum, Yorkville, New York, 63
St. Joseph's Orphan Asylum, Philadelphia, 24, 90
St. Louis, 22, 23, 24, 59, 116, 131, 136

St. Mary's Home for Children, Chicago, 47, 69, 98, 119, 141, 152, 153, 177, 186

St. Mary's Orphanage, Nashville, 26, 96

St. Mary's Orphanage, Providence, 82, 117, 139, 203

St. Paul, Minnesota, 125

St. Paul's Orphan Society, Pittsburgh, 24

St. Peter's Orphan Asylum, Cincinnati, 23

St. Stephen's Home for Children, New York City, 63

St. Vincent de Paul Orphan Asylum, New York City, 138

St. Vincent's Orphan Asylum, Philadelphia, 23, 82, 84, 96, 99, 120, 127, 130, 135–136, 150, 163–164, 165, 170, 178, 181, 185, 192, 194, 199, 203

Salem, Virginia, Lutheran Children's Home of, 114, 150, 164, 167, 179, 180, 183, 190

Sandusky, Ohio, 24

San Francisco, 26, 109, 132; before the 1830s, 20, 24; Maria Kip Orphanage of, 63, 64, 93, 94, 95, 97, 124, 130, 135, 142, 161, 177, 178, 190, 207; Presbyterian Orphanage and Farm of, 70, 100, 119, 120, 129, 168, 184, 191, 193, 206; Community Chest of, 100; Protestant Orphanage of, 120, 125, 131, 143–144, 164, 167–168, 203, 204, 206, 211; Hebrew Orphan Asylum of, 206

Savannah, Georgia, 20

Scarlet fever, 152–153, 164–165

Schedule, 149–155

Schneider, Eric, 3

Schools. *See* Education; Public schools

School Sisters of Notre Dame, 79, 82–83

Scientific philanthropy, 64

Scott, Anne Firor, 19

Scott, Lillian, 213

Sectarian orphan asylums: religious training and, 71; placement of children in, 110; chores in, 174

Settlement house workers, 116

Sheltering Home for Jewish Children, Denver, 71

Sisters of Charity, 18–19, 23, 24, 26, 38–39, 79, 96

Sisters of Mercy, 86

Sisters of Notre Dame, 79, 82–83

Skocpol, Theda, 8, 216, 218, 244n87

Small group system, 73

Social service agencies, 216; funding and, 98–99; placement of children in asylums and, 104–105, 110–113, 120, 146

Social workers, 217; approach to dependent children, 4; anti-institutional attitudes of, in the 1920s and 1940s, 13; public funding of private orphan asylums and, 43; care of children with behavioral problems and, 46–47; staffing of orphan asylums and, 87; boarding out and, 140; criticism of asylums by, 164

Society for the Prevention of Cruelty to Children (SPCC), 110, 165

Soldiers' orphans' homes, 12, 76, 84

South Carolina: orphan asylums in, 18, 99, 100, 119; foster care in, 47

Southern states: attitudes toward poverty in, 15; almshouses in, 17; Catholic institutions in, 26; male and female roles in asylums in, 75; admission policies in, 114

Sports, 68, 196, 200, 205–207

Staffing: men's and women's roles in, 79–80; in Protestant orphan asylums, 79–80, 82; in Catholic orphan asylums, 80, 82–83; hiring of former inmates and, 81, 85; in Jewish orphan asylums, 83–84; child-staff ratio in, 87–88; quality of, 88–89, 101–102

State aid to families, 13

State boards of charities, 100

State Colony and Training School, Louisiana, 48

State government: mothers' pensions and, 43–44; shift from orphan asylums to foster care by, 47–48; support for institutions for dependent children from, 75, 76; building of orphan asylums and, 91; funding of orphan asylums

by, 93, 98–101; regulatory bodies and, 100; placement of children in asylums by, 110, 113, 125
State Industrial School for Girls, Lancaster, Massachusetts, 108, 166, 258n5
State Orphans' Home, Montana, 41, 69, 116, 158, 168, 183, 186, 193
State Reform School for Boys, Massachusetts, 150–151
State-run asylums: placement of children in, 113; admission policies of, 123; placing out by, 137
Strayer College, 194
Subscription lists, 89
Summer vacations, 209–211
Sunday schools, 178–179
Superintendents, 81–82, 88, 159; parental role of, 60; asylum management and, 81, 84; employment of families of, 81; county asylums and, 100; cottage system and, 167; as teachers, 188; play and, 198
Surrender agreements, 126–127, 138
Syracuse, New York, 20

Teachers, 82, 84, 188–189
Tennessee, 100
Texas, 22
Thomas Asylum for Orphans and Destitute Indian Children, New York City, 25
Tiffin, Susan, 223n7
Troy, New York, 19
Trustees, 88, 202; in Catholic orphan asylums, 79; asylum management and, 81, 84, 86; fund-raising and, 97
Tuberculosis, 24

Unemployment: placement in asylums related to, 106–108; length of stay related to, 131–132
Uniforms, 148, 154
Urbanization, and poverty, 15, 21–22, 76, 240n35
Ursulines, 17
Utica, New York, 20

Vacations, 209–211
Vermont, 22
Veterans, children of, 12
Virginia, 16, 100; Lutheran Children's Home of, 114, 150, 164, 167, 179, 180, 183, 190
Visitation rights, 128–129
Voluntarism, 76

Wage labor, 21–22
Ward, David, 20
War of 1812, 19
Washington, D.C. *See* District of Columbia
Weir, Margaret, 8, 21, 218
Welfare state, 7–9
West Virginia State Board of Children's Guardians, 100
Whitefield, George, 18
White House Conference on Dependent Children (1909), 4, 37–40, 43, 49, 218
Whooping cough, 153
Widows' pensions, 104; state support for, 43, 45. *See also* Mothers' pensions
Willard Asylum for the Chronic Insane, 166
Wisconsin, 137
Wisner, Elizabeth, 18
Women: as founders and managers of asylums, 75, 76–78; funding and asylum management and, 79–80; staffing after the Civil War and, 81–85; in Catholic orphan asylums, 82–83, 86; in Jewish orphan asylums, 83–84. *See also* Gender
Working-class families: orphan asylums as aids to, 69; placement of children in asylums and, 106–108

Yellow fever, 18, 21, 24
YMCA, 206
Yorkville, New York, St. Joseph's Asylum, 63

Zmora, Nurith, 83, 234n10
Zunz, Olivier, 28